ACCLAIM FOR

THE STRAW GIANT

"Offers good ideas to improve
U.S. fighting capabilities...
A highly credible analysis"
BusinessWeek

"People who are concerned about national defense
must read this book."
General James M. Gavin

"An insightful examination...
Hadley's criticisms are well taken."
Kirkus

"REQUIRED READING!"
Congressman Les Aspin, Chairman
Armed Services Committee

"DEVASTATING"
Publishers Weekly

A Report from the Field

THE STRAW GIANT

AMERICA'S ARMED FORCES: TRIUMPHS AND FAILURES

Arthur T. Hadley

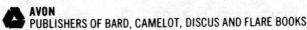

AVON
PUBLISHERS OF BARD, CAMELOT, DISCUS AND FLARE BOOKS

Portions of this work were originally published in *Playboy* and *The New Republic*.

AVON BOOKS
A division of
The Hearst Corporation
105 Madison Avenue
New York, New York 10016

The Random House edition contains the following Library of Congress Cataloging in Publication Data:

Hadley, Arthur Twining, 1924–
   The straw giant.

   1. United States—Armed Forces.   I. Title.
UA23.H23   1986   355'.00973   85-19328

First Avon Books Trade Printing: November 1987

The truth must lie in the facts.

    —Judge Learned Hand

THE STRAW GIANT

CONTENTS

PREFACE

This book is the result of forty-three years of experience with the military. Four were served inside, as a soldier; the rest have been spent outside, as a reporter, though occasionally I returned inside again as a lecturer or member of a task force or committee. As I stood before the Army recruiter in June 1942, the day after my eighteenth birthday, and raised my right hand, I knew as little of the armed services as most other Americans. My family had no military background. One year before, I had been writing antimilitary articles for my school magazine. Then Pearl Harbor was attacked midway through my senior year in high school, and on graduation I joined up.

America's armed forces were expanding rapidly. I spent seven months in the ranks as a tanker and then, after three months in Officer Candidate School, became a "ninety-day wonder," a second lieutenant. My first orders sent me to a tank batallion, where I remained for a time, and then chance struck. A new type of unit was being formed to shoot propaganda leaflets in artillery shells and make loudspeaker broadcasts to the enemy. For reasons I still cannot comprehend, I was sent to one of these units. Not wishing to stop being a combat platoon leader, I

xiii

protested loudly about the change, but to no avail. However, when later I became a military reporter, this unwanted assignment turned out to have been a great advantage. Since I was responsible for the firing of leaflets and the making of loudspeaker broadcasts for an entire army (which usually consists of at least nine divisions covering some thirty miles of front), I was able to travel widely, though only a young and very junior officer.

I would watch an attack being prepared at the highest levels and then finally jump off with the lead platoon. The experience was not entirely beneficial. Too much responsibility too young made me rather arrogant for a time. But I had the opportunity to see the military from various vantage points that the average officer, restricted to his more limited sphere, would not gain until he became very senior. So my first debt in the writing of this book is to all those who helped me then.

The making of loudspeaker broadcasts, particularly from tanks, was occasionally spectacularly successful; but I never had any illusions about the risks I faced compared with those of the average infantryman. The chief emotional residue of my wartime experience remains compassion for those who do the fighting and the dying. That too is part of this book.

After the war I entered Yale. The university then had a number of experimental programs in which selected undergraduates could take graduate courses. In one of these I was able to study for two years in Arnold Wolfers's graduate seminar on international relations. After graduation I joined the Washington bureau of *Newsweek*. I was the junior reporter in that bureau in 1950 and as such was not entitled to a summer vacation; so I was on duty that Sunday in June when the Korean War began. By the time the more senior members of the bureau returned from their vacations, I was firmly ensconced as a Pentagon correspondent. In writing this book I am indebted to a number of people from this period of my life. At Yale there was Arnold Wolfers and my fellow students in his seminar. In the Pentagon there were the reporters who taught me their craft and the officers on whom I reported back then and who shared their insights with me.

For a period in the 1950s and early 1960s the late General George A. Lincoln, then chairman of the social science department at West Point, used to invite me up to lecture on the relationship between the press and public policy. I made a number of friends in the next generation inside the armed services while delivering these talks, and many of them have contributed in one way or another to this book. For example, my Vietnam reporting benefited from their willingness to tell me the truth, often at some personal risk, or even better, to allow me to visit places where I could see for myself.

About ten years after World War II, a number of British military leaders, clergymen, and men of affairs became concerned about the lack of strategic thought in the nuclear age and began corresponding with each other. After a time a few in America were included in this circle. From this informal interchange came the Brighton Conference in January 1957. At the conference's close a handful of us, including Professor Michael Howard, the late Alistair Buchan, and I, were deputized to write the charter for the Brighton Conference Association, which later became the International Institute of Strategic Studies. The institute's annual conferences, continuing deliberations, and papers have been invaluable in keeping my ideas current, disturbing my more complacent thoughts, and testing my wilder theories.

In 1959 a group of scientists, largely physicists, of whom the guiding spirits were Victor F. Weisskopf and Jerome B. Wiesner, held a Summer Study on the problems and feasibility of arms control, under the umbrella sponsorship of the National Academy of Arts and Sciences. I was invited to attend and write a book that would explain the new science of arms control. My debt to the conference participants and others I met through them is gratefully acknowledged.

No journalist can survive without outlets for what he writes. These are not always easy to obtain, for often audiences do not wish to be disturbed by reports from the field. I am therefore grateful to a number of editors who have given me space. In the 1950s the late Max Ascoli of *The Reporter* provided a forum. Arthur Kretschmer at *Playboy* and Robert Manning at *The Atlantic* published my Vietnam pieces in the late 1960s. Recently the *New Republic* has taken my contributions. Most important, starting in 1976, when military reporting was anathema, Harry Rosenfeld, then assistant managing editor of the *Washington Post*, fought to provide room for me to describe the chaos inside America's armed services and the "revolution" caused by new, far more accurate weapons.

It is impossible for me to write anything about defense without acknowledging the impact made upon my life by the friendship of Robert A. Lovett, for many years General George C. Marshall's right hand. Lovett combines an understanding of people, vast intelligence, a legendary memory, wily bureaucratic and political skills, and a personality lit by roman-candle bursts of humor. His career measures his stature: World War I naval aviation hero, Secretary of War for Air during World War II, Under Secretary of State during the Marshall Plan's inception, then Deputy Secretary of Defense, and finally Secretary of Defense in the closing period of the Korean War. "He was a man, take him for all in all. I shall not look upon his like again."

People from all three services have kindly undertaken the labor of reading this manuscript. These include General James M. Gavin, parachute commander in Italy, Normandy, Holland, and Germany who later became an author of distinction and a reasoned, early critic of the Vietnam War. Air Force General John A. Ralph and Admiral Thor Hansen, two recently retired flag officers respected for their strategic insights, gave invaluable help. Other readers providing assistance were Logan D. Fitch, formerly the Assault Commander of Delta Force on the Iranian mission; and Peter Braestrup, editor of the *Woodrow Wilson Quarterly*, whose high standards of reporting are equaled only by his courage as a Marine officer. In a special category is a former Army officer of the Vietnam era, Dr. Lewis Sorley. His help, not just with this manuscript but with much of my military writing, has been both a pleasure and an education for many years. It is important to add that while all those mentioned have aided me greatly, none of them are responsible for my errors and conclusions, nor need they be in agreement with anything I have said.

In addition to personal observation, this book is the product of literally hundreds of interviews. To most of those interviewed I promised anonymity because the military is touchy about the press. Some of the interviewees are now retired, yet it seems wiser to leave the original stipulations in place. Industry and even academia are not always tolerant of divergent views. Where possible, the notes at the book's end give more details about sources.

I am—how I wish I were not—a slightly dyslexic, ambidextrous mirror reader with little patience. Those who check my manuscripts and do my typing bear a horrible burden. The research for this book was begun by Felicity Swayze; Olga Barbi took over next; and the whole was finally completed, along with the bibliographical notes, by Caroline Danish, with an assist from Karen Springen. All worked with skill, good humor, and incredible patience. A wizard at the word processor, Ann Charbonneau, saw the manuscript successfully through its myriad changes.

I am all too well aware that the military, and those who report on them, are sometimes accused of being war lovers. I have not found this true of most of those I know inside America's armed forces. I saw my first man die violently in Brittany when I was twenty, my last, so I hope and pray, in Vietnam at age forty-six. One of my sisters was murdered when Arab terrorists placed a bomb on the airliner in which she was flying. I have experienced warfare and violence and hate them both. But like it or not, some form of warfare and the need for efficient, rational military power are here to stay. And so is writing about the military, even if we reporters sometimes receive the treatment traditionally reserved for bearers of bad tidings.

Finally, in a work such as this, written for both the generally informed and those with a deeper knowledge of the subject, the problem of which examples to include and how much detail to employ always arises. No one has described this dilemma with more eloquence than Jeeves's employer, Bertram Wooster, when introducing his friend the newt-keeper, Augustus Fink-Nottle. "I mean to say," muses Wooster, "if I take it for granted that my public knows all about Gussie Fink-Nottle and just breeze ahead, those publicans who weren't hanging on my lips the first time are apt to be fogged. Whereas, if before kicking off I give about eight volumes of the man's life and history, other bimboes, who were so hanging, will stifle yawns and murmur, 'Old stuff. Get on with it.'" I can only ask all readers to give my efforts to cope with my own "Fink-Nottle dilemma" their tolerant understanding.

THE STRAW GIANT

ONE

Prologue:
Disaster in the Desert

From the command pilot's seat in the cockpit of the four-engine C-130 transport plane, which was coated with special paint to render it less visible, Colonel James H. Kyle keyed the correct code. The radio and light beacons implanted in the Iranian desert began to flash and transmit. The beacons had been concealed on the thirty-first of March, twenty-four days before, by two CIA agents who had flown in, dodging beneath the Iranian radar screen, and landed a specially equipped plane. After testing the soil and setting the beacons, they had taken off undetected. On course and on time, Kyle's command aircraft picked up the lights, circled, and landed as planned. This was about all that went as planned that disastrous night.

Night operations have a deserved reputation for difficulty. Even when they have been meticulously rehearsed by men who trust one another and have fought together, things tend to go wrong. On that twenty-fourth of April, 1980, at this lonely stretch of desert, code-named Desert One, some of the units and men about to come together had not even seen one another before. Other units in the mission profoundly distrusted one another. Nine different groups of men had to meld together in the hostile dark, harassed by constant noise and sand blown from the aircraft engines, which were deliberately left running all night for immediate takeoff.

There was Delta Force itself, the ninety-three commandoes who were to perform the main mission of rescuing the hostages from the U.S. embassy. There was a thirteen-man Army Ranger detachment from Europe, who were going to free the four American hostages held separately from the others in the Iranian Foreign Ministry. These men had barely met other parts of the rescue force. There were some dozen Army antiaircraft experts with Redeye antiaircraft missiles. There were eleven men fluent in Farsi, who were going to drive the trucks in the final attack phase of the operation. Şome of these were in the armed forces, some were intelligence agents, some were civilians. One was even a Navy captain from the Naval War College. They had rehearsed with other parts of the force for only a few weeks.

There were the Marine pilots and crews of eight Navy helicopters. (Six of these were necessary for the mission; the other two were backups.) Unlike the rest who are arriving in the C-130s from Masirah Island, these have flown off the carrier *Nimitz* operating in the Gulf of Oman. The helicopters were to refuel at Desert One and take on board the rescue force and then fly to Desert Two, a hiding place outside Teheran. After five months of rehearsal the commandoes and marines were hardly speaking to each other. The commandoes regarded the piloting skills of the marines as wanting and believed some of the pilots lacked aggressiveness. The marines saw Delta Force as a bunch of gun-happy crazies who were likely to get them all killed.

There was another group of twelve Rangers, who were going to guard Desert One while the choppers refueled and Delta Force loaded on the choppers. There was the Air Force Special Operations Control Team, who were to manage the refueling site. There were two Iranian generals, who were friends of someone or other in Washington. Finally there were the Air Force pilots and crews of three tanker aircraft and three transports flying Delta Force and the Rangers to Desert One.

After they had reached Desert Two in the refueled Marine helicopters, the plan called for the rescue force and choppers to hide out for the day. The next night the attackers would drive into Teheran in trucks provided by secret agents already in that city and rescue the hostages. The freed hostages and their rescuers would be picked up at different points in Teheran by the helicopters and flown a short distance to an abandoned air base south of the city near Manzariyeh, which would have been seized just before by another Ranger force. From there all would fly out on Air Force transports.

This multi-unit complexity was dictated by two factors. First, the United States did not possess a military organization that had the planes, helicopters, and other equipment necessary to conduct long-range antiterrorist operations. So when the hostages were seized in Teheran, such a force had to be hastily cobbled together from bits and pieces obtained all over the armed services. The second problem was Teheran's distance from the coast. There were no helicopters with enough range to fly in one leap from the carrier to. Teheran, carrying Delta's commandoes, and then perform the rest of the rescue mission. There were four Air Force helicopters capable of being refueled while flying, as bombers and fighters are. But these were brand-new aircraft, experience with them was limited, and if one failed, the remaining three could not do the job.

The solution was to take Navy long-range helicopters and fly them with maximum fuel to Desert One, which was as close to the Iranian capital as secrecy and terrain permitted. There they would refuel on the ground and take on Delta Force, the Army Rangers, and those others involved in the rescue phase itself. They could then fly the shorter distance from Desert One to Desert Two, just outside of Teheran, carrying both the commandoes and sufficient fuel for the rescue operation. The whole concept, code-named Eagle Claw, was tricky, complex, and triservice. In fact, it was more penta-service, as the marines considered themselves a separate service and the CIA was involved. Historically, since before World War II, this is precisely the type of operation at which the armed forces of the United States have not performed at their best.

There had been no full rehearsal of the operation to bring all its disparate parts together. Equally unbelievable, no written plan existed covering what each part was to do. Some of the men had not known for months who actually commanded them; nor were they certain from whom they were to take orders. The Pentagon's after-action report on the disaster, known as the Holloway Report after the senior admiral who led the investigative board, blamed such omissions on an obsession with secrecy. Overconcern with secrecy was certainly a problem. It was several months before the weather experts for the mission—who came from the Strategic Air Command, where they had been briefing bomber pilots for top secret nuclear warfare operations—were cleared to learn sufficient details about the Iranian mission to be fully effective, or before those on the mission were able to learn the professional credentials of their weather briefers. However, it seems probable that the failure to hold a joint rehearsal and to draw up a written plan was caused as much by a combination of interservice rivalry and the committee system at the apex of America's flawed defense structure as by security concerns. The writing of a detailed plan would have created endless hours of interservice disputes and caused such delays that the operation would have been jeopardized.

Because there had been no rehearsal or detailed plan, small problems would become large ones. The various unit commanders at Desert One bore no markings by which they could be recognized in the dark. Nor did the radios of the various units have meshing frequencies on which they could talk to each other. Delta Force could talk by relay to the White House in seconds but not to the Marine helicopters or the Rangers guarding the desert strip. On the battlefield every little thing works either for you or against you. Events, chances, gains, losses, commissions, omissions, planning, command, morale, physical condition, all combine to bring about victory or defeat. Before the rescue force even landed, certain recurring weaknesses inside America's armed forces were combining to give the rescue mission less than its best chance.

Colonel Kyle's C-130, the first to land, was called the Blackbird because it contained the Farsi speakers and secret radios and radar-jamming equipment. Also aboard the plane was Colonel Charlie Alvin Beckwith, fifty-one, a six foot one, 215-pound Georgian with vast combat experience, who commanded Delta Force. With him was the lead section of Delta's commandoes, led by Major Logan Fitch. The Ranger force and Air Force Combat Control Team shared the cramped rear of the plane with Major Fitch's commandoes. The men from all three units were volunteers who had sought out and trained for this type of mission. Now, flying in, they all got on well, jammed together in the heat inside the plane, which zigzagged at 800 feet above the desert to avoid the Iranian radar screen. Afterward, all the groups on board were to call one another "real professionals," the highest accolade those at the cutting edge of defense award. (The lowest printable denegration is "medal-heavy, water walker.")

For Delta Force the long, hot, crowded ride from Masirah to Desert One seemed more familiar than exciting. The commandoes, with roughly 120 pounds of equipment apiece, were lying on scrounged mattresses and checking their weapons. They had been practicing for such a challenge for close to two years. In interviews and after-action reports many of them recalled that they merely grabbed some sleep. Contrary to press reports, their weapons were not brand-new space-age stuff specially designed for antiterrorist activity. For the most part Delta Force carried regular equipment: U.S. M-16 rifles, German machine pistols, explosives, rockets, and shoes identical with those of other U.S. and NATO outfits.

The four-engine Blackbird landed hard, harder than usual, and one of the secure radios was disabled. Still, the landing was nothing to be alarmed about, and the plane was in exactly the planned position. The ramps and side doors opened and the Rangers raced off first on their jeeps and motorcycles. Then the men of Delta Force ran off the plane. Many immediately relieved themselves into the sand. To avoid jet lag and combat the heat the men had been told to drink a great deal of Gatorade as they waited at their secret bases, first in Egypt and finally in Oman.

Before Delta Force had gotten organized—indeed some members were still inside the plane—a large Mercedes bus, its headlights on, came driving along the desert road that traversed the landing zone. The rescue force was prepared for such traffic because when the two CIA agents had landed to set the beacons and take soil samples they had seen vehicles drive by. Still, to have the brightly lit bus arrive just as they debouched surprised everyone. "It seemed just like a movie"—several of the force used the identical phrase to me later in describing their feelings. Reacting immediately and as rehearsed, a Ranger stopped the bus but had trouble getting the passengers to leave. He was just about to shoot through the roof when Fitch and several of Delta Force came up panting with their Farsi speakers to evacuate the bus peacefully.

While the bus was being unloaded, the first small nudge toward disaster began several thousand yards away at the west end of the landing zone. A Ranger blocking team and a small group from Delta were still racing to get into position when an Iranian gasoline truck followed by a small pickup drove toward them. Efforts to stop the gas truck by shooting at the tires failed. A Ranger fired an antitank rocket at the truck, which exploded and burst into flames. The driver of the gas truck leaped from his cab, raced to the pickup, and escaped. Those back at the bus and standing about the Blackbird immediately thought that the mission had been betrayed to the Iranians and that they were now under attack. In that black night, amid the noise, dust, and sand from four aircraft engines and the patches of fog drifting by, the men of Delta began frantically readying their weapons to repel the attack they believed moments away.

"Christ, things are happening too fast," one of the commandoes later reported thinking. "Here is the war starting and my rifle is still wrapped in blankets to protect it from sand." Others felt that they were reacting too slowly because they had regarded themselves merely as passengers during this part of the operation. Their jobs, as they saw it, would not begin until the Marine helicopters had delivered them to their mountain hideout on the outskirts of Teheran.

The Rangers knew the explosion was merely a gas truck, but their radios could not talk to those of Delta or the Air Force pilots. So the hostage rescue force burrowed into the warm sand, ready, like Custer's doomed cavalry, to fight it out. In after-action reports many recall the same thought: "Welcome to World War III." Beckwith and Kyle were about to get on the secure radio and warn the other C-130s to turn back, when the Delta Force team with the Rangers reported what had actually happened. All returned to the job of preparing for the helicopters they believed were thirty-five minutes away. No other vehicles came by the landing zone that night. But the truck and bus had established a mind-set that the operation was beleaguered: that things were out of control, not going according to plan. And battles are won and lost on mind-set as much as anything else.

The burning gas truck also created a visual problem for the pilots of the five following planes. Again because of secrecy, there were no plans for other than emergency communication between the Blackbird and the other C-130s. As a result, when these planes arrived at Desert One four minutes later, their pilots were still, correctly, wearing their night-vision goggles. Bright light causes these goggles to "fog up"; and the glare of the burning gasoline truck did just that. With their night vision impaired, the pilots had difficulty landing their planes as intended. The two troop carriers and three tanker aircraft landed far more spread out in the desert than planned.

Though this meant more confusion and greater distances to carry heavy equipment, there was nothing yet to indicate that the mission would end in disaster. Listening on the secure Pentagon channel, Beckwith had learned several hours before that the planned eight helicopters had departed the *Nimitz* on schedule. All believed the helicopters would soon arrive, be refueled, then load up and fly forward. Nobody could be sure, of course, because the force had not been equipped with radios that could communicate securely via satellite between Desert One and the helicopters (although such radios existed). Those at Desert One waited, knowing nothing. Ten minutes went by. Finally an hour. Where were the marines?

Since problems with the helicopters were the immediate and most visible cause of the rescue mission's disastrous failure, that part of the operation repays wider examination. The stage should be set by recalling that the date was 1980. In the immediate past Presidents Lyndon Johnson and Richard Nixon had disguised the cost of the Vietnam War by paying for it with funds shifted from other parts of the armed services. The agony and eventual defeat in Vietnam had led to public disgust with all things military, the defense budget had been drastically cut, and the draft had been stopped. Equipment deteriorated, discipline was absent, and able leaders left in droves. The armed forces were a disaster area from 1976 to 1978; in constant dollars, these were the years of their lowest funding since immediately after World War II. Some of the incredible happenings then, such as bombers shedding engines in flight, are described in future chapters. By 1980 there had been only slight improvement.

It was in such an atmosphere that the search began for helicopters with enough range to ferry the rescue force to Teheran from somewhere outside Iran. The only operational helicopters capable of accomplishing this, even with one stop to refuel en route, were the RH-53s normally used by the Navy for mine-sweeping. These were stripped of their minesweeping gear and six (later two more were added) were positioned on a carrier operating in the vicinity of the Gulf of Oman. In the months that the helicopters were on the carrier, few knew why these particular choppers were on board. Maintenance on them was routine and they were not flown regularly. The eighth helicopter, a "hangar queen," became operational only a few days before the mission, owing to special efforts by the Joint Chiefs back in Washington. On the day of the mission, six of the choppers were doused with seawater when a seaman pulled the wrong lever on the carrier's hangar deck.

Meanwhile the joint task force that was to carry out the operation began training with other RH-53s. The first set of helicopter pilots picked to fly the dangerous mission had come from the Navy. Again because of concerns over secrecy, neither the pilots nor the Atlantic Fleet commander who supplied them was told what the mission was to be. Indeed, these pilots thought they would be needed for only three days. Not surprisingly, the Atlantic Fleet commander, whose main concern was minesweeping in the Indian Ocean in the event of a crisis in Afghanistan, did not allow his best men to "volunteer." When these Navy pilots finally learned what the mission was, two of them simply refused to fly, saying they felt the mission was beyond their abilities; and it is true that they and some others lacked the skills for long-range night operations. A few even broke security and told their wives or girl friends about the mission. The first group of pilots were sent back to their units and another call for "volunteers" went out.*

This time, because of political pressures within the Joint Chiefs of Staff, the Marine Corps was selected to supply the volunteers. Until that point the Marines had been the only part of the armed forces without a role in this prestigious undertaking. The Navy was supplying the ships, the Air Force the planes, the Army the Rangers and commandoes. Again, the pilots were not told in-

---

* During World War II, units would frequently volunteer men who were absent without leave or in jail, merely to get such troublemakers off their rolls and sent somewhere else.

itially what the mission was for. The old military joke "I need three volunteers—you, you, and you" repeated itself. Though some aircrews were good, anxious for a chance to prove themselves and see action, others were not outstanding. A distinctly motley group ended up flying the helicopters for this most difficult and demanding mission.

Because of the diffuse structure at the level of and just beneath the Joint Chiefs of Staff these "volunteer" Marine helicopter crews were never formed into a true military unit; they had no commander who would be rewarded for success or take responsibility for failure. In service parlance, "there was nowhere to pin the tail on the donkey"—no one person to keep track of what skills needed to be developed, who should be rewarded for good work or relieved for poor performance, what mechanical problems were most likely on the helicopters.

In addition to the amorphous organization of the Marine contingent, the three main parts of the force that were going to have to mesh together in the foreign dark did not even live together as they trained. The Army antiterrorist unit, the ninety-three-man Delta Force, lived in huts in the Arizona desert. The Air Force C-130 pilots, a highly professional unit who had trained for just such missions, lived at their base in Florida. And the marines lived in barracks outside of Yuma, and to the annoyance of Delta Force, went into town at night. All parts of the force were uncertain as to who was in overall command of the mission.

The situation was bound to lead to tensions and misunderstandings. By and large, the Air Force unit and its fliers and the Army's antiterrorist Delta Force got on well together. Both were highly professional and had volunteered some years before for units they knew performed this type of dangerous, lonely work. The outfits that the fliers and commandoes belonged to were established units; they had a service home. There were the usual kinks that had to be ironed out, but progress here was satisfactory.

The Marine pilots and aircrews were a different story. Through no fault of their own they had not been trained for missions requiring such complex flying skills, nor did they possess that necessary, particular type of continuous, self-motivating courage. Many were not happy about the nature of the mission for which they had "volunteered." Because they were not an actual unit with a designated commander, their discipline grew lax. The marines did a lot of drinking and blew some dope. In the Arizona desert town of Yuma, near the training area for the combined force, several marines told some of the local girls about the secret rescue attempt. That finally exploded the problems of the rescue force all the way up to the Joint Chiefs.

Right then one powerful General officer should have been brought in to unify the force and make certain all were properly trained. But under the Defense Department's committee system no one had the authority to order this obviously necessary step. Defense Secretary Harold Brown, an able physicist with long Pentagon experience, had the legal power to exert the pressure to change both the command structure and the commanders. But in reality he was powerless because of his cold and distant personality, his lack of combat experience, and his past service under Robert McNamara, the Defense Secretary during the Vietnam War and a man most of the military despise. Indeed, as we shall see, the very history of the Pentagon had isolated Harold Brown from the armed services.

Even the Defense Department's own official after-action report of the disaster was to criticize the organization of the training, though it did so in Orwellian newspeak: "The review group recognizes that joint doctrine assigns the Service component commanders unit training and support responsibilities; however, for this mission, forces were so interdependent that complete force integration was essential." Sadly, complete force integration was not achieved. (Nor was it achieved in Beirut, where in October 1983, 241 marines died in the carnage of their headquarters, largely because, again, no one knew who was in command.)

Possibly the able Chairman of the Joint Chiefs of Staff, General David C. Jones, an Air Force officer, might, through sheer force of personality, have cleared up the organizational problem. But Jones was already struggling with the Marines on what was to him an even more important issue: interservice control of airplanes. The only result of the security breach in Yuma was that the FBI was called in to blanket the town's bars. The Joint Chiefs made plans to cancel the hostage rescue mission if the FBI reported the Iranians had learned of the plans. Fortunately, the patriotism of the women proved stronger than the discipline of the marines.

But though disaster had been avoided, the basic problems remained. Out in the Arizona practice ground things continued as before, the vital parts of the force living, and often training, apart. Several times the marines refused to fly because the night was too dark and dusty, the very conditions later to be encountered in Iran. By now both the Air Force and the Army lacked confidence in the Marine pilots' ability to fly the mission or to keep secrets. But in spite of constant reports of trouble, neither the Joint Chiefs nor the National Security Council took action. At the White House National Security Council level, alert officers did recognize that the helicopters and the pilots were the part of the rescue mission most likely to fail. They were finally able to add two extra helicopters to the mission. The internal politics of the Pentagon prevented them from doing more than this. One cannot wholly exonerate the marines for the failure that was to follow, and the Holloway Report did not. Still, the chief blame should be marked against the system that selected these men and left them an unorganized group. It is quite literally as if one had asked a group of Army gas-decontamination experts to go on a dangerous mission as underwater frogmen simply because both groups work in rubber suits.

Nominally in command of the whole disparate rescue force, but without authority to order any significant changes, was a rather conservative Army general. The reason for his selection remains as much a mystery as that for the selection of marines to fly the choppers. He lacked experience in this type of operation and had never been regarded as inventive.

Another reason the helicopter problem did not receive adequate attention was that there were always hopes that some alternative method could be found to get Delta Force into Teheran. The mission continually had difficulty getting enough hard intelligence out of Iran on which to base any realistic plan. The national revolt against all forms of violent power had hit the CIA even harder than the military. Recruitment was down, many able people had left, others had been fired or "riffed" by reduced budgets. The agency had been further tarnished by its perceived part in Watergate and later damaged by congressional investigations and the disclosure of some uncontrolled and dubious operations. Successive Congresses and Presidents Ford and Carter had greatly reduced the CIA's budgets. The cover of some agents was blown by extremists in the peace movement, while Hollywood depicted CIA employees as murderous thugs.

President Carter had placed in charge of the CIA Admiral

Stansfield Turner, a friend and Naval Academy classmate. Turner, a rigid, powerful man, lacked experience or understanding of intelligence. He had further weakened the CIA by firing many seasoned field agents and other intelligence specialists. He then brought in a small coterie of naval officers at the top to make most vital CIA decisions. He had kept his commission when he became the head of the CIA, getting special congressional approval to do so. Admiral Turner's reported secret agenda was to become Chairman of the Joint Chiefs of Staff when his friend President Carter was reelected. Many who dealt with him found him excessively anxious to offend no one. For over a year Turner had no agents in Iran who could contribute hard information, and he resisted attempts by others to insert agents.

In the words of an intelligence operative I have known most of my life, "We had zero intelligence about the target. Zero." The man traced a zero in the air with his index finger. "The CIA had first been stiffed by the Church Committee in the aftermath of Watergate and then Turner, with his reliance on a few naval insiders and technical means of information rather than humint [human intelligence, i.e., secret agents], stiffed it further."

Charlie Beckwith, the commander of Delta Force, kept telling everyone that intelligence was just fine. Why he did so is an interesting question, as that opinion was not shared by other operators on the mission. For example, no one even knew how thick the U.S. embassy wall in Teheran was or for certain of what that wall was made. Nor did they know where the hostages were being held inside, or the number of their guards. Finally a few old agents were reactivated and sent into Iran and the Army in Europe found some others.

In such an atmosphere all sorts of wild plans flourished inside the most secret confines of the Pentagon. It wasn't just a question of constructing a good plan; it never is in such situations. A workable plan had to be formed while numerous crazy plans were fought off. And many such plans were backed by powerful officers who saw in them means to advance their professional careers. The situation was further complicated because the White House had claimed a year earlier that the force now being created had already existed. Everything had to be done in a manner designed not to embarrass the President.

For example, one such plan called for jumping an airborne

division on the Teheran airport to seize the field. After that a second division would be airlanded, and with the help of naval air power, the two divisions would attack through the city to rescue the hostages. What the Iranian guards would be doing to the hostages meanwhile was never made quite clear. Another plan called for a secret airborne attack on a partially abandoned military airfield, Na'in, outside Teheran, holding the field for a day, and then driving into Teheran the next night and rescuing the hostages. This plan was championed by a very persuasive officer who saw himself as commander at the base, which would ensure a promotion. His detractors called him the John Wayne of Na'in.

Not all the plans were so patently outrageous. Detailed and serious consideration was given to sneaking the rescue force into Iran inside specially constructed trucks that had been built to resemble the huge trailers hauling frozen meat from Germany to Iran. The Iranian guards at the Turkish-Iranian border were rather lax, and if they did open up the rear doors of the trucks, they would see nothing but meat carcasses. But hidden in chambers beneath the frozen meat would be Delta Force and their weapons. This plan had definite advantages because, freed of the need to carry Delta Force, the helicopters could carry more fuel. Fewer helicopters would be necessary and these could be used in a more flexible manner; perhaps helicopters could be dispensed with altogether. However, the truck plan was finally abandoned because the trucks would have to drive through Turkey to reach the Iranian border, and both the State Department and CIA feared that if the mission was successful, Iran might conclude that Turkey was part of the plot and declare war on that nation.

In the end it became obvious that the best possible plan was to airlift the rescue force close in to Teheran. Those who were actually to carry out the rescue had believed it their best option all along. Now the helicopters were critical.

The helicopters' part in the actual mission began with a fine example of seamanship as they were launched from the nuclear carrier. The *Nimitz* had sailed at top speed for a day and a half and successfully lost the Soviet trawler tracking her. After that success the unnecessary disasters began to strike. The first occurred an hour after the launching.

Nitrogen under pressure is used in the main blades of some helicopter rotors to help them keep their shape while remaining flexible. On the instrument panel of one of the helicopters a warning light flashed, indicating that nitrogen was leaking out of one of the rotor blades. While the helicopters were in Arizona training for the rescue mission this had happened often enough to have been identified as an important problem. Sikorsky, the helicopter manufacturer, and the Air Force had conducted experiments and discovered that after the warning light went on, the chopper had a minimum of fifteen additional hours of routine operation before blade failure. Further, out of the forty-three blades from the RH-53 helicopters returned for inspection after the warning light went on, not one had had an actual blade crack and leak. Since flying time for the rescue mission was way under fifteen hours, there was no reason why this helicopter could not have continued to Desert One and then to Teheran. However, either this carefully accumulated information had not been passed to the helicopter pilots or under pressure of the actual operation they forgot it. In any event, the crew landed in the desert, abandoned their helicopter unnecessarily, and were picked up by the next helicopter in line.

An hour later the seven remaining helicopters encountered a dust cloud their pilots had not expected. The dust was so thick that the choppers could not fly by reference to the ground. Instead they had to rely on the artificial horizon and other gauges on the helicopter instrument panels. IFR, or instrument flying, is difficult, especially in a helicopter, though many pilots do it routinely. These particular pilots had not been adequately trained to fly IFR, any more than they had been trained for complex long-range missions. They had been told the weather would be clear on the way to Desert One and had trained in that type of night flying in the Arizona desert. The National Intelligence Summary on Iran prepared by the CIA specifically mentioned the probability of low-level dust clouds in the flight area. This report had reached the Air Force pilots but not the marines.

Becoming disoriented in the unexpected weather and experiencing instrument problems, one of the senior Marine pilots turned and flew back to the carrier. A short while later the flight leader and his wingman also reversed course, flew out of the cloud, and landed in the desert, expecting the rest of the pilots to follow them. After twenty minutes it became obvious that he and his wingman had turned back by themselves, while the rest of the choppers were continuing the mission. The Marine commander then took off in pursuit of those he led.

There was no reason for the helicopters to be flying just above the desert floor on instruments. They could safely have climbed to 400 feet, where the air was more clear of the dust, because the zigzag courses that both the C-130s and the helicopters were following had been carefully laid out to fly through holes in the Iranian radar. The Air Force pilots knew this. The Army Delta Force knew this. Again, no one had told the marines. Even worse, the marines had heard a rumor that the whole area was blanketed with radar and that they had to stay low. Unable to communicate with each other or with the Air Force, and down to the minimum number of helicopters required for the mission, the pilots of the six remaining choppers plowed on through the sandy gunk they had not expected and in which they were not adequately trained to fly. There was no way for them to learn that the dust storm would end after roughly an hour and that at Desert One it was a relatively clear and starlit night.

By the time the last helicopter arrived at the Desert One rendezvous site, they were one hour and twenty-five minutes late because of the dust storm. Of the six that arrived, one had landed flashing far more serious panel warning lights than the chopper unnecessarily abandoned. That bird was flown by an officer who all along, in the judgment of his peers, had been the most gung ho of the marines. He had pressed on, hoping the lights merely indicated something that could be repaired on the ground while he was refueling. Unfortunately, his courage and dedication were not rewarded. A hydraulic pump had failed and was unrepairable. That left five helicopters.* Exactly why so many people were taking part in the mission that six helicopters were necessary—whether the force had grown far too large because too many cooks were stirring the pot—is a complex and technical question. But to lift the force at Desert One on to Teheran, six helicopters were necessary. The mission had to abort.

That April night in the Iranian desert no sudden bugle peel or

* Whether the sixth helicopter could or could not have flown the mission remains a subject of intense debate. In hindsight, the helicopter could most probably have completed the operation.

stutter of sad drum recalled those there from the high hopes of their start to the despair of failure. Two false reports had circulated that the mission was being aborted, so now the true cancellation order was often disbelieved. A bunch of men yelling uncertainly into one another's ears ran about the desert floor in the dark, dust, and noise, trying to locate everyone and get them safely out. Since elaborate plans had been made to continue by helicopter but none to evacuate on the tanker aircraft, orders were given and countermanded. Troops lined up for one aircraft and then marched to another. No one was quite certain where they were to go.

Imagine the hostile, alien darkness; the blowing sand from the six helicopters and the four transport aircraft still on the ground, all with their engines going to guarantee a restart; the heat and sweat and noise; the piles of heavy equipment like camouflage nets; and the fear and the haste and the disappointment. At this confused moment, who is giving orders to whom? What is the command picture, as they call it in the Pentagon? There were four commanders there on the desert floor, wearing no identification marks, equipped with radios that did not work together, and having no agreed-upon plan of operation. Each did not even have a designated place to stand.

There was the exceptionally able Air Force colonel, James Kyle. He was known as the On-Site Force Commander. If there was one man who stood out that night, there is unanimous agreement among all there as to who was that man. Kyle was that calming and forceful presence toward whom confused men turned and to whom enraged men listened. Another commander there was Army colonel Charlie A. Beckwith, Delta Force leader. He was known as the Rescue Force Commander. There was a Marine lieutenant colonel, Edward Seiffert, who arrived last. He was called the Helicopter Force Commander. Finally there was an Army Ranger commander, a major. He was known as the Refueling Site Security Force Commander. With confusion such as this, unless the mission was blessed with luck, trouble would follow. The force had no such luck. Horror came.

One of the helicopters, after refueling from a tanker C-130, needed to reposition itself for the trip back to the carrier. All through the night the Marine pilots had had trouble moving their helicopters about in the dark. Two of them had blown their front tires as they maneuvered. Now, as the pilot started to fly his bird out from behind the C-130, he became disoriented in the blackness thickened by dust stirred up by his and the tanker's engines. His helicopter tilted right. Its blade cut into the flight deck and left side of the C-130 and flames spurted out. Inside that C-130, exhausted after lugging their equipment from helicopter to helicopter, were the Redeye antiaircraft artillerymen and Major Fitch's commando section.

The men in the plane had their equipment off and were lying down on the rubbery, waterbedlike, partially full gasoline bladders. They felt a slight *thunk, thunk*. Most felt relief at first, thinking, Here we go at last, leaving the tension and the failure behind, finally taking off. Then a shower of sparks came tumbling aft into the body of the plane from the pilot's compartment. Seeing the flames coming from the forward part of the aircraft triggered among those in the rear the previous mind-set that the operation was beleaguered. Everyone's thought was "My God, we are being attacked."

The tanker crew chief and Major Fitch tried to get the left-hand plane door open. When they had forced it slightly ajar, they found nothing but a wall of fire, and hastily slammed the door shut. Other commandoes were trying without success to work the right-hand door. The ammunition, the explosive to blow a hole in the embassy wall, the antiaircraft missiles, the extra gasoline were all on board this plane and would blow at any moment. Many in the plane, particularly those farthest from the door, thought that this was the end. The Air Force crew chief calmly and professionally reached over the men of Delta Force and threw the switch sequence that placed the tanker door on manual. The crew chief and the two nearest commandoes kicked at the door. It flew open. Miraculously, in the bare minute before the plane turned into flaming fragments, all those in the rear leaped safely through the door onto the desert. Even as the plane began to explode, some commandoes were tugging at the burning forms of the airmen in the C-130's front cockpit, who were still struggling unsuccessfully to get out.

The reports of the survivors about what happened next become confused and even contradictory. Those who had escaped the burning aircraft searched out the other two C-130s and the Blackbird and began to board them, though by now these planes were dangerously overloaded. Some way off in the dark stood several helicopters with their rotors still turning, and men explored these to see if they could fly out on them. However, though the helicopter motors were still running, there were no aircrews on board. The marines had abandoned their helicopters so rapidly they had not even shut off their engines. Nor had they destroyed, as planned, the secret equipment on board.

Checking the desert darkness to make certain no survivors of the burning C-130 had been abandoned, the last members of the mission boarded the Blackbird. The plane's doors closed and the aircraft slowly accelerated on its takeoff run over the desert floor. The pilot slightly misjudged his direction, and just before flying speed was reached, the C-130's wheels slammed into the shoulder of the dirt road that paralleled Desert One. The aircraft shuddered, seemed to rise for an instant, then settled toward the ground. There was a second thud as the wheels hit the sand. The plane bounced into the air again, staggered, then became airborne. Of the long flight back to Masirah off Oman, what many of those in the tanker C-130 with the seriously wounded remember most is the peculiar, sweet, cloying smell of burned flesh.

At Masirah, as the wounded lay under the wing of an aircraft, some headquarters colonels from Washington began to take snapshots of them and were almost physically assaulted by several men from Delta Force.

One is reminded of Harry Hotspur's description of a staff officer:

> . . . he made me mad
> To see him shine so brisk and smell so sweet
> And talk so like a waiting-gentlewoman
> Of guns and drums and wounds,—God save the mark!—
> And telling me . . .
> . . . but for these vile guns,
> He would himself have been a soldier.

Back in Washington, the Marines rushed out a report, which they leaked to the press, highly critical of the Air Force and Army planning for the operation. This further fed the fires of inter-service warfare. The Air Force responded with the information that the marines had abandoned their helicopters without even turning off their engines, let alone destroying the aircraft, and that top secret papers, which the Marine pilots should not have been carrying, had fallen into Iranian hands as a result. Not willing to admit to failure, the military spent millions devising impossible plans to go back into Iran and rescue the hostages, even though by then the hostages had been moved and no one was certain where they were.

Cyrus R. Vance, President Carter's Secretary of State, who had been against the mission from the beginning, resigned, and the President's popularity continued the downward slide that was to end with Ronald Reagan in the White House. American prestige, already shaky as a result of the lost war in Vietnam, took another blow. Americans and their friends and enemies alike asked themselves, after Vietnam and now Iran, How reliable and powerful is the United States? What kind of armed forces did we have? Thirty-five years before, having along with our allies defeated the Germans and the Japanese, we were the most powerful nation in the world. How had it happened that without a shot being fired, we had failed to rescue our hostages from a disintegrating tenth-rate power?

The Pentagon answered such disturbing questions by handing out medals to many of the participants and then discouraging them from talking to the press. An official board of inquiry, called the Holloway Board after its chairman, retired admiral J. L. Holloway III, was convened to look into the disaster. In its public report the board gently chided the military for certain failures. The classified report was more specific but still soft in tone. In particular, when it came to criticizing the organization at the top of the Pentagon, both the civilian bureaucracy and the committee-ridden Joint Chiefs and their Joint Staff, the report walked with cats' feet—and a quiet, polite cat from the same club, at that. As for reforms, a new antiterrorist unit that had its own long-range helicopters was later created. Other systemic problems were either denied or treated by hand-wringing or hope.

The Beirut disaster followed in 1983, with 241 marines unnecessarily dying when the building in which they were asleep was successfully demolished by a truck bomb. Next, during the U.S. invasion of Grenada in 1983, American forces in the north commanded by a Marine colonel could not communicate with those in the south commanded by an Army general. An Army officer had to call the Pentagon on his credit card to try to talk to the Navy offshore. Army helicopters ferrying wounded to a ship offshore for treatment were forbidden to land on the ship because the pilots had not trained in Navy techniques. Men died unnecessarily again. Obviously there are serious problems inside the American military. What are they?*

When one looks hard at American defense, six basic themes appear and reappear. Sometimes these six are separate, sometimes they weave together. All of them helped create the disaster at Desert One. All of them will be present at our next defeat. I have named these key factors: the Great Divorce, Interservice/ Intraservice Rivalry, Flawed Organization, Readiness, Overcontrol, and finally, Keeping the Able From Contributing to the Action, or KAFCA.

The first recurring theme is what I term the Great Divorce. The Great Divorce is the less-than-amicable separation of the military from the financial, business, political, and intellectual elites of this country, particularly from the last two. Important sections of America regard those who serve in today's armed forces as at best unwanted stepchildren, at worst stepchildren not only unwanted but inclined to be vicious. Indeed, the gulf between the armed services and the rest of society appears so vast that the armed forces are close to becoming an "Other America," the "Other America of Defense."

This has two results. The first and most obvious is that since our armed forces recruit mostly from a limited economic and social cross section of society, the able people inside them are often perilously thin on the ground. The second, equally important but less obvious, is that those civilians in positions of power inside the government and outside tend to lack hands-on experience of the armed services. These leaders fail to identify the problems correctly, and their solutions to what they perceive as the problems often worsen the actual situation in the field.

With firsthand knowledge of the armed services, key civilians would have known that the Marine Corps was not the service to supply the helicopter pilots. Marine helicopter pilots specialize in short-range, preplanned flights, such as ferrying supplies from

---

* The successful diversion of the Egyptian plane carrying the shipjackers of the *Achille Lauro* to Sicily involved only one service, the Navy. Further, the mission was a traditional one, sea control.

ship to shore or flying the President to Camp David from the White House. The Marines give priority to fielding stand-up, gravel-crunching infantry who will charge straight ahead through a brick wall under intense fire. For helicopter pilots you look to either the Army or the Air Force. As a result of Vietnam, both these services have a great deal of experience in carrying people great distances to tiny clearings inside hostile places. (I stood in one such clearing in a part of Vietnam where we assured the world and our citizens that we had no one. A lieutenant colonel was decorating some of his men. As he lined them up he said, "It is my great pleasure to give you these medals, which, since we are not here, you cannot possibly have earned.")

There were 143 such Air Force chopper pilots, many of whom had been in and out of such places, and all of whom had been flying and training for years for just such a mission as the Iranian rescue. They were not considered when fliers for the mission were chosen. The reason given afterward was that the secrecy of the mission would have been compromised if Air Force pilots had appeared on board the carrier in the Indian Ocean. Even the mild Holloway Report criticized that "reasoning." Experienced and respected civilian leaders would have understood exactly why the marines had been picked and been able to take the next step.

The second recurring fault inside our armed services comes like Leda's sons, Castor and Pollux, as a pair of mighty twins. The first twin, Interservice Rivalry, is well known. But the second, Intraservice Rivalry, though referred to less, does almost as much damage. Interservice Rivalry dictated that either Marine or Navy helicopter pilots would be selected for the Iranian mission because the planes were to fly from Navy carriers. Admirals believe their control over naval aviation would be jeopardized if Army or Air Force pilots were permitted to fly off carriers—or any other ship. Next, Interservice Rivalry created the conditions whereby the Army Delta Force and the marines lived far apart in the desert training area, enjoyed different privileges, and in a short time grew to distrust each other.

That there were too few helicopters able to refuel in the air was caused in large part by Intraservice Rivalry. Dominant parts of all three services did not consider hostage rescue operations important enough to fund such helicopters in the lean years following Vietnam. Congress and the Executive had wished such antiterrorist operations to have priority; but the services spent their funds on areas they considered more important. Inside the Army, Delta Force had great trouble recruiting necessary specialists from other parts of that service because special operations were not and still are not considered a priority by many senior Army generals.

Unfortunately, Interservice/Intraservice Rivalry is an area where the armed services often march backward at the very moment when the arrival of new weapons increases the need for all forms of cooperation. For example, until ten years ago, officers who graduated from the three service academies could choose the service in which they wished to serve. They no longer can. An officer who graduates from West Point and wants to serve in submarines has no recourse, nor does an Air Force Academy graduate who would like to lead combat troops.

The next theme, Flawed Organization, is seldom understood and, being deemed bureaucratic and dull, is often dismissed as unimportant. But the dull ax is the one most apt to glance off the log and remove your foot. Flawed Organization is particularly damaging at the apex of the Defense Department: the Joint Chiefs of Staff, the Joint Staff, and the multitiered office of the Secretary of Defense. Few realize that the four-starred Chairman of the Joint Chiefs, the country's senior military figure, for all his prestige, has little actual power. He has no deputy. He does not command a single man, not even his driver. He cannot promote those officers on the Joint Staff who serve him well. Their promotions come from their service home.

By law the Joint Chiefs of Staff themselves cannot act unless all three members (four, if the Marines are involved) are in agreement. As a result, our defenses are managed by a series of committees whose membership, by law, constantly changes. Logrolling, political trades, papered-over disagreements, and lobbying are the constants. When reports from the Arizona desert training area apprised the Joint Staff that the mission was in jeopardy, no one had the authority to act. When flawed plans to free the hostages were advanced, plans that favored a particular career or service, these could not simply be turned down by the Chairman or someone selected as mission commander. There was no such commander. Each plan had to be studied by the staff and discussed until it died a slow bureaucratic death and could be buried in the files. So genuine problems, like that of the helicopters, never got full attention.

After the Falklands war had been won by the British, Michael Heseltine, the British Secretary of Defense, visited Washington. A year before the Falklands, the British had changed their Joint Chiefs organization from one like America's to one in which the Chairman had more actual command. "You know," said Heseltine, "we never could have won with our old organization." In the Iranian mission the Flawed Organization we still have did its damaging work.

The fourth recurring theme that weakens American defenses goes under several names: Readiness, Tooth-to-Tail, Supply versus Combat. The basic question here can be thought of as one of balance: How does a commander, from the President through the Secretary of Defense and the Joint Chiefs on down to the lowest lieutenant and noncommissioned officer, divide up the money and time available to produce the most efficient fighting force? America's armed forces are constantly criticized for being out of balance: having too much tail (supporting, rear-area forces) and too few teeth (combat forces). But in the complex military world, judging what is tooth and what tail becomes difficult. While stored on the carrier, the rescue helicopters were accidentally sprayed with seawater the day before the mission. In flight, three of them developed mechanical problems. This reflects on the quality of the mechanics aboard the aircraft carrier. Were those mechanics and the money for their training part of the tooth or the tail?

Other armed forces judge the division between tooth and tail differently. The Israelis issue their tank brigades powerful mobile showers to clean the battle grime off tanks, and spray cans full of an aerosol that takes the stench of the burned flesh and lacerated bowels out of hit tanks. The Israelis find that soldiers repair battle-damaged tanks slowly and fight in them inefficiently if the tanks smell of gore and have dirt and filth caked on them. The American Congress has not authorized the buying of such supplies, preferring to spend money on more tanks, guns, and ammunition. Generals don't want to challenge Congress on this one because they know they will be whipsawed on the Readiness/Tooth-to-Tail argument. "Showers for the tanks, general, ha, ha, ha. And are you going to have aftershave lotion for the drivers, too, ha, ha, ha." But if the showers and deodorant spray cans mean that the Israelis can return battle-damaged tanks to combat in three-quarters of the time it takes U.S. forces, are such items really tail or as much tooth as the ammunition? Which force is the more ready force?

Readiness is how prepared to fight a unit is at a given moment. Readiness judgments are difficult to make because military units don't know the date of their World Series or Super Bowl. If they spend today getting totally prepared for the day after tomorrow, today's readiness suffers. If they are 100 percent ready today, like an overtrained athlete they are going to be off peak for performance next week. Readiness is profoundly affected by the Great Divorce. If those entering the armed services are below average in intelligence, more time and money must be spent to make them ready. At the same time the hard and sometimes risky training necessary to make a unit ready may be forbidden by public attitudes toward the military.

For example, in 1952 Lieutenant Colonel Creighton Abrams, later Commander in Chief in Vietnam and still later Chief of Staff of the Army, trained his tank battalion in Europe by having his tankers fire live machine-gun ammunition at one another. He painted the tips of the bullets yellow, so all could learn which tanks were taking hits. During the Vietnam War it is doubtful that such hard training to make soldiers truly ready for combat would have been permitted by the public and Congress. After-action reports on the Iranian disaster stressed that some of the forces did not appear mentally ready for the mission. In Beirut, the Marine sentries around the building where 241 marines were killed by a truck bomb stood guard with unloaded weapons. Their commanders felt they were not well enough trained to handle loaded weapons. If the Navy had spent less money restoring battleships and more on training marines, would the United States have been more or less ready for Lebanon? Would the Straw Giant have been stronger overall or weaker? Some of the most harrowing decisions that must be made inside the armed forces deal with Readiness/Tooth-to-Tail problems.

Overcontrol, or the "Russification of the American Armed Forces," is the fifth constant problem. With modern electronic communications, senior commanders from the President on down can talk to anyone they wish. And they can get any set of facts they wish from the humblest lieutenant at the bottom of the defense totem pole. Soon they may even be able to get a TV picture of the lieutenant's battle. But when does this help and when does it hurt America's might? Marshal Foch, French hero of the First World War, pronounced a much-quoted dictum: "Don't telephone. Go see." Yet in American military actions, real and simulated, the air is jammed with electronic chatter as those at the top try to keep control over the tiniest details. In the Iranian action, those waiting at Desert One for the helicopters could and did communicate with the White House; but they could not explain the weather to the oncoming helicopters or talk to the Rangers guarding the desert airstrip.

In Vietnam, Overcontrol led to disasters large and small. On the last day of the American involvement there, the White House was requesting the tail numbers of the helicopters being used to lift the Americans off the embassy roof in Saigon. Mired in such gnat-sized details, those at the command summit had lost control over the strategic direction of American policy, while those at the bottom were robbed of initiative and lost flexibility and confidence in themselves.

The final theme present in the Iranian desert and throughout the armed forces today is KAFCA, pronounced Kafka (since this is a military book I have made up an acronym). KAFCA is Keeping the Able From Contributing to the Action. Inside the armed services this problem is more politely referred to as "personnel mismanagement." In part, KAFCA is an outgrowth of the Intraservice part of Interservice/Intraservice Rivalry; but it is destructive enough to merit consideration on its own.

The armed services not only fund first those missions that they consider most vital to their self-interest, they also place their ablest people in those missions. Other tasks get second and even third call on able people. Areas that those in command deem less important, such as buying weapons, or military intelligence, or training foreign troops, or, for the Navy, service on joint staffs, become pastures for the marginally competent. KAFCA was present at the selection of the helicopter pilots and contributed to the difficulty the CIA and the armed services had in finding people with the necessary information about Iran.

In 1971 I was standing in a line of Iranians who were winding their way into a second-floor cafeteria in Isfahan, central Iran. As I inched upstairs, waiting my turn for some lamb and yogurt, a voice asked if I was an American. I said yes. Behind me in line, dressed in civilian clothes, were two Iranian Air Force pilots who had learned English during jet training at an Air Force base in Texas. We had dinner together, and I asked them if they had made many friends in the States. A few, they said, but mostly they were left on their own. One told this story: In his second week in training, before he knew much English, the Air Force colonel who commanded the base came up to him, held out his hand, and said with a smile, "Howdie."

"No," replied the Iranian pilot, "I'm Omar. Haudi is in the class ahead of me."

"I can't understand a damn thing you foreigners say," said the colonel and walked off.

Contrast this with the practice of the British Army, where each foreign officer going through British military schools is assigned a fellow British student whose duty it is to make friends with that foreign officer, make sure he meets people and sees the country. There's even an allowance for whisky. And as part of his school performance, the British officer is graded on his ability to make the foreigner feel welcome.

Such are the six damaging strands, some heavier than others, that weave and have woven through the pattern of our defenses. Starting in colonial times, America's military history is a more complex and intriguing subject than is generally realized. However, there is no need to begin this examination of the Giant's posture that far back. By and large, America's recent military triumphs and failures have their roots in the armed services of the depression years, just prior to World War II.

TWO

Getting
to the Beginning

The present Defense Department was created in 1947, at the close of World War II, out of the myths, pressures, and victories of that war. Those who created and led America's triumphant armed forces formed their basic beliefs and attitudes in the years of peace immediately prior to the war. Those beliefs and attitudes changed little during the course of combat. Indeed, if anything, with victory they hardened into the reinforced concrete of complete conviction. An understanding of the Defense Department and the present state of our armed forces begins in these prewar years.

The Navy and the Army of the late depression years were of minuscule size. There was no Air Force; that service-to-be was then part of the Army, called the Army Air Corps, and had received equality with the Army's other combat arms only in 1926. Five years before Pearl Harbor you could have put the officers of the armed forces of the United States inside the present John F. Kennedy Stadium in Philadelphia for the Army-Navy game and still sold tickets to the general public. The military budget in 1985 dollars was $6.4 billion, compared with $306 billion today.

Those few men then in the armed services lived inside a world of their own. The United States was far more rural and the average military post more isolated physically from the rest of society. The Great Divorce raged bitterly, with the United States in an anti-military period.

The fluctuations of the United States' attitudes toward its military constitute interesting social history. At first, the colonists looked to the British standing armies for protection from Indians, Spanish, and French. Then a series of ill-fated campaigns in which both American militiamen and British regulars took part, such as Cartagena in 1740, caused the colonists to distrust the regulars. Remembering the successes of their local militia forces in a battle such as Louisbourg, while forgetting failures like Phips's Quebec campaign, Americans came to believe militia forces alone sufficient for colonial defense. Before and during the Revolution British regular forces abused the power they held. A grave distrust of regular military forces, both Army and Navy, developed in early America. "We conceive," said the Albany City Council, "that his Majesties Paternal Cares to Release us [from fears of French and Indians] have in Great Measure been Made use of to oppress us."

Many framers of the Constitution held eighteenth-century beliefs on the perfectability of man and so were philosophically opposed to military force. Thomas Jefferson himself was anti the professional military and was against the formation of the Revolutionary officer veterans' organization, the Society of the Cincinnati. One of Jefferson's followers, Elbridge Gerry of Massachusetts, had tried at the Continental Congress to limit the regular Army to 300 men. This move was defeated only by Washington's rare, personal intervention.

The breach between the civilian elites and the military began to narrow during the war of 1812. With the exception of Andrew Jackson's triumph at the battle of New Orleans, that war was a disaster for the United States. The British regular forces were victorious everywhere over the American militia units. It became obvious that for national security America needed professional armed forces of her own, so she began to build up a professional navy and army.

From then on through the Civil War the military were fairly well integrated into society, and military service was considered a prestigious profession, particularly in the South and West. For example, all those in Andrew Jackson's cabinet who had been in the armed services used their military rank as titles, as did General Jackson himself. The military remained an honored and valued branch of society for a time after the Civil War. In those years, being a veteran was almost the sine qua non of a successful political career, though the South continually voted against military appropriations. In part this was Southern distaste for voting funds for an army that had recently defeated them. In part, it was because the monies paid for Yankee soldiers still stationed on southern territory. Then, as the West was settled, the Indians were vanquished, and society was industrialized, the gap between the armed forces and other parts of America opened up again.

By the time of the Spanish-American War the military had become a derided profession. The performance of the regular army in Cuba was poor. General William Shafter, fat and gout-ridden, lay in his hammock, oblivious to the hardship of his troops. The Spanish often had better weapons than the Americans. From Cuba Theodore Roosevelt, the future president, sent home stinging criticisms of the professional officers, the supply system, and the corruption within the services. Though America was victorious in World Wars I and II, and some of the military leaders of those wars, such as Generals Pershing and Eisenhower, were immensely popular, the military continued to remain divided from much of national life. By the end of the Korean War, when America was far less united than portrayed in historic legend, the gap had widened further. Since the Vietnam War this split has enlarged to almost become Milton's "gulf profound . . . where armies whole have sunk."

In my time in Vietnam I found only four junior officers from prestigious East Coast or West Coast universities. The Massachusetts Institute of Technology went through the entire Vietnam War reportedly without sustaining a single fatality among its graduates. Just before joining the 1983 NATO fall maneuvers I spent a week with the British Officer Selection Board. Applying to the board in that one week were an Oxford blue and an honor student in languages from Bristol. In America, such men are extremely unlikely to elect the armed services today.

How many times have I been asked recently by otherwise thoughtful and intelligent officers; "Do you think it is possible to graduate from Harvard today and still be a patriot?"

On the other side a friend, a widely respected writer and professor whose views often grace editorial pages, asked me, "How is your eldest son doing?" I replied that he was doing just fine, that he had remained in the service and was an astronaut candidate. "Isn't that the son who did so well at college and went to medical school?" the professor asked. "Yes," I replied. "He must be a great disappointment to you," my friend said. For an instant, I thought he was joking.

While the gap between the civilian elites and the military was not as wide before World War II as it is today, it was nevertheless huge. In the thirties the Nye Committee of the Senate had castigated international financiers, munitions makers, and generals for unnecessarily leading the United States into World War I. Walter Millis's *Road to War*, which in 1935 argued the same thesis, became, in Frederick L. Allen's words, "an influential best seller among highbrows." Harry Hopkins, one of Roosevelt's closest advisors, was a pacifist. Influential educators, such as Professor Charles Beard and Robert M. Hutchins, president of the University of Chicago, were isolationist and antimilitary. With Hitler and Stalin then allied in the Nazi-Soviet Non-Aggression Pact, the American Communist Party and its many fronts had ably organized to keep America neutral. "The only way to fight war is to begin by fighting the warmongers in our own land," Party leader Earl Browder stated in 1936.

In 1937 the Gallup poll found that 71 percent of Americans thought it had been a mistake for the United States to enter World War I. As war approached closer, the America First Committee, of which the American hero Charles A. Lindbergh and Senator Gerald P. Nye were prominent members and which was supported by many clergymen, particularly in the Midwest, and the Hearst and Patterson/McCormick newspapers, inveighed against career officers as warmongers who wanted to gain glory by sending American boys overseas to die. This committee drew additional strength from the many professors among its members from such prestigious institutions as Yale and Harvard.

The military distrusted the scholars, intellectuals, and politicians right back. The average service officer saw in the intellectual elite the reasons for his country's unpreparedness, both in the present and before World War I. He resented the way these groups had tried to depict him and the munitions makers as conspiring to promote World War I. Inside the Navy there was an additional reason for distrust. Many naval officers felt that disarmament efforts had left them with dangerous, undergunned ships. These were the "treaty cruisers" built in the late twenties to limitations imposed by the 1922 Washington naval conference. They lacked the proper size antiaircraft and main guns and were not completely watertight because internal bulkheads and armaments had been reduced to save weight.

General George C. Marshall, who led the wartime Army, General Henry H. ("Hap") Arnold, who led the Army Air Corps, Admiral Ernest J. King, who led the Navy, and their brother officers grew up in this isolated, budget-starved atmosphere, which produced in many of these men that fierce family/service loyalty usually bred by poverty and exclusion. Practically to a man the leaders of all three services—for the Army Air Corps was by the close of the war separate and powerful enough to be called a service—ended the war convinced that peace would have come sooner at less cost if they had received the lion's share of men and funds and been allowed to fight their war their way.

Interservice/Intraservice Rivalry was destructively present in those lean years. Admiral King, a man so competitive he became petulant when he lost to his children at Monopoly, had spent his life battling his aviators and the Bureau of Naval Personnel, which he felt was filled with "fixers." One of King's many adversaries, Admiral John H. Towers, Chief of the Bureau of Naval Aviation, is described by contemporaries as being "almost paranoid," seeing most of his fellow naval officers as out to get him and to scupper naval aviation. Towers wanted only those who had been with naval aviation from the "beginning" to command carriers.

This battle continued into World War II, when naval aviators even regarded as enemy those pilots who had learned to fly late in life. One of their presumed foes was Admiral Raymond A. Spruance, victor at Midway and by all odds the ablest carrier task force commander of the war. The "real" aviators, led by Admiral John S. McCain, claimed Spruance had downgraded carriers to a supporting arm of the Marines. Undeterred by problems of logistics or Japanese shore-based aircraft, they wanted to go haring into Japanese home waters on Light Brigade–like charges. This internecine naval warfare—known as the brown-shoe, black-shoe battle because aviators wore brown shoes, surface sailors black—

dominated ship procurement, officer assignments, and promotions before, during, and after the war.

Today, the Navy is the most seriously divided service. A new faction, or union, as the warring parties are known inside the Navy, the submariners, has joined the battle. Submariners belong to the "felt shoe" union because they wear felt shoes to cut down on noise. The portion of our nuclear deterrent that is carried by submarines now goes underfunded because the dominant carrier admirals divert to surface ships money Congress has authorized for submarine programs. Shortly after the war the Navy tried unsuccessfully to retire then Captain Hyman Rickover, one of that service's most brilliant officers, and the dominant force behind the nuclear submarine program.

Before World War II submariners were too low in the naval hierarchy to count. The Navy back then was the most anti-Semitic of the three services (there is no way to put a good face on this), and submarines were sometimes referred to as the "Jewish service" and were often used as dumping grounds for marginal officers. When war came, serious failures of both men and equipment followed. The Mark XIV torpedo usually ran beneath its target, and when it did hit the target, it failed to explode. Many submarine captains fought their battles in a timid and conservative fashion. During the war's first year more than a third of them were relieved. Meanwhile, inside the prewar Navy, the Marine Corps, frustrated and forgotten, could not even get amphibious tactics taught at the Naval War College.

In terms of America's military future, the most destructive prewar intraservice rivalry was that inside the old Army Air Corps between the bomber pilots and the fighter pilots. Already in the thirties, bomber pilots dominated the world's three major air forces: the RAF in Britain, the Luftwaffe in Germany, and the Army Air Corps of the United States. In 1937, the Office of the Chief of the Army Air Corps adopted as its slogan: "Fighters are obsolete." The reason for the bomber generals triumph was bureaucratic. The fighter is largely a defensive weapon and closely wedded to the ground battle. The bomber is independent and offensive. If fighter pilots were to be dominant, the need for a separate air force would be diminished. Men who see a diminishing future for themselves, or can be tagged as seeing one, tend to lose organizational battles.

The bomber became the future, particularly for the Luftwaffe and the U.S. Army Air Corps. In Britain, though the bomber pilots were dominant, British traditions of defending their island caused that nation to pay more attention to fighter development and doctrine. The results of the differing German, American, and British perceptions of air power were predictable. The Germans and the Americans neglected the development of radar, fighters, and antiaircraft. The British did not. In the mid-thirties they pushed the development of radar and of fast, single-wing, multi-gunned fighters. Indeed, in 1937 the British government gave priority to fighter production over bombers, though the bomber generals fought the decision all the way. Air Marshal Hugh M. Trenchard said it "might well lose us the war." Three years later, the Spitfire fighters and radar nets ordered in the mid-thirties won the Battle of Britain.

Fighters had beaten bombers. British purchasing decisions, as well as their tactics and extraordinary courage, had changed the course of history. Perhaps in the whole world, only the U.S. Army Air Corps leaders failed to understand the lesson of the Battle of Britain: that bombers alone could not survive in sufficient numbers to be effective. Finally, one clear afternoon over Schweinfurt in 1943 the American Air Corps lost sixty Flying Fortresses and their crews in three hours. Then by the light of burning pilots, martyrs to the cause of blind belief, strong, rigid men began a partial reexamination of their fixed ideas. They yelled for long-range fighters, P-51s, as escorts for the bombers. After the war they forgot that lesson. Generals are as prone to selective memory as any other adults.

This bitter Air Force battle for dollars, doctrine, people, and promotions continues, now waged between TAC (the Tactical Air Command, the fighter pilots) and SAC (the Strategic Air Command, the bomber pilots). This warfare has been so desperate and the domination of the bomber pilots so complete that until General Charles A. Gabriel became Chief of the Air Staff in 1982, a fighter pilot had never commanded the Air Force. When you consider that the dominant Air Force image is that of a lonely fighter pilot patrolling the skies, the intensity of this internecine bloodletting becomes apparent. A number of excellent men had their ideas scorned and were kept from high command because they were on the wrong (fighter) side (Generals Chennault, Quesada, Griswold, Saville, to single out a few). The country as a whole still pays for the loss of such talent and the domination of doctrine, procurement, and promotions by the "bomber mafia."

While it was fighting within itself, the Army Air Corps was also fighting for both its ideas and organization within the Army. Take the case of Captain Laurence S. Kuter, who as General Kuter in 1947 became one of the chief architects of the present military organization. Kuter, dark, driving, and driven, had graduated forty-fourth out of 203 at West Point in 1927. He found his love after transferring from the Artillery to the Air Corps. He graduated first out of 60 from the Air Corps Tactical School at Maxwell Air Force Base, and though only a lieutenant (the rest of his class were captains and majors), he was asked to remain as an instructor.

Kuter, now in his element and full of ideas, found himself unable to publish his thoughts on the future of air power in any of the Army journals, which were dominated by ground-bound conservatives. General Perry McCoy Smith, in his brilliant book *The Air Force Plans for Peace*, details the ways in which the Coast Artillery, a branch without a mission, was particularly hostile to Kuter. The Coast Artillery wished to take over antiaircraft artillery to give their branch a fresh reason for existence, so they killed articles by Kuter on the employment and potential of bombers. As a result Kuter's formative years were spent battling conservative ground commanders over his ideas. He never forgot this. When in 1943 General Arnold entrusted him with future planning for the postwar separate Air Force, Kuter failed to see that during the war the Army attitude had changed, and that the Army staff had supported many of his plans. Personal proof of the new atmosphere was before his eyes every time he pulled his uniform from the closet and looked at his epaulets. Marshall, who admired his drive if not always his judgment, had selected him as chief Air Corps planner and by 1942 had made him the youngest general in the Army, double-jumping him from lieutenant colonel to brigadier general.

Locked in his previous beliefs, General Kuter positioned the postwar Air Corps for battle against the Army over the shape of the postwar Defense Department. He and his staff believed, wrongly as it would turn out, that the naval aviators, and therefore the Navy, would support a separate Air Force and a strong Defense Department. Within that new department aviators, Air

Force and Navy, working together, would control future budgets and through these the department itself. When at war's end the Navy fought against defense unification, while the Army gave the Air Force support, the Air Staff's arguments and political alliances were all in the wrong places.

The Army too was fighting intraservice battles that would affect American postwar policy. Infantry and armored (tank) officers were battling each other over the development and employment of tanks, with the cavalrymen, a third and less powerful group, now on one side, now on the other. The cavalry and the armored officers lost practically all the battles to the dominant infantry officers. The Tank Corps had been abolished at the end of World War I, and the few remaining tanks were given to the infantry. The infantry officers, who saw the main mission of the tanks as supporting infantry, kept the tanks small, lightly armored, and equipped only with machine guns. The Ordnance Department of the Army tried several times to put bigger guns on tanks, as the Russians, Germans, and British were doing, but the infantry kept on saying no.

Brigadier General Adna R. Chaffee finally got an Experimental Mechanized Force organized in 1929; but General Douglas MacArthur, a World War I infantryman, killed that project in 1931, when he was Chief of Staff. MacArthur turned the mechanized force—men and vehicles—over to the cavalry, who wanted only light tanks for reconnaissance. MacArthur's bureaucratic ploy was all the more destructive because by law only the infantry could have tanks, the cavalry being restricted to "combat cars." The tankers got around this simply by calling those tanklike things with tracks going clank-clank over the fields "combat cars." But as an Army poor relation, American tanks remained few, small, and undergunned. In 1940 the U.S. army had 464 tanks in all, armed mostly with machine guns. The Germans had over 5,000, armed mostly with 75-mm cannon.

When in 1940 the American army finally began to build a tank with a 75-mm gun, they put that gun down on the side where it was too low to shoot effectively, and set a much smaller, obsolete 37-mm gun way up on top of the tank in a sort of gazebo. This tank had been designed in 1938, with World War II less than a year away, by a committee that had concluded that since another Philippine revolt was possible (the last one had ended in 1905), a primary requirement of any new American tank must be the ability to shoot over ripe sugarcane. These two-story monsters with the 75-mm gun stuck on the side were called General Grants (the tank must have been so named by a Southerner).

The Army finally came to its senses and in 1940 designed another tank, the adequate—it cannot be rated higher than that—General Sherman. The Grants were palmed off on the British to replace the catastrophic British tank losses inflicted in the desert by Rommel's Afrika Korps. "The British Eighth Army welcomed the Grant as a godsend," writes a respected historian. Well, yes and no. The high silhouette of the Grant, with the ineffective 37-mm at the top, meant that the Germans could hit them with their bigger guns before the Grant could get its side-slung 75 into play. "Brewing up in a Grant" became a British euphemism for burning to death in one.

Keith Douglas (probably the finest poet of the war) described desert fighting in a Grant: "The 75 is firing. The 37 is firing, but it is traversed round the wrong way. The Browning [machine gun] is jammed. I am saying: 'Driver, advance on the A set, and the driver, who can't hear me, is reversing. And as I look over the top of the turret and see twelve enemy tanks 50 yards away, someone hands me a cheese sandwich." It all seems funny to read now. But Douglas and other young men are dead. And after the war, at the time of the creation of the Defense Department, armor and infantry officers would be devoting still more of their time to battling each other and too little to overall policies of defense.

Today electronic warfare specialists, though much talked about, are not in favor. In a maneuver in Texas in 1978, the 1st Cavalry Division had to be loaned electronic equipment from three other U.S. divisions and one U.S. corps to begin to have adequate electronic equipment to imitate a Soviet division. Yet the United States is the country where the electronic revolution began. Similarly, prior to World War II, America, the country where the automotive revolution began, had but a few inadequate tanks.

Fortunately for the country, as war approached the Army Chief of Staff, General George C. Marshall, had the stature to remain above both service rivalries and the distrust of intellectuals. He established at Army headquarters in Washington his Advance Planning Group, a collection of military Rhodes scholars and instructors from the Department of Government, Economics, and History at West Point. Unfortunately, the Army Air Corps Long-Range Planning Group contained no such collection of scholars and indeed showed an anti-intellectual bias. The Navy felt no need for an advanced planning group at all.

Prewar America provided one plus to offset its military problems. The old saw " 'Tis an ill wind that blows nobody any good" was at work when the frigid blasts of the Great Depression drove into the Army and Navy a group of officers of marked ability. Some of these men were there because they wanted a free education and needed every penny of the slim cadet allowance. Others saw their military education as the route to a secure job. "Things were rough, I'll tell you, in Madison County as I grew up," said Andrew Goodpaster, a captain at the start of World War II, who was finally to rise to full general by 1969 and become NATO commander.

Other able men had entered the military during World War I— when, unlike the situation during World War II, Korea, and more especially Vietnam, the draft was reasonably fair and equitable. After the war these men found they liked military life and decided to stay in for a while. About the time their second six-year hitch was up, the depression made the services seem an attractive place to stay. The same thing happened, though to a lesser degree, in 1979, when the caliber of those in the services went up during the recession of 1978–1983.

The best of these men had not only intellectual ability and physical courage but moral courage also. Again, take the example of Captain Kuter (General Kuter by the middle of World War II, and a passionate believer, as we have seen, not just in air power but particularly in the bomber). In the summer of 1943 Kuter's superior, General Henry H. Arnold, commander of the Army Air Corps, asked him to have the Air Staff change its estimated figures of German aircraft production, which showed an increase in production in spite of the American bombing campaign against Germany. (After the war these figures turned out to be correct.) Even though the staff figures cast doubt on Kuter's own theories about the supreme dominance of the bomber, he wrote Arnold:

> The paper in question is staff advice to the Commanders. I cannot subscribe to putting in that paper any advice that cannot be supported. Consequently, this particular paper will not be rewritten in the manner in which you expect.
>
> It is very clearly the prerogative of the commander to throw the advice away and place any figure he may choose in a command paper.

America's defeat at the hands of the Japanese at Pearl Harbor forced on the armed services some measure of cooperation and opened the ladder of rapid promotion for many of the able. Before we examine some of the bureaucratic battles inside the strange organization with which Washington fought World War II, the intelligence failure at Pearl Harbor deserves brief attention because American failures in this area still occur with alarming frequency.

A constant, little-understood obstacle to effective military intelligence is known in service argot as the Green Door problem. An item of intelligence is often considered so secret that it can be known only to insiders. That knowledge may save your life; but it is hidden from you behind a magic Green Door. Since the possession of secrets enhances the power of those who know them, intelligence information is often unnecessarily restricted for reasons of bureaucratic prestige rather than national security. Air Force General John Ralph, now retired, once complained succinctly, "I'm going to be dying over Germany while some dumb s.o.b. worried about his parking slot at the Pentagon decides which satellite pictures I need."

Deciding who should know what secret information poses an extremely difficult question of degree. There are secrets, such as the fact that we and the British had broken the German and Japanese codes (the Ultra or Enigma secret), that have to be highly protected. Vice President Harry Truman learned of the atomic bomb only on becoming President. Some intelligence, to be valuable, must be shared with one's allies; and allies are suspicious of one another's ability to keep secrets. The British feel we let our politicians in Congress know too much. We feel the British were lax in not discovering sooner that Philby, Burgess, Maclean, and Blount were Soviet agents.

The classic example of the Green Door problem was the sinking of the cruiser *Indianapolis* at 12:05 A.M. on 30 July 1945. Eight hundred and eighty officers and men were lost out of a crew of 1,196, the greatest loss of life of any naval ship in our history. The *Indianapolis* was sunk by a Japanese submarine while en route to the Philippines from Tinian Island, where she had delivered the atomic bomb later dropped by the *Enola Gay*. Naval intelligence knew that there were four Japanese submarines along her route but had neither changed the ship's course nor told her captain of the danger. The information about the submarines came from code-breaking and was therefore highly classified. The *Indianapolis*'s captain and the shore-based officer who could have altered her course were not cleared for such information. As a result, the ship was not even zigzagging as she steamed into the danger zone. Then, in an ironic reverse twist on the Green Door problem, Rear Admiral Lynde D. McCormick, the commander of Task Group 95.7, to which the *Indianapolis* was to report, never learned she was coming, and therefore had no way of knowing the cruiser was overdue and probably sunk. The message about the *Indianapolis*'s date of arrival was only marked restricted, the next to lowest form of military classification. Admiral McCormick's message center was so busy decoding secret and top secret messages, most of them of lesser importance, that they never got around to reading the merely restricted transmission.

The Green Door problem continues. In Vietnam, Air Force colonels assigning targets for the fighter bombers could not learn whether or not the targets they assigned had been successfully hit. The information on target destruction came from satellites, and the target assigners were not cleared for that information. Lieutenant General Frederick C. Weyand, the commander of the U.S. forces around Saigon, could not fully persuade his colleagues about the date and focus of the 1968 Tet offensive. Weyand, an experienced intelligence officer, had figured out the details of TET through his own private back-door channels into signal intelligence. But he could not make his knowledge understood; and he was one of the most senior commanders in Vietnam. General William Westmoreland, the Commander in Chief in Vietnam, had spent so much of his military career outside the Green Door that he had no experience in interpreting signal intelligence's often complex indications.

In the basement of NATO's headquarters near Mons, Belgium, is a walled-off section where U.S. officers sit pondering intelligence they cannot share with their allies. The walls are to come down in wartime. Granted, there is always highly secret intelligence that must be closely held. Still one must question whether more damage is not being done by excessive secrecy than by too full disclosure.

Besides the Green Door problem, there exists a social attitude, both inside and outside the armed forces, that restricts American intelligence. This is the belief that America is somehow better than the rest of the world. We often scold other nations and act as if we were the world's nanny, too wise and good to do dirty things like spy on people. When he was Secretary of State in the thirties, Colonel Henry S. Stimson, later Secretary of War during World War II, abolished the code-cracking section of the State Department with his famous phrase that gentlemen did not read other people's mail.

This belief in American goodness goes hand in hand with the idea of warfare as a game. If warfare is a sport, then it follows that to win we should fight square and not hit below the belt by performing such unseemly acts as stealing the other fellow's signals. To use intelligence is somehow to cheat, to take unfair advantage. The armed services have tended not to assign able people to intelligence; and recently Congress has certainly underfunded and probably overrestricted the CIA.

Paul Fussell has perceptively noted an extreme extension of this principle of American perfection. This is the proposition one occasionally hears that America was "wrong" to use atomic bombs against Japan, that it would have been better to allow thousands on thousands of American and Japanese infantrymen to die in honest hand-to-hand combat on the beaches than to drop those two bombs. Such views are also products of the Great Divorce. Those holding them do not come from the ranks of society that produce infantrymen or pilots. The belief that good governments should not practice intelligence is like the belief that good Victorians shouldn't perform sex. The consequences of such unnatural behavior lead to unfortunate lapses. America was surprised by the seizure of the U.S. embassy in Teheran, though the planned attack had been the talk of the bazaars for several weeks.

The three armed services are today altering their attitude toward intelligence more rapidly than Congress and the rest of America, with the Navy taking the lead. I believe the present superiority of naval intelligence results in part from the fact that the prewar Navy, with its schedule of calling at foreign ports, was traditionally the least insular service. In addition, the Navy's code-breaking efforts during World War II were superior, leading to such successes as the destruction of the Japanese carriers at the battle of Midway. Bobby Inman, a brilliant man who made his career in naval intelligence, was promoted to admiral in the seventies and ended up as deputy director of the CIA. Admiral

Noel A. Gaylor became Commander in Chief of the Pacific, one of the Navy's most prestigious commands, after heading the National Security (code-breaking) Agency.

The Air Force and the Army bounce around about in the middle in their production and use of intelligence, with the Air Force probably a bit stronger, particularly when it comes to satellite information. In the last several years the general officer lists of both the Army and the Air Force have begun to contain more men whose principal careers have been in intelligence.

At the bottom of the class come the Marines, traditionally contemptuous of intelligence. In World War II their failure to heed the evidence that there were reefs at Tarawa on which their amphibious vehicles would founder resulted in horrendous casualties. Recently, when a truck bomb wiped out the sleeping marines in their Beirut headquarters, Marine Corps Commandant General P. X. Kelley told Congress that the truck bomb was a "new and unexpected weapon" and one that "no one anticipated." Yet the U.S. embassy in Beirut had been attacked in this fashion a few weeks earlier, and plastic explosives in a small truck killed people at the U.S. embassy in Saigon in a similar attack during the Vietnam War. A Marine lieutenant, landing on Grenada during that action, inquired of a *Washington Post* reporter what language the natives spoke. One cannot blame the lieutenant here, but rather the senior officers who sent him on a mission without such knowledge.

From the beginning the Green Door problem was in operation at Pearl Harbor. Those in Washington were so interested in keeping secret the fact that we had broken the Japanese codes that the information they passed on to the commanders at Pearl Harbor was guardedly minimal. At the same time, the commanders and their staffs in Hawaii had so little experience with secret intelligence that they misinterpreted the information they received. The Army Air Corps commander, for example, thought he was receiving a warning against sabotage and so had his planes all lined up so they could be more easily watched.

The intelligence failures at Pearl Harbor were exacerbated by Interservice Rivalry. Both the Army and the Navy had been patrolling the skies around the islands, but each service thought the other was responsible for overflying the area from which the unbelievable attack came. In the Philippines, Admiral Thomas C. Hart and General MacArthur were barely on speaking terms. Hart thought that MacArthur's plans for the defense of the islands were illegal, "going far beyond his war plans." MacArthur, arguing that Hart's few ships were of slight importance to the islands' defense, found the admiral's proposals "objectionable . . . the term 'Fleet' cannot be applied to the surface elements of your command." The air commander also felt himself excluded. There were no air patrols and no common plans for defense. As a result, several hours after the attack on Pearl Harbor, planes in the Philippines were caught on the ground and destroyed. There were, of course, other serious problems. Many commanders were hardly better than third-rate; and through a bureaucratic bungle, naval headquarters in Washington thought that the fleet was at sea when in fact it was tied up at the docks of Pearl Harbor.

Under the pressure of the disaster at Pearl Harbor and the series of defeats that followed, the Army and the Navy found the bureaucratic will to reorganize themselves. In December 1941, sixty-one Army officers had the right of direct access to Army Chief of Staff General Marshall. By March 1942 he had reduced this number to six, though many of those so displaced carried their grievances to Congress. Inside the Navy, Admiral Ernest J. King, who in the spring of 1939 had wept because he thought he would be retired as a junior admiral, became, the day after Pearl Harbor, Commander in Chief of the U.S. Atlantic Fleet, a suddenly resurrected title. He also persuaded President Roosevelt to give him, by executive order, control of the naval bureaus, which had successfully maintained their independence since their creation in 1915. By March, King had also assumed the title and position of Chief of Naval Operations, CNO, taking total command of the Navy.

Meanwhile, at the apex of the armed services a change occurred which realigned interservice management in a manner that gravely cripples today's Defense Department. The four senior service officers (Admiral King, General Marshall, Admiral Harold R. Stark, then the Chief of Naval Operations, and General Arnold of the Air Corps) had been meeting off and on before hostilities as something called the Joint Board. The Navy didn't want to continue meeting that way because, by law, news of what went on inside the Joint Board had to be shared with the civilian secretaries, and Admiral King distrusted his civilian naval leaders. (Under Secretary of the Navy Ralph A. Bard was never able to invite King for lunch during the entire war.) Since the Navy didn't want to meet officially, the four senior officers started meeting unofficially and decided to call themselves the Joint Chiefs of Staff (JCS). When Stark proved not up to the job and was passed off to an honorary post in London, Admiral William D. Leahy joined the JCS as Roosevelt's personal representative. However, at no time did a formal order ever create the JCS or define its functions.

This suited President Roosevelt, who liked informal, slightly messy arrangements because they gave him more control over the people involved. However, the fact that during the war the JCS functioned merely as a committee without formal bureaucratic standing created serious wartime problems. For example, there were a number of legally created wartime boards and agencies, as disparate as the Office of Strategic Services, which handled spies, and the War Production Board, which handled supplies. Since the JCS had no official existence, it could neither control nor influence these vital bodies and the questions they were deciding. Not until 1944 did President Roosevelt even refer the Navy's requests for aircraft to the JCS for comment. The President just accepted the Navy figures and passed them on to the War Production Board.

When the Defense Department was created after the war, this lack of a legally established Joint Chiefs of Staff worked pernicious mischief. Those who wished to protect their own service by keeping the three armed services as separate as possible were able to say, "Well, look how well the informal arrangement functioned during the war." The wartime Joint Chiefs had not functioned particularly well, but even today that fact is not generally known, and back then it was successfully hidden behind the banners of victory, often artfully waved for just that purpose. In the peacetime world, with the urgent need for cooperation gone, the old Joint Chiefs arrangement based on informal agreement and committee operations immediately broke down, and it continues in disarray.

The Joint Chiefs remain a committee and must agree unanimously in order to accomplish anything. As a body they command nothing; rather, they advise the President. If the President orders something done, now, as back then, there is no one person in charge who can ensure that the order is carried through. If Marshall, who is generally regarded by history as the first among equals, was able to set the nation's military goals, it was because, as Winston Churchill remarked of him, "This was the noblest Roman of them all." There was a force of personality there, a flood tide of selfless energy, which, though often written about, had to be felt to be believed. I particularly remember his intense blue eyes, whose strength seemed to approach wizardry.

When Marshall finally retired from public service for good in 1951, worn out in the middle of the Korean War, he called five or six of us regular Pentagon correspondents into his modest E-ring Pentagon office to make his announcement. His chair was at the right of his desk and he rocked back and forth in it while he talked, hands behind his head, elbows back. "I have passed almost all of my life in the service of the United States," he said, "and it has given me some satisfaction." He paused, rocked back and forth some more, smiled, and repeated, "some satisfaction."

The radiant look in those light-blue eyes, reflecting the appreciation and the happiness of a life well and fully lived, of risks taken, of gains and losses, and of the final balance, could light up a nation. I had seen such eyes only once before, when a man who had risked himself to save my life, turned to smile at me. When people who I think are serious ask me, "Why would anyone want to go into the armed services?," I try to tell them about Marshall's eyes.

Still, for all Marshall's strength of character, the JCS functioned only as a committee; and powerful men fought through it and around it for what they believed. To get the Navy to retreat from this or that cherished tenet of sea power, Marshall would use the threat of going to Congress while the war was on to ask for a unified Defense Department and a separate Air Force. If the Navy cooperated, he would agree to delay the question of a separate Air Force until the war's end. The strength of this threat lay in the fact that a separate Air Force, created during the war, might well have included naval aviation.

When King particularly wanted something his way, he used his standing with the President, for Roosevelt, a former Assistant Secretary of the Navy and a maritime buff, respected the crusty King and usually had a warmer welcome for Admiral King than for General Marshall. So King used White House pressure to overcome decisions he saw as detrimental to the war, even as Marshall used pressure from Congress.

If, in addition to going to the President, the Navy tried to thwart Marshall by going to Congress, Marshall's constant ally, Robert A. Lovett, the prescient Assistant Secretary of War for Air, would be there first, using the same threat of a separate Air Force that should command naval air. In the main, Lovett and Marshall were more successful with their pressure tactics than the Navy was, and unified war plans advanced. But such constant battles fought because the JCS was not a legally constituted body made unification of the postwar Defense Department far more difficult.

Ironically, it was the Navy that, as World War II loomed, first pressed for a unified Defense Department. In June 1941, the Navy General Board recommended unanimously that "unification" take place, proposing a single Defense Department under a Joint Chiefs of Staff. But by a year later, when that proposal had finally reached the service secretaries by way of the Joint War Plans Committee and the Joint Board, the Navy had reversed itself and was against any type of unification. On the Joint War Plans Committee a new Army brigadier general, Dwight Eisenhower, who hadn't thought much about service relationships before, examined the first Navy proposals for complete unification and "strongly endorsed" them for the Army. Throughout his life his view never changed.

The Joint Chiefs of Staff remains an impotent committee today, and one can learn about today's failures by examining some wartime disputes. Coping with the German submarine menace produced an early World War II JCS impasse. Major problems usually occur when services feel threatened at their boundaries. By February 1942, two months after Pearl Harbor, thirty-one ships had been sunk off the East Coast of the United States, while not a single German submarine had been damaged. In the peaceful early thirties Congress had ordered the services to decide who controlled what air space in terms of what the airplane in that air space landed on. If the plane took off from and landed on a carrier or was a seaplane, then the Navy owned the space it flew in. If the plane came off an air base, then the Army Air Corps owned the air space.

Where land and sea met—the defense of the coast—there the problem arose. A doctrinal statement produced by the Joint Board on Aeronautics in 1919 had said that both Army and Navy planes might be involved in attacking an enemy invading the coast. The board ducked any further details of who and how. The problem was particularly intense because coastal defense was a major area in which Colonel William ("Billy") Mitchell, the air-power pioneer, had attacked the Navy. To protect the coast, the Navy wanted to come ashore and fly land-based bombers. The Army Air Corps said that was its territory. The Congress, true to its own logic, agreed with the Army Air Corps. The Army Air Corps offered to go after submarines with its land-based bombers. The Navy insisted that what happened over the seas was its responsibility and restricted the Air Corps to close-in patrol of the coast. At the same time the Navy began to build inefficient, expensive seaplanes. When war came, there were not enough of these seaplanes, and the waters off the East Coast were soon bright with the flames of burning tankers.

The Navy argued that it would soon get a convoy system organized and that with more sea and carrier planes, everything would be fine. Marshall and Lovett again offered Army planes to do the job. The Navy accepted some of them, but then went further and asked a sympathetic Congress to transfer 200 Army bombers to the Navy, to be used on convoy duty. The planes would be armed with torpedoes, definitely a Navy weapon. These were planes that Marshall and Arnold had counted on for the strategic bomber campaign against Germany. When the Congress agreed to the transfer and Roosevelt supported the Navy, Marshall and Lovett countered by asking in the JCS for a Unified Joint Command for antisubmarine warfare. The Army Air Corps did not help its case when its pilots, not trained to fly over water, got lost more often than did the Navy pilots. And the Navy did not help its case by taking the bombers given it to be used against submarines and flying these planes in support of the marines at Guadalcanal.

Increasingly desperate over their lost planes, Marshall and Lovett took their proposal for a unified antisubmarine command under the Army Air Corps back to the President in a paper that argued, among other items: "We have available for command men whose offensive spirit and initiative have been amply demonstrated. . . . The absence of such an offensive spirit in antisubmarine warfare is our major obstacle today for success." Should you have any trouble translating that, it says the commander of the

Army and his civilian counterpart for air are calling the admirals cowards. The admirals reacted as one would expect. Their choler was further heightened because the Army Air Force claimed to have sunk Japanese ships at the battle of Midway that had actually been sunk by naval carriers. It is hard to remember when recalling such disputes that Germany and Japan were the presumptive enemy.

As the dying continued, the Army withdrew all its planes from antisubmarine warfare. The Navy, with Admiral King holding firm, refused a compromise that would have given antisubmarine warfare exclusively to the Navy in return for Army Air Corps control over all other land-based heavy bombers. King continued to insist that his service should possess any aircraft it wanted, including heavy land-based bombers. Marshall warned King personally once again that he would break their informal truce over discussion of an independent Air Force while the war was on, and would urge Congress to create such a force right away and to consider including naval air in the force, a course of action that had been recommended by air-power pioneer General Billy Mitchell.

Finally, President Roosevelt seemed to swing to Marshall's side as, for the first time, he referred the Navy aircraft procurement plans to the JCS for approval, instead of merely approving the Navy's figures, as he had done in the past. Thereupon, Marshall refused to agree to King's aircraft request and continued to threaten to ask Congress for an independent Air Force. Under such pressure King finally agreed to the compromise. All went back to fighting the war. I am aware this makes dreary reading. But these feuds still flaw today's forces.

Another disruptive wartime JCS dispute that still weakens the Giant was the Interservice/Intraservice Rivalry over manpower. There never was enough manpower to go around, and educated manpower was in particularly short supply. Each of the three services bid constantly for the small pool of what they considered the best, often without knowing for what exactly they wanted such men. For example, in 1939 the Air Force was training only two hundred aviation cadets a year. They had to be college graduates, be recommended by three prominent persons in their communities, and pass a rigorous written examination. There was a continuous shortage of pilots, many people were failing the exam, and Congress was upset at the low numbers of cadets.

Secretary for Air Lovett became convinced that the written examination had nothing to do with flying ability; but the Air Force staff, led by General Arnold, insisted it measured skills they must have. Lovett, a World War I hero as a naval aviator, took the aviation cadet exam and failed. He next gave it to Julius Stratton, the president of MIT, who failed. The two of them then gave it to ten MIT students at random, and the only one to get a high grade was a female chemistry wizard from a family of musicians. When Lovett threatened to go public with this tidbit, the Air Staff wisely threw in the towel. The service lowered its education requirements for pilots to high school graduation, and changed the written test. The number of those entering the Air Force increased five times.

The manpower contest between the Army, Navy, Marines, and Army Air Corps and the wartime defense industries would have been worse had not Roosevelt felt that he had been pressured by the admirals during the first war into taking more men than the Navy needed. "Those dear delightful officers of the regular Navy are doing to you today just what other officers were trying to do to me a quarter of a century ago," he wrote Secretary of the Navy Frank Knox. Convinced of this, the President continually cut the Navy's manpower requests. These requests were already low because Admiral King, who had a tendency to overcontrol everything, had for a series of complex personal reasons underestimated the manpower needs of his service. But though the situation could have been worse, severe manpower shortages developed. Industry solved part of this problem by admitting women into the work force in large numbers for the first time. In 1939 women were only 1 percent of the work force in the defense aircraft industry. By 1944 they were 39 percent. The armed services themselves made scant use of women during the war.

Unlike the Navy, the Army overstated its manpower needs. Right after Pearl Harbor the JCS estimated that an army of 334 divisions would be needed to defeat Germany and Japan. God knows how they arrived at such a figure, where they thought the manpower for such a force would come from, or where they believed the divisions would train and who would train them. In the winter of 1942–1943, when the Army had grown from 190,000 men in 1939 to 5,067,000 (of which 1,270,000 were in the Army Air Corps), the Army had to stop creating divisions as it ran out of space and trained cadres. Those in the Army before Pearl Harbor were then known as "old soldiers." The Army started creating divisions again the next summer, finally producing a total of 90.

By 1944 all expansion of the armed forces stopped, with the Army plus the Army Air Corps at 8,000,000 and the Navy and Marines at just under 4,000,000. Even with women in the work force, the civilian economy creaked along under great strain. When one realizes that the Russians raised over 400 divisions, and the Germans fielded around 300, despite their limited manpower base, 90 divisions seems slim. Granted that U.S. divisions were slightly larger than German or Russian divisions; still, the judgment of historian Russell F. Weigley in his insightful exposition of the European war remains: Creating 90 divisions was "not an impressive performance for a super power."

Inside the Army itself Intraservice Rivalry crippled America's combat abilities. In that battle for skilled, motivated men, the Army's most important branch, the infantry, lost out. That America possessed good infantry is one of the myths of World War II. This is not to belittle those who were there, but to fault the system that sent too few able men to that vital part of combat. This continuing Tooth-to-Tail/Readiness problem is still with us today, accounting for reverses suffered in both Korea and Vietnam.

Shortly after D day, as the fighting got heavy in Europe, the maldistribution of manpower began seriously to hurt the battle for Europe. Severe shortages of infantrymen and tankers had caused the Army to up the monthly total of these combat replacements going to Europe to 54,000 men, an increase of 18,000 men a month. Army headquarters cut back on the leave granted to men going overseas, shortened the basic training time, and began to comb the rear areas for combat-fit men. Still the Army never seemed able to handle its manpower efficiently. The replacement system was described by a frustrated combat general as "an invisible horde of people going here and there but seemingly never arriving." Then came dark December and the Battle of the Bulge, with 138,400 casualties in one month. Divisions averaged 78 percent of strength, and the combat replacement barrel was bare. "The two things that bother us are replacements and ammunition," wrote General George S. Patton in his diaries.

In particular, infantry casualties were far heavier than foreseen.

To give some examples: In the first week of the Battle of the Bulge, the 12th Army Group suffered 50,000 casualties; 40,000 of these were infantrymen. Riflemen make up 68.5 percent of the strength of an infantry division. Statistics from fifty-seven World War II infantry divisions showed that these riflemen suffered 94.5 percent of the division's casualties. In an armored division the infantry and armored regiments fight roughly the same battles. Yet in the 2nd Armored Division, the 41st Infantry Regiment had 2,444 casualties during the war, including 482 KIA (killed in action). The most heavily engaged tank regiment, the 66th, had 961 casualties, including 257 KIA. "Upon such sacrifices, my Cordelia, the gods themselves throw incense." The disproportionate dying among the infantry created bitter tensions at the close of World War II, both inside the Army and more particularly between the Army, the Navy, and the fledgling Air Force. These rancorous tensions were reinforced in Korea and Vietnam.

(The British, who had been fighting longer with less manpower, experienced more drastic problems. They were forced to merge some of their veteran organizations. With casualties in Normandy running to 80 percent in some infantry units, the British lacked any replacements whatsoever. Even in some of their famous battle formations, such as the Desert Rats, the British and Canadians began to be plagued by morale problems that hindered unit effectiveness.)

To fill its combat replacement needs after the Battle of the Bulge the U.S. Army scraped its own hide, as it was to do later in Korea and in Vietnam. All military prisoners who volunteered for combat were pardoned. Men were pulled from the Army Air Corps, over 30,000 of them, with the Air Corps finally apologizing for the quality of what they dumped on the infantry. (Remember those "volunteer" Marine pilots in the Iranian desert?) Men were scrounged from rear supply areas, from noncombat Army units in the States, and rushed to the front. Infantry training centers and officer candidate schools were set up in Europe.

The pool of deferred students in college was dipped into. In their bidding for the best qualified, all three armed services were offering programs under which able-bodied Americans were granted deferments to go through college. So pervasive was this practice of college deferment that the chief of Selective Service, General Lewis B. Hershey, bitterly remarked: "In the Civil War it required $300 to escape service. In this war it requires sufficient funds to attend college." By the time of Vietnam, military deferment via the college and graduate-school route had become one of the most divisive factors in American society.

So severe was the World War II manpower shortage that the Army even did the unthinkable for those times and began to tap the pool of black soldiers serving in segregated noncombat units. Many black soldiers wished to volunteer out of these units for combat, and after some stuttering hesitation, the Army began to accept them as infantry replacements. These black soldiers were still segregated, both by order and usually in actual practice, into platoon-size units of roughly 35 men. Still, for all this, as it fought toward the Rhine the Army was some 82,000 infantry replacements and 5,000 tanker replacements short each month.

Unfortunately, we are not just talking numbers. There is a question of quality, which is usually avoided. Since the dying was so predominantly among the infantry, many historians and journalists have felt it unfair, perhaps even disloyal, to raise questions about the standards used to select riflemen, the basic fighting unit of the Army. Yet these questions of manpower assignment are part of both Intraservice Rivalry and KAFCA, and they must be examined because in the Korean War and the Vietnamese War the practice of assigning below-average manpower to the infantry, and to some extent to the tank forces, killed people.

During World War II the average infantry division got as riflemen those the rest of the armed services (specifically including the Army Air Corps) did not want. I am criticizing not the infantrymen themselves, the lonely doughs out front, but the lack of strategic planning and enforcement that relegated such a high percentage of leftovers to the rifle companies. And then kept them there. In World War II, members of the Army Air Corps, the future Air Force, rotated home after a certain number of missions. In the Vietnam War and to some extent the Korean War, infantrymen came home after a year of service. For the World War II infantryman there was no such rotation. These men stayed, like Housman's mercenaries, and "took their wages." Most infantry officers can quote the next three words.

The unfair selection process began with a policy that let all those who volunteered pick where they wanted to serve. Not surprisingly, only 5 percent of those volunteering elected to become infantrymen or tankers. The American bent toward mechanical and technical solutions to problems, plus the relative safety of the Navy, assured that the Navy and the Army technical services gained a high percentage of the more able. This was particularly true of officers; the Navy ROTCs and other such programs at selected universities attracted a large number of above-average volunteers. The Army's official history gloomily reports: "By the end of 1943 the operations of this priority [the ability of volunteers to choose to serve where they wanted] and a number of other factors had reduced to a dangerously low level the number of men allotted to the ground forces who seemed likely to perform effectively in combat."

Everyone on the inside with eyes and the will to see knew what was going on. Everyone was aware not only that the initial allotment was unfair, but that commanders in the States held back the best men and officers for the training centers and school systems in order to make their own performance look good.

"I wish you'd been around before," I said to a new mechanic who, shortly before the war's close, skillfully fixed a persistent problem in one of my trucks.

"I've been trying to get overseas for two years," he replied.

"I believe you. Where have you been?"

"The Field Artillery School."

So it went. The infantry that stormed ashore on D day were an inch shorter than the average soldier in the Army. This gives you some idea of their physical profile. Three months before D day the Army transferred some 30,000 protesting aviation cadets into the ground forces. I remember looking at some of these men as they arrived at Camp Shelby, Mississippi, where I was then a tank officer. I thought how tall and alert these ex-cadets looked and how much I would like to get some of them into my outfit. First, though, these men had to be persuaded to fight. A large number of the ex-cadets mutinied, refused to accept training, and had to be herded into a theater and threatened with imprisonment before they agreed to serve in the ground forces. This was in World War II, when the country was united; but we had forgotten such actions by the time of Vietnam.

During World War II, veteran infantrymen in several battle-tested divisions were asked to identify and describe the outstanding enlisted combat performers. Twenty-four percent of those named as outstanding performers had some college education or were college graduates. Forty percent were at least high school graduates. When you consider these percentages together with the fact that at the time of Pearl Harbor only 30 percent of the men in the World War II infantry companies were high school graduates and only 11 percent were college graduates or had some college, the importance of education in ground combat becomes overwhelmingly apparent. And by the time of D day and the Battle of the Bulge, the percentages of educated men had drastically declined. By then, 40 percent of those in the combat divisions were classified as below average in intelligence.

When General Abrams was Chief of Staff of the Army in the early seventies, he used to be asked how the tank battalions in Vietnam and in NATO compared with his World War II battalion. He always replied that as a lieutenant colonel he really commanded two tank battalions: the superb unit he took into action in Normandy, and what that same battalion became later, after it had been filled up with the mediocre personnel provided by the Army to replace his casualties. Further evidence of the shortness of skilled personnel in the average infantry unit is provided by our enemies. While greatly fearing the American artillery, the Germans downgraded the American infantry. Again the artillery was allotted a higher-priority call upon the pool of talented men.

To try to overcome the assignment of the least able to the infantry and armor, veteran divisions, like the 1st or 9th Infantry or the 2nd Armored—outfits people wanted to join and whose commanders had enough clout to buck the system—kept officers at the replacement depots, illegally plucking the best replacements. Then they ran their own training programs inside the division to try to bring those they received up to their higher standards of performance. You could easily spot the men from such divisions: their equipment was cleaner; they even walked differently; their spacing on the march was safely spread out; they knew when to hit the dirt, when to run forward; when they paused, they didn't lie down, they set up fire positions and dug holes. Their officers were out front. They were also the most imaginative, attacking at night without artillery, being among the first to use loudspeakers. You might well get killed in such units, but you would seldom get killed doing something stupid. But such divisions were not typical. By the second month after D day senior American commanders had sacked a large number of officers, from lieutenants up to generals, including two corps commanders, in an effort to improve the aggressiveness of the general run of U.S. infantry and armored divisions.

The existence of such elite outfits as the four airborne divisions and the Rangers also tended to lower the quality of the average infantry division. Such special units were composed largely of infantry volunteers. This meant that an inordinate number of fine soldiers were concentrated in one place, weakening other divisions. Such volunteer units are necessary. As a journalist, I was part of the battle to save the airborne from deep cuts before the Korean War and to create an antiterrorist unit in the Carter years; but there is seldom a gain without loss, and the elite units meant the average infantry division lost again.

A month and a half after D day the American high command discovered it had only six divisions in Normandy on which it could consistently rely to beat the Germans—two airborne divisions, the 82nd and 101st; three infantry divisions, the 1st, 4th, and 9th; plus one tank division, the 2nd Armored. (The 3rd Infantry division, fighting in Italy and southern France, was the final member of this exclusive club.) Though some of the other divisions, such as the 4th and 7th Armored or 30th and 8th Infantry, later became consistent performers, the number of such units remained far too small.

The pioneering historian of small-unit actions, General S.L.A. ("Slam") Marshall, discovered that less than 15 percent of the riflemen in an average infantry company were actually firing their weapons. In a few of the exceptionally well-trained outfits—the paratroopers or the Rangers—those firing might reach 25 percent, never more. Further, those who fired were the same few who moved forward. Other combat studies, notably those of Stouffer et al., found that these battle leaders had more education than the average soldier. Not since the 1960s have our tankers and infantrymen in NATO won any of the prizes given to outstanding units. With embarrassing regularity these are won by our allies. Our defenses continue to be crippled by a Defense Department that cannot force an equitable distribution of skilled manpower, and a Congress that will not draft the educated.

The Battle of the Bulge provided dramatic evidence of what it meant to shortchange the infantry. Every historian writing about that battle has noted the heroic work of small, isolated engineer units in stopping the German advance. S. L. A. Marshall, John Eisenhower, Russell Weigley, all cite the extraordinary bravery of such outfits as:

> A squad of the 241st Engineer Combat Battalion, at Stavelot Bridge
> Company C, 51st Engineer Combat Battalion, at Trois Points
> Company A, 291st Engineer Combat Battalion, at Lienne Creek
> Headquarters and Service Companies of the 81st and 168th Engineer Combat Battalion
> The 44th Engineer Combat Battalion, at the Clerf River

General James M. Gavin, whose 82nd Airborne successfully held out on the northeastern sector of the Bulge (along with, as you might guess, the 1st Infantry and 2nd Armored), remarked after the war that he felt the scattered engineer units, probably amounting in manpower to about one-third of a division, had been "worth three divisions." The German S.S. commander of the Bulge northern armored spearhead, Obersturmbannführer Joachim Peiper, the officer responsible for the Malmedy massacre, told interrogators after the war that it was the "God-damned engineers" who had blunted his spearheads.

Why did these units hold when so often infantry and armor units were disintegrating around them? Because they had had first call upon the abler men; and this pool of superior talent had not been so drained by heavy casualties.

Considering the personnel assigned to them, the performance of the World War II infantry divisions, while deserving criticism, also breaks your heart. At a crossroad near Merzenhausen, about five miles southwest of Aachen, I sat in my loudspeaker jeep and watched in impotence and fury as two tired columns of "doughs" from the 29th Infantry Division trudged past me to make another attack into Merzenhausen. I knew I could get the Germans in the town to surrender with my loudspeakers, for the 2nd Armored almost had the town outflanked. But I was a young lieutenant, loudspeakers were new, and I couldn't get permission to broadcast from the colonel running the attack. So the infantry went in and did their unaided best, succeeding with heavy casualties. That was one of the worst moments of my life. Just about the time I had forgotten it, or thought I had, I went to Vietnam and saw the unfair, war-losing, deadly pattern again.

Turning from manpower problems to cooperation between the services, specifically between air and ground forces in Europe, one finds Interservice Rivalry and Flawed Organization unnecessarily killing people. On the morning of 24 July 1944, a month and a half after D day, the Americans were finally prepared to break out from their portion of the Normandy beachhead in an operation called Cobra. To aid the breakout, heavy bombers were to fly from England and drop 3,300 tons of bombs in front of the American troops just before they advanced. Getting the bombers to participate at all had been difficult. General Carl A. Spaatz, the American Air Force commander, had resisted, fearing that the use of his bombers to support anything connected with D day might prejudice the future establishment of a separate Air Force.

Spaatz and his deputy, General Hoyt Vandenberg, who would be Chief of the Air Staff after the war, had not fully believed in D day. In this they were supported by the Royal Air Force commander, Air Marshall Arthur ("Bomber") Harris. These men felt that the vast preparations to invade Europe merely detracted from their strategic bombing campaign, which they still believed could win the war by itself. Vandenberg, a handsome, political general who was not too bright, advocated abandoning the invasion of France, to concentrate on more bombing. This was to be followed by the invasion of Norway, so Sweden would come into the war.

The night before the planned Cobra breakout, the weather forecast, though marginal, was adequate and the overall air commander for the operation, British Air Marshal Trafford Leigh-Mallory, ordered the operation. H-hour was to be 1:00 P.M., to give the weather further time to clear. Finding the weather less good than forecast the next morning, Leigh-Mallory flew from England to Normandy to take a look for himself.

That he should have been in England is of itself interesting, showing the difference in psychological perspective between ground and air commanders. Leigh-Mallory felt that he had to remain in England because most of his aircraft remained based there until airfields for them could be captured in Normandy. Yet both British and American ground commanders resented that he was not with them to understand what they were facing. "Obviously he is a gutless bugger," wrote General Bernard L. Montgomery, "who refuses to take a chance and plays for safety on all occasions. I have no use for him." Disasters breed from such different perceptions and animosities. A major Allied disaster now came whistling down.

Arriving in France, Leigh-Mallory found the weather so poor that he called off the attack. But about 1,600 heavy bombers had already taken off; and less than half of these received the recall order. The other planes that plowed on cannot be faulted for this failure. No command channels had been designated, and the recall order was merely broadcast on several channels to which the aircraft commanders might happen to be listening. Of the roughly 800 planes that kept on, most found the cloud cover so dense that they didn't drop their loads. But some 300 planes released through the overcast, killing 25 and wounding 131 soldiers of the 30th Infantry Division.

That was a regrettable accident. What happened on the morrow punishes belief. The planes on the twenty-fourth had come in over the American infantry at right angles to the road that marked the front line. The plan, as the ground forces had understood it, was for the planes to come in parallel to the road so that the danger of premature bomb release would be avoided. The Air Force said this would be too dangerous for their pilots. Nor would they change the plan, even after the disaster of the first day. The infantry, assuming that the first day's bombing would have alerted the enemy to the intended attack, wanted the bombing the next day and so reluctantly agreed to have the Air Force again begin the bomb run above the ground troops. At 9:38 A.M. on the twenty-fifth, a beautifully clear day with a light breeze blowing from the south, 87 bombers let go short. The 30th Division was clobbered again, this time along with the 9th and 4th. One hundred eleven ground troops were dead and 450 wounded. Again there had been no way to communicate by radio and halt the bombing. (Does this sound like the Iranian desert, like Grenada, like Beirut?)

This bitter fruit grew from the Air versus Ground battles of the thirties. Its taste would poison the minds of those who created the postwar armed forces organization. Fortunately, under the driving impetus of Air Force Major General Elwood R. ("Pete") Quesada, the fighters in Europe were soon working closely with the ground forces. Quesada's fighters even accepted orders from officers on the ground who were not Army Air Corps. The bombers continued to fight their private war. Air/ground coordination is another area in which we have marched backward since World War II. In Korea and Vietnam, and on maneuvers today, Air Force doctrine all but prohibits accepting targets provided by other than Air Force officers, who tend not to be present on the ground. Whereas Army antiaircraft units lock their missiles on any blip their radars detect.

One cannot lay all the blame for present divisions at the door of the Air Corps of those days or today's Air Force. I fought with one World War II infantry unit that had shot down so many of our own planes that its antiaircraft machine guns all had little tags on their triggers saying, "This gun will only be fired under command of an officer." The infantryman, face down beneath bullets, would like to have the entire Air Force bombing the machine gun that has him pinned. The bomber general in World War II, convinced, and correctly so, that his campaign against German oil supplies was bringing their entire war machine to a halt, reluctantly would sacrifice the infantryman. The problem was there was no commander or body who could mediate between such claims. Nor is there now.

The Navy also had problems coordinating its aviators and surface sailors. However, the Navy's problem was not as acute because naval air was less independent of the Navy than the Army Air Corps was of the Army; and senior naval aviators had also held nonaviation commands.

Successfully combining the various forces necessary for victory remains one of the supreme challenges of command. Even where a single head can theoretically order something done, great difficulties remain. As Lieutenant General James Hollingsworth was wont to remark in Vietnam: "Any damned fool can write a plan. It's the execution that gets you all screwed up." Military historians have noted that at Waterloo Wellington was more surely in command of his mixed force of British, Irish, Germans, and Belgians than Napoleon was of his French forces. Unfortunately the challenge to produce unity was not always met in World War II. And we have seen that, years later and on a far smaller scale, the disparate elements of the Iranian hostage rescue mission never truly fused.

. . .

In spite of all our errors, America's vast reserves of industry and manpower, combined with the daily, lonely heroism of the British, the tenacity of the Russian armed forces, and the genius of the Allied scientists, produced victory. The very magnitude of our total victory blinded us to how close we had come to failure and masked the fundamental reasons for our triumph.

We won and instantly demobilized. No, "demobilized" is too mild a word; we fell apart, as we did after Vietnam. That vicious metaphor of sport that so dominates our strategic thinking struck again. The ball game was over and we raced home, holding almost unchanged the attitudes we had learned before the war. I was as anxious to get out as all the rest. Wartime service was one thing; but peacetime service and the problems of military power could be left to others.

Between 30 June 1945 and 30 June 1946, the strength of the U.S. Army dropped from over 8 million men to less than 2 million. The Marine Corps shrunk from 475,000 to 156,000. Overall, of the 12 million men and women under arms in 1945, less than 1,600,000 remained in the service by 1947. The draft had stopped. In the rush to "bring the boys home," thousands of tons of supplies were given away to our allies, left to rust in huge stacks overseas, or shipped back to the United States, where they were put in storage, sold as surplus, or cannibalized for parts. Destroyers, mothballed in antirust gunk, swung in the Hudson River, acres and acres of airplanes weathered on southwestern airfields, tanks in small clusters turned rust-red all over Germany and France. I stared at them in amazement alongside the road in Normandy when I went back in 1948.

In such a chaotic situation, morale plummeted. At Fort Bragg, home of the airborne, a regiment of the 11th Airborne Division refused to jump. The press sympathized with the nonjumpers, for the Great Divorce opened up again. Reporters turned from stories of the invincible war machine to tales of boondoggle and corruption. There were riots in the replacement depots overseas as men felt the government too slow in bringing them home.

General James Gavin climbed on a drill platform to confront one such group and he remembers this as one of the most challenging moments of the war. The Army, faced with the task of policing Germany, had to create a special unit, the Constabulary, because the morale of the rest of the ground troops was considered too fragile even for riot control. The Constabulary was given first call on the best men and what workable vehicles were left and was then isolated from the press so that it could be brought up to some approximation at least of prewar standards.

I was in the military hospital system in France and the United States during the wind-down and watched in pop-eyed wonder as officers were admitted to our ward who had been beaten up by enlisted men. I remember one of these was a captain who had won the Medal of Honor with the 9th Division. Some rear-area troops who didn't like officers had jumped him as he was waiting to sail for home. All this happened after a war about·which there was close to total national agreement. But over the years we forgot these things, or, more accurately, refused to look at them, as they were in conflict with our national self-image. So we were surprised when the breakdown of authority and consensus came, first during Korea and later at the end of our unpopular, losing war in Vietnam.

In the rapid demobilization, the combination of bombers and atomic weapons on which the defense of America supposedly rested existed mainly in the press releases. By 1946 there were just ten B-29s flying that were equipped with the necessary complex equipment to drop the primitive atomic bombs of those days. As trained mechanics quit the Air Force, on any given day less than five of these planes were able to fly. With serious training stopped, the forerunner of the Strategic Air Command became largely a ferry service, flying pilots home.

Bases from which the bombers theoretically would be launched became indefensible. In 1946 General Marshall pointed out to the Congress that he lacked the troops even to defend the vital strategic bomber bases in Alaska. As for the atomic bombs themselves, production of them had ceased, and in 1946 only twelve were in the stockpile. These bombs were in pieces, and the scientists who knew how to assemble them had gone home, like everyone else.

General George C. Marshall had shifted from being Chief of Staff to being Secretary of State for the latter part of this period. He later reminisced: "When I was Secretary of State, I was pressed constantly . . . to give the Russians hell. At this time, my facilities for giving them hell—and I am a soldier and I know something about the ability to give hell—was one and one-third divisions over the entire United States. That is quite a proposition when you have to deal with somebody with over 260 divisions and you have one and a third."

Meanwhile, inside the armed services the prewar parochialisms and feuds, like the Theban dragon's teeth, sprang up with vigor. In the Army, the infantry branch successfully moved to assert its control over the rest of that service. A most unfortunate effect of this internal battle was the downgrading of the artillery, the part of the U.S. ground forces that had particularly excelled. Inside the division, the artillery officer was no longer a general but merely a colonel, while an additional infantry general was created. The results of this were to prove disastrous in Vietnam. The artillery fire became less accurate than in World War II; while the infantry were more often lost, because the artillery observer, with his map-reading skill, was no longer so ubiquitously present.

In the Army Air Corps, the bomber generals moved fast and ruthlessly to exclude fighter generals such as Quesada from any approach to the levers of power. Here the battle was particularly bitter as the bomber generals believed any emphasis on fighters detracted from their demand for a separate Air Force.

The prewar regulars in the Navy searched for a legal formula to remove from their service the many excellent reserve officers who, having found they enjoyed wartime naval service, now wished to remain on board. The regular naval officers did not contest the worth of the reservists; but they felt that the next war was far away, and they doubted that the reservists could truly stomach the boredom and discipline of the peacetime Navy. Meanwhile the reservists held down jobs and received promotions that would otherwise have gone to regulars who would stay the course.

Everywhere the battle standard of the American armed services, though triumphant, was in tatters, while inside the services the recent victors now fought over crumbs. Today's defense organization was created in this atmosphere. At that time most Americans believed planning for defense was at best unnecessary, at worst immoral and destructive of world peace. The defense organization then established was deeply flawed, but those who created it had remained behind to bear the heat of the day for a while longer, while most of America ran home to play. Let that too be entered in register beside their names.

Certain vital intangibles were present at the close of World War II. These hidden forces deserve closer attention than they have had, for like invisible puppet strings, they caused the players to dance about the board in ways not realized even by the performers themselves.

Begin with tiredness. At the war's end everyone was so damn tired. Those who had been in combat were undoubtedly the most exhausted but there had also been strain in Washington. Secretary of War for Air Robert Lovett had three officers suffer heart attacks while briefing him. He remembers vividly the first one: the young pilot, a colonel, was talking about the pilot shortage right after Pearl Harbor, when suddenly his face became ashen, his form crumbled. General Spaatz leaped forward from his chair to catch the body before it fully hit the floor. They pounded on the colonel's chest, they raced for oxygen, but too late. Several wartime leaders, including Admiral McCain, died of heart attacks almost immediately at war's end. Others at their own request took billets far removed from legislative action or postwar planning, in order to get on with the business of seeing their wives and meeting those young strangers, their children.

When the war was over General Sir Brian Horrocks, who had led the Thirty British Corps in the unsuccessful ground attack toward the parachutists trapped at Arnhem, was talking to General James M. Gavin, who had commanded the 82nd Airborne there. "If only I'd had a green division, Jim, a green division." In 1947 the State Department Planning Staff, assembled by George Kennan to lay the groundwork for what was to become the Marshall Plan, began its report by noting "the physical and psychic exhaustion of people everywhere." In my own small picture, officers of the 2nd Armored, which had fought in Africa, Sicily, and France, used to say to me in November of 1944, "If you had just known us in the summer, before we were all so goddamned tired."

One had to possess Marshall's selfless view of duty or Admiral King's passionate belief in the rightness of his service to be willing at war's end to spend grueling hours in legislative battle over matters of armed service organization. Sheer exhaustion kept many of the best and most experienced minds out of the postwar military debates, while those who remained, like many tired people, were often impatient of compromise and full of short-fused anger.

The next hidden force was the powerful feeling of self-confidence among the victors. Strong men had done their this or their that, often in conditions of danger and deprivation, and were convinced that their particular action had won the war. One seldom reaches the rank of general or admiral without definite convictions of self-worth. Further, and this is seldom realized outside the Other America of Defense, generals and admirals are the most undisciplined of men. They have succeeded ever since their junior years by bending orders.

You are a young lieutenant in Vietnam. The rules of engagement say that you can call in air support if you are confronted with more than twenty of the enemy. Less than twenty enemy you and your men have to handle by yourselves. One morning you count fifteen "Charlies" advancing through the rice paddy in front of you. I can tell you with total assurance that Lieutenant Future General claims he sees thirty enemy, calls in an air strike, kills the enemy with less effort, and saves his men. The overall war effort may suffer because somewhere else Lieutenant Total Honesty, facing nineteen Viet Cong, is still counting and hoping to get twenty. Or maybe he faces twenty-five but his request has been denied because our future general has seen thirty. So it goes. And those who condemn Lieutenant Future General as they read this had best ask themselves quickly which officer they would prefer to walk with on patrol.

After the loudspeaking tank became really successful on the other side of the Rhine, there were demands for it everywhere. One day over my radio an order reached me from the corps commander, a three-star general, to proceed with the talking tank from the 2nd Armored Division and go to the 83rd Infantry Division, then attacking toward the Harz Mountains. Naturally obedient, Lieutenant Hadley complied. As my little unit was clanking down the road away from the 2nd Armored's battle, I was stopped by the commander of the 2nd Armored, two-star General I. D. White, who was directly under the corps commander, bound by law and military training to carry out the corps commander's orders. The following conversation ensued:

I render my most obsequious and snappy salute, and leap from the tank.

"Where the hell are you going, Hadley?"

"Sir, I have been ordered by the corps commander to take this tank and my other loudspeakers south to the 83rd Division."

"You turn that tank around; you take it back into battle here;

you break your radio so you can't hear anything from corps; and when this battle is over you throw a track or something so you have to stay with my division."

"Yes, sir."

Observing the Aristotelian dramatic unities the scene closes as it opens. I render my most obsequious and snappy salute and clank back in the direction from which I have come.

Lest people think I exaggerate, let me turn to wider history. On December 24, during the Battle of the Bulge, Lieutenant General J. Lawton Collins, VII Corps commander, was passed an order from his superior, the Army commander, full General Courtney Hodges, guardedly over the phone, to "roll with the punch" and look on his map for a town beginning with *H* and another with *A* and rest his front lines there.

"Lightning Joe" Collins was a man who felt, correctly, that his Army commander often lost both opportunities and soldiers' lives by being too cautious. Behind Collins's lines were two large towns: Huy and Andenne. In front, his staff was finally able to locate two small towns: Le Houisse and Achene. Guess which way Collins rolled with the punch, forward or backward? And was he punished for so ingeniously disobeying orders and launching an attack that worked? After the war General Collins became Army Chief of Staff. For years I have been hearing Defense Secretaries and Assistant Secretaries talk about how they are going to "order the military to get on the team." I smile and hope they are wearing helmets when the roof falls in.

Making the postwar problem more complex was a certain set of qualities—what one might call "son-of-a-bitch doggedness"—that produces successful wartime leadership but poor peacetime leaders. Some fortunate officers—Generals Dwight Eisenhower, Omar Bradley, Lauris Norstad, Matthew Ridgway, and James Gavin, along with Admirals Forrest Sherman and Harry Train, spring immediately to mind—can be successful in both worlds. Their command presence combines resolution with flexibility, toughness with compassion, or as the British say, sangfroid without bloody-mindedness. But many wartime commanders had succeeded by the more usual method: "Damn the torpedoes, full speed ahead."

After the war, the outsider, specifically the press and the Congress, saw the much-decorated, successful commanders but could not judge which of them to listen to. The gulf between pride in service and mere parochialism, while vast in effect, is often invisible to those within and without the Defense establishment. How could one tell which commander had successfully snapped the mental shackles that had been welded in place on so many during the lean prewar years? Admiral King, a great wartime naval leader, was to be a disaster as a postwar organizer. General Curtis E. LeMay, a courageous bomber commander who revived and immeasurably strengthened the Strategic Air Command in the fifties, was overwhelmed by the complexities of Vietnam when he was the Air Force member of the Joint Chiefs of Staff. "He sat there at the end of the table," one of the highest Defense officials said of him, and "it didn't matter if his hearing aid was on or off. He didn't understand a thing."

The final invisible force at work was the differing psychological attitudes stamped on each officer, first by his early service and then by his personal wartime experience. Our ideals and attitudes about our work are largely formed in our first job experiences. For example, the reporters of my generation learned their trade when news was more accessible and public officials and the press felt that, though they practiced different professions, they were part of a shared process, with common bonds and beliefs. Our job standards, practices, and expectations differ from those of reporters who broke in during and after the Kennedy-Johnson-Nixon press manipulations and the Vietnam War. (I place no value judgments on this; I merely use it as handy example.) Similarly, a close friend of mine who runs her own computer research firm can tell within two or three minutes of conversation if the executive with whom she is talking received his or her early training at IBM, Hewlett-Packard, Digital Equipment, Apple, etc. The different styles of these firms, picked up early in a person's career, never leave.

So it is within the armed services. The new-fledged Army lieutenant soon learns that he can make no movement without coordination. He cannot go right, left, backward, or forward without informing units on his right and left, artillery, tanks, supply trains, his superiors—all in detail. He is, for all his command authority, a rather restricted part of a whole. His unit's success, indeed its survival, rests on the efforts not just of himself, but of outsiders. If he advances too aggressively, his own artillery may fall on him, or the enemy can sneak between him and the next unit to attack his rear. This tends to make the Army officer more conscious of the needs of others, more supportive of teamwork than are officers in the other services. The Army officer is also apt to be more disciplined. Given an order, he salutes and says "yes, sir" the most readily—which is not always an advantage. We reporters in Vietnam, who saw both the folly of that war *and* the worth of those fighting it, used to lament over what we called "the can-do Army."

The new Army officer's command is also an open book. He is seldom off by himself for any length of time; and on maneuvers he is usually surrounded by the civilian environment. His superiors continually drop by to inspect him. He sees that his battalion and regimental commanders, even his division's commanding general, are themselves restricted in certain ways because they are parts of a whole, whose combined functions produce success. Even when the Army officer, after ten or fifteen years' time, reaches the rank of major or lieutenant colonel and runs a battalion, he still finds teamwork as important to his job as leadership. So early habits of coordination and attention to the abilities of those around him are reinforced. I believe this is why Army officers, even when they may not be as able as officers from another service, tend to perform better in positions of interservice and allied command.

The young naval lieutenant experiences a completely different psychological environment. He is part of a self-contained unit, his ship, that can and often does go off by itself for long periods of time. He does not have to be concerned that his ship will run over a baby carriage or that his crew will steal someone's apples. While his own functions are rigidly prescribed—he cannot, for example, move his guns farther down the road; they are fastened to the ship—he sees that his superiors have tremendous leeway. The commander of a ship puts the wheel to the right, or commands a starboard turn, and, self-contained within the ship, all the paraphernalia of battle—ammunition, men, food, fuel—turn right also. There is no coordination necessary, no requesting permission, no letting people know. While the ship must return to base or conform to formation if maneuvering with a task force, it remains totally independent in ways no Army unit attains. (Even commandoes have to get another service to fly them places.) It may be months before a superior "comes aboard" for an inspection.

The young naval officer sees that, while juniors must rigidly conform, seniors, far from relishing coordination and assisting the function of larger units, glory in independence. They like to be off by themselves, or perhaps with a few other ships, "putting themselves in harm's way." Traditionally, naval officers, more than officers in other services, fight assignments to the Pentagon. They tend to regard shore duty, including study at civilian colleges for graduate degrees, as time wasted. So from the very beginning there is bred into the naval officer an independence of operation, a sense of isolation from other parts of the defense world, indeed from the world itself, for the naval officer puts in more time away from his family than do officers in the other services.

This physical isolation, plus the fact that the naval officer has maintained the aura of being a gentleman more than the officers of the other two services have, makes him more doggedly independent than his Army or Air Force counterpart. Perhaps this is part of the reason why, while the overall quality of the naval officer corps is probably the highest, it seldom produces senior commanders with the breadth of those found in the Air Force and the Army. Nor do naval officers usually do as well in positions of joint or allied command. These early lessons of independence help explain why today the Navy, unfortunately for itself and the country, is most embroiled in Intraservice Warfare: submariners versus surface ship officers versus pilots versus staff bureaus versus Marines versus Atlantic fleets versus Pacific fleets. Such naval parochialism is not merely an American phenomenon. In their perceptive book on the Falklands battle, Max Hastings and Simon Jenkins tax the British Navy with the same arrogance toward the needs of other services.

If at the close of World War II the naval officer had been an aviator, he, like the fliers of the Army Air Corps, would have been promoted a lot faster than officers in the ground or surface forces. Naval aviation and the Army Air Corps began the war with fewer officers and both units expanded faster relative to their numbers. This meant that at the close of World War II the dominant Navy faction, the aviators, shared with their Army Air Corps brethren a belief that life was sweet; they were supersuccessful people to whom good things happened. Aviators, Air Corps and Navy, tended to be expansive, to be certain their strategies were right. Officers in the surface Navy or the Army ground officers, whose promotions had been far, far slower, held less optimistic and certain attitudes about the world.

I remember John R. Norton, one of the leaders of his class at West Point and a highly decorated paratrooper who ended the war as a lieutenant colonel, the top rank reached by any of his ground-bound classmates, going down the list of Air Force officers in his own class and the classes following his who were then brigadier generals. "I'll get ahead of them in about fifteen years," he remarked. (He did.) "But in the meantime, think of all the things they can buy their wives that I can't." On intangibles such as these the new defense structure rose.

The emotional forces that mold a young Air Force officer are more complex and difficult to discern. First, the Air Force is so new a service that the psychological profiles of its members are less historically defined. Then too, the experiences of the bomber pilot and the fighter pilot, to say nothing of the missile engineer, are in many ways markedly different. Still, there are certain psychological constants that distinguish most Air Force officers from those in other services. They are more exuberant, have about them more of the feeling that the future is theirs for the taking. They are apt to have a more passionate attachment to machinery and a very different sense of time. After all, pilots can be in Moscow for lunch. An Army officer measures an hour's progress in yards, a naval officer in miles, an Air Force officer in continents.

Even the way officers in the Army and Air Force use the same metaphor is indicative. When an Army officer says "down among the weeds," he means flat on his belly in the mud with nicks in his helmet, not able to see what is going on, and the stuff cracking by overhead so close the very sound seems to wound. When an Air Force officer says "down among the weeds," he means under 4,000 feet and slightly lost with his wingman missing and those awful red balls of fire zapping up at him out of unseen places and his little "sweat, you're on hostile radar" light going ape. Neither place is pleasant; but you come out of each one, if you do, with different perceptions of time, distance, strategy, technology, warfare, and the world.

Air Force officers are, like naval officers, physically and psychologically further distanced from their killing than Army officers. At the same time their form of warfare is more brutal than that of the other two services, often involving more civilian deaths.

While highly dangerous for short periods of time, an Air Force officer's life is on the whole more pleasant; and in his moments of peril he relies more on machinery, on technocracy, to see him through. (Experts in flying safety believe that the reason some pilots fail to eject from the cockpit of a damaged fighter is not just their refusal to admit failure but also a psychological identification of the cockpit with the womb.) Finally, Air Force officers from the beginning of their careers are more intimately involved with nuclear weapons than are officers in the other services (with the exception of the submariners), training to use them, and in some instances handling them, almost daily.

As a result, what seems important to officers in the other services often appears to Air Force officers as unimportant, "Mickey Mouse." It tends—I repeat, tends—to make them impatient. They have the airplane and often the bomb; they use science, which is the future; they have conquered distance, even space itself—what besides themselves can be necessary for victory? Churchill's jest "With the atom bomb the Air Forces of the world have achieved their final goal. They can destroy the entire human race without the loss of a single pilot" is unfair in the extreme. Still, as in many jests, the barb of slight truth is used to hook the laugh. However, Air Force officers know that they must return in a short period of time to a vulnerable base where they are entirely dependent on those who service their planes, and this tends to mitigate the feeling of isolation they experienced while airborne.

I believe the Air Force marriage with technocracy produces a strong trace of anti-intellectualism, which is more noticeable in that service than in the others. Navy and Army officers at their worst suffer from ridigity. Air Force officers at their worst suffer from lack of brains. (One of their advance planning colonels spent a half hour expounding present-day weapons development to me through a historical analogy that placed Alexander the Great after Julius Caesar.) But at the same time, because of their involvement with strategic warfare, science, procurement of complex weapons, and by now the frontier of space, outstanding Air Force officers have thought a great deal. Of all three services, Air Force officers are the most uneven lot.

Such broad generalizations are always open to challenge. People in the Other America of Defense themselves seldom talk of them.

How can a service that includes carrier pilots and submariners have an integrated personality? How can one that includes missile engineers and fighter jocks? Yet they most certainly do, though there are important subsets of attitudes within each service.

For example, to interpret a fighter pilot's evaluation of a new airplane, one has to know what aircraft he first flew. Fighter pilots who started in single-pilot fighter aircraft, like the F-16, are apt to recommend simpler, faster, more maneuverable aircraft, whereas those with initial service in two-pilot aircraft, like the F-4, lean toward endurance, sophistication, and survivability. What is interesting here is that pilots who have served in single-pilot fighters occasionally, after flying in more complex two-pilot fighter aircraft, switch to preferring such planes. But I have never found a two-pilot fighter pilot who changed to preferring single-pilot models. A great deal that has been written about the value of this or that fighter aircraft has failed to take into account the psychological motivations of those flying officers backing or condemning a particular plane.

For years, in the Army, tank design was in part a contest between those who in World War II had fought in Italy and those who had fought in France and Germany. In Italy, with narrow twisting roads and many mountains, armor protection was more important than mobility. In France and Germany mobility was more important than armor protection.

Many of the bitterest divisions inside the Defense Department happen because of these different service-wide psychological attitudes. To be aware of them is to understand why during the Korean and Vietnam wars naval carrier officers like Admiral Arthur Radford and bomber generals like Curtis LeMay were the most enthusiastic about battle and optimistic of easy victory. Also, one could correctly predict that the three chief military opponents of the Vietnam War would be, as they were, Army airborne Generals Ridgway and Gavin and Marine General David M. Shoup. As Gavin remarked then, "No man who has spent much time in a foxhole is eager for the next war." By now such service attitudes appear to be bred into personnel selection. The Air Force seems set to remain the most bellicose service. In 1974 over 50 percent of the cadets at the Air Force Academy did not approve of detente, while detente was supported by the majority of cadets at Annapolis and West Point. In the battles at the end of World War II over the creation of the Department of Defense this little-understood invisible baggage was often the most important presence in the room.

At war's end those who had served at the front, behind the front, in the defense industries and scientific laboratories, came home, each with his or her own memories. But the very force of their individual recollections created a collective amnesia about the basis of Allied triumph. Nations of differing politics and outlook had worked together, if at times with bristling unwillingness, toward the common goal. Almost all of America had united to strive for victory. In Washington, in spite of crippling interservice battles, a strategy had been agreed upon and the necessary decisions made and carried forward. American industry had mobilized and women had joined the work force in large numbers. Men accepted the rigors and dangers of military life, if not with joy, certainly without massive attempts at evasion. At the dying edge, the three services joined together to fight one war. On the battlefields of air, sea, and land the whole nation produced those junior leaders whose brains, energy, and leadership, given often at final cost, won the war.

Meanwhile, on the home front the Great Divorce began to heal. Leading scientists and other scholars, to whom the very thought of regimentation was anathema, put themselves under military orders and worked. From this unity of society came such war-winning successes as radar, the proximity fuse, the cracking of the German and Japanese codes, and, finally, the atom bomb itself. I am not trying to say that everyone gave 200 percent, that the world shone like the sun, that all bore equally the heat of the day. But there was more than an approach to unity; there was a genuine working national unity that produced victory. This was the war's true glory. And our self-inflicted defeat was that such unity vanished almost immediately upon victory.

THREE

The
Chaotic Creation

I n the fall of 1946 *Life* magazine ran a picture showing all that was left of the famed 2nd Armored Division drawn up in a Texas field. There are 60 officers and men in the picture. No tanks. Two years before, when, having fought from Africa through Sicily and France into Germany, that veteran division pinched off the German thrust in the Battle of the Bulge, it had boasted 14,620 officers and men and 390 tanks. No matter that historically, the aftermaths of major wars have been times of particular turmoil, or that the Soviets had overrun countries for whose freedom we had fought. "Never again!" and "No More War!" were not slogans but certainties. America posted with dexterity to give the alien country of Defense back to the natives, the regulars. The same pattern of political and civil behavior had occurred after World War I, then only twenty-seven years away, when the United States virtually renounced all armed force excepting a small Navy.

Rereading reports and proposals on defense from those days and remembering what it was like to walk the corridors of the Pentagon back then, one is struck by how poorly the future was understood. The dominant belief was that the Pentagon would soon be so empty that other parts of the government would be able to work inside it. I thought I would never see another dead American soldier. If there was to be another war, which we doubted, then it would certainly be all-out and atomic. Overlooked was the fact that between the war's end and the time the Defense Department was finally voted into existence in September 1947, America had already used limited military force, or its threat, as an instrument of policy sixteen times.

In neither political, military, nor academic circles was there serious discussion of the strength necessary to reach various political objectives, because the objectives were ill-defined and the strengths unevaluated. The slogan around Washington, "To keep the peace, we must be strong enough to win a war," typified the level of thought on military affairs. It was not until late 1946 that a few reasoned books on strategic thought, such as Bernard Brodie's *Absolute Weapon* and James M. Gavin's *Airborne Warfare*, began to appear.

The press, which then as now played a major part in setting the nation's agenda, mirrored this lack of strategic thought. Military reporting was considered a dead end. Most of the famous war correspondents had left to become editors, political reporters, or foreign correspondents, the traditional roads to prestige and promotion. When I began regularly covering the Pentagon in 1949 there were roughly fourteen correspondents accredited to the Pentagon, as against some two hundred accredited to the State Department. And we reporters saw the strategic and organizational battles in the same simplistic terms as did those in the armed services and Congress. That writing about defense, like writing about finance, might require some special training was never considered. Many of us reporters were veterans and deemed that experience enough.

After the Vietnam War a particularly able correspondent, Neil Sheehan, wrote: "The techniques of the government propagandist and the public relations man . . . long ago outraced a tired community of hemmed-in reporters, editors who ask the wrong questions and publishers who are more interested in profits than accuracy. Scribbling a few details in a notebook, hustling them into something readable on a typewriter, and then rushing on to another story the next day, was appropriate to police-beat reporting in Chicago in the 1920s. It is an anachronism today."

It was an anachronism back then, too, only we weren't so intro-spective.

In this zeitgeist, the dominant theme in the creation of a new defense organization was how to hold down expenditures, not how to build an efficient structure to secure American interests. Both legislative and executive branches of the government accurately reflected the desires of the American people to shrink military forces and budgets, lower taxes, and fulfill social expectations that had gone unmet in the depression and wartime years. President Truman's 1945 message to Congress on military reorganization exemplified these priorities. His message began by stating:

> I had not fully realized the extent of the waste and inefficiency existing as a result of the operation of two separate and un-coordinated military departments until I became chairman of the special Senate committee created in 1941 to check up on the national defense program. I had long believed that a coordinated defense organization was an absolute necessity. The duplications of time, materiel, and manpower resulting from independent Army and Navy operations which were paraded before my committee intensified this conviction.

It was only in later paragraphs that Truman considered the benefits of a unified command on the applications of armed force.

> In the theaters of operation, meanwhile, we went further in the direction of unity by establishing unified commands. We came to the conclusion, soon confirmed by experience, that any extended military effort required overall coordinated control in order to get the most out of the three armed forces. Had we not early in the war adopted this principle of a unified command for operations, our efforts, no matter how heroic, might have failed.

Here President Truman was echoing the constant theme of General Marshall. As early as the Arcadia Conference in 1942, two weeks after Pearl Harbor, Marshall had told Roosevelt and Churchill: "I am convinced that there must be one man in command of the entire theater, air, ground and ships. We cannot manage by cooperation. Human frailties are such that there would be an emphatic unwillingness to place portions of troops under another service. If we make a plan for unified command now, it will solve nine-tenths of our troubles."

From the time of Truman's first message until today, unification has been presented to the armed forces primarily as a method of saving money. Such words as "we need more military efficiency" are most apt to mean more efficiency in buying weapons rather than in applying violence. This attitude created then and continues to create added resistance on the part of the military to the acceptance of reforms. Senior officers are sensitive to budgetary considerations. They have been to management schools; they work with budgets all the time (albeit often with the same results as the rest of us); they know there must be limits on defense spending. But they resent an argument based almost exclusively on the bottom line, whereas national need, something of a nonstarter in the business world, is often an effective lever inside the Other America of Defense. Where the outsider sees mere profligate spending, the true culprit is more likely to be failure to differentiate between the national interest and a service interest.

As the battles over the new form of defense organization began, the key service role was played by the fledgling Air Force. By the war's end, that service, though under nominal Army control, was already perceived by the public and Congress as independent, and indeed as the dominant service. And within the Air Force the careful prewar and wartime campaigns of the bomber generals to maintain control had been successful. The Air Force was now a bomber service, whose commanders were certain that air power alone could keep the peace or, if necessary, win unaided any future wars. The recently arrived long-range bombers plus the atom bomb made these proponents of strategic air warfare seem prophets whose vision had proved correct. Fighter-plane generals and air-transport officers who were for both an independent Air Force and close cooperation with other services, particularly the ground forces, were placed in military Siberias far from where the press or Congress could hear the questions they raised.

In their drive to become a separate service and play the major role in America's defense, the Air Force generals were greatly aided by the postwar desire to severely restrict military spending. Then, as today, one of the featured attractions of strategic nuclear weapons, whether missiles or bombers, was that they are cheap. No gorgeous Lorelei upon her perilous rock can sing the siren song of defense funds saved and real economies made as sweetly as those who advocate reliance on strategic nuclear weapons alone. In debates over America's postwar defenses, those who most wanted to cut the military budget, who really were, many of them, against most things military, turned to the most violent military answer: strategic bombing.*

The economic argument was particularly compelling in the years immediately after the war, for then we and the British were briefly blessed with an atomic monopoly. That gap between ourselves with nuclear weapons and the rest of the world without them was indeed vast, wider than any prewar ocean, and behind that barrier the most skinflint could feel safe armed with merely a few nuclear weapons. Before Korea, Vietnam, and the years of terrorism and mutual nuclear plenty, those who saw the "absolute weapon" as less than absolute were a forlorn handful.

Air Force efforts to be both separate and dominant were also aided by the rich vein of American isolationism, by no means mined out just because it had proved so disastrous in the prewar years. In our secret hearts are not most of us part isolationist, closet Richelieus, who want to see the fighting and the dying done elsewhere than on our territory? Decked in postwar clothes, the old isolationist arguments powerfully affected the Defense Department's creation. They ran this way: Since the Industrial Revolution, increasing numbers of machines and amounts of steel had been substituted in warfare for men. American bombers, the best in the world, exemplified this historic trend. Ground forces had suffered appalling casualties in World Wars I and II. Strategic bombing, almost decisive in the late war, would now, with the atomic weapon, be decisive in any future war. Nuclear bombing was not only cheaper in dollars; it was cheaper in American lives. And it took place far away from American soil. Was any military power other than air power necessary?

* There is an argument against a nuclear defense policy today that stresses the high cost of nuclear weapons. This has been true particularly in Britain, where the expense of missile submarines is criticized by Left sections of the Labour Party. But this argument, which has interesting points, applies to smaller countries who rely on the U.S. nuclear deterrent for general overall strategic protection, while they maintain other forces for more conventional actions, like regaining the Falklands. For ourselves, strategic nuclear weapons are still the cheap "answer," though they grow ever more expensive. (A 1948 B-36 wing cost $132 million, a 1955 B-52 wing $500 million, a Minuteman wing $1 billion, while the cost of an MX wing still goes unmeasured.)

There was never any doubt that the Air Force would become the separate service that technology and wartime success demonstrated it should be. The issue was how powerful within the armed services this new power would become. To what degree would the Air Force influence or even control the policies and budgets of the other services? Here the monolithic and rigid outlook imposed by the "bomber mafia" on Air Force thought and doctrine worked against even the mildest forms of unification. By concentrating exclusively on the strategic mission and downgrading other air-power functions, the Air Force aroused the distrust of its supporters in the Army and incurred the full wrath of the Navy.

The Navy had been America's strategic service and continued to think of itself that way. Blockade, freedom of the seas, and showing the flag are strategic concepts and naval missions. More Air Force flexibility and respect for interservice missions, such as air defense or support of ground troops, could well have lessened the Navy's feeling of direct challenge. As it was, naval officers believed that, in the words of one admiral, "We would become a taxi-cab service, hauling somebody else's team into battle." They feared that the powerful emergent Air Force would seek additional missions, such as antisubmarine warfare, perhaps even the air transport of naval supplies.

The Navy did not seek to remain dominant by trying to block the Air Force's becoming a separate service. Instead, the admirals strove to make certain that the policies, funds, promotions, and weapons of each service would remain totally under that service's control. In arguing so, the Navy faced several problems. The first of these was the Richardson Report.

Toward the end of the war a team led by Admiral James D. Richardson had asked combat naval commanders for their thoughts on postwar military organization. These men, to whom the lessons of battle were daily realities, insisted that any postwar military organization must be tightly unified, probably in a single department. In 1945, when the Senate Military Affairs Committee began to hold hearings on unification, these admirals changed their minds. They gave a number of not-too-convincing reasons, the principal burden of their testimony being that they had been too busy fighting the war to consider the total problem. But senior Air Force and Army officers had come out of both their warfare experience and their Washington experience with viewpoints diametrically opposed to those of the Navy. Why? The senators wanted to know. The whole episode made the admirals appear intransigent at best.

Further, a principal naval argument in favor of complete automony was the effectiveness of the Navy as a fully integrated service. The Navy had its own fighting ships, its own air force with its carrier air arm, its own supply ships and supply aircraft; it even had its own ground forces, the marines, with their own aviation. The Navy should be left free to operate independently precisely because it was a self-contained, unified force operating under a single command.

But when it came to overall command in Washington, the Navy argued the reverse, that unity of command at that level led to abuses of power, threatened civilian control, and was less efficient. The admirals opposed Air Force actions over water, because all battles on the surface of the oceans, beneath the oceans, and in the air above the oceans were one and required complete unity of command by the Navy. However, such rules did not apply if the Navy wanted to project air power ashore, because over land the air battles and the surface battles were completely different and should be controlled by different services. The only exception to this revealed truth was made if the marines happened to be involved, in which instance the surface battle and the air battle became one and indivisible. Amen.

The Navy had some legitimate fears about the survival of the service in effective form. The atomic bomb made surface ships extremely vulnerable, and it would be several years before people applied the same logic to strategic air bases. The newly created Air Force, no matter how independent in fact, was after all still the old Army Air Corps with bigger wings. One can understand naval anxieties that in any committee the Air Force and the Army would outvote the Navy two to one.

Army and Air Force generals had come out of the war with more prestige than Navy admirals. King, Spruance, and Halsey were legitimate war heroes and so regarded; but they lacked the wide public appeal and press support of such superstars as Omar Bradley, "Tooey" Spaatz, "Hap" Arnold, "Matt" Ridgway, and of course "Ike" Eisenhower. There was an ex–Army officer in the White House, the former artillery battery commander Captain Harry S. Truman. The Navy felt all this would influence Congress and the people against naval programs. Finally, as we have seen, during the war the Navy had come to rely on its legal right of access to the President as its hole card in budget and doctrinal wars. Under complete unification, the three services would be reduced to sub-cabinet level and the Navy would lose its historic lifeline of presidential access.

Tough old Admiral King spelled it out bluntly when he told the senators, "If the Navy's welfare is one of the prerequisites to the Nation's welfare—and I sincerely believe that to be the case—any step that is not good for the Navy is not good for the Nation."

But the Navy neither publicly admitted nor privately faced these very legitimate and important fears. No responsible debate materialized between flexible-power advocates in the Army and Navy on one side and ultimate-response advocates in the Air Force on the other. Instead of serious considerations about the limits of strategic and tactical nuclear power and proper defense organization, the arguments degenerated into allegations, animosity, and leaks.

Before Congress and in the press, the Navy attacked the policy of strategic nuclear bombardment by claiming that nuclear weapons had not really changed warfare, would not be decisive, and were immoral. I recall some admiral—I have mercifully not got his name in my notebook—announcing to a group of us in the Pentagon press that he was using in his mess, with no harmful effects, the silverware recovered from the battleship *Nevada*. The *Nevada*, along with a number of other naval ships placed in the target area, had been sunk during the 1948 Eniwetok atom bomb tests. While establishing his boldness with knife and fork, his announcement did not make the instant converts he seemed to expect.

The Navy then had no planes or aircraft carriers capable of dropping the atomic weapon. The early atom bombs were very heavy and required aircraft too large to be carrier-launched. The Navy's moral problem was that while publicly denigrating the strategic-bombardment doctrine as unworkable and immoral, it was secretly spending major portions of its budget to build super-carriers and airplanes able to handle the few atomic weapons then available. Those of us who knew of the difference between the Navy's public pronouncements and its secret preparations developed an overall distrust of naval policy.

Nor was the Air Force playing by the Marquis of Queensberry rules. Though advocating total reliance on nuclear warfare, it was carefully keeping secret the number of weapons in the nuclear arsenal. It is now known that there were only six, in various stages of assembly. The hydrogen bomb had not then been invented; and the basic ingredient of nuclear weapons, uranium, was still in short supply, with much of it wasted in inefficient methods of weapons manufacture. Many of those taking part in the debate knew this but were constrained from saying so, not merely by the awesome classification placed upon such information, but also by genuine fear that if the Russians learned of this weakness, they would immediately march into Western Europe. To have one side exaggerating the available strategic airpower while the other was gagged by patriotism further enraged the partisans and poisoned rational consideration of defense questions.

Those intangibles mentioned at the close of the last chapter now played their vital part. Naval officers remained angry at Air Force officers for claiming successes against the Japanese Navy that had been achieved by naval aviators. And these hard feelings were directed primarily at the dominant bomber generals who had made the claims. Navy pilots regarded the Air Force pilots as inferior to them socially and intellectually, as high school rah-rah guys with no college education. (Hollywood reflected American and service preconceptions. In the Academy Award winner for 1946, *The Best Years of Our Lives*, both the Navy seaman and the Army sergeant are shown, on return home, to be educationally and socially above their military superior, the Air Force lieutenant, who was a soda jerk before he got wings.) It was not that both Air Force and naval pilots didn't love to chase girls and drink whiskey. But the Navy pilots saw the Air Force pilots as people who chewed bubble gum and scratched themselves while they chased girls and drank whiskey.

During the war the Air Force had been proud of its democratic, dirt-beneath-the-fingernails approach to command. There was no Air Force Academy until the late fifties; and while top Army Air Corps commanders were largely West Pointers, many senior Air Force officers were pure fliers from land grant colleges, or men who had not gone beyond high school. When the Air Force became an independent service in 1947, only 50 percent of its officers had attended college, as against 77 percent in the Army and 85 percent in the Navy.

This flexible attitude, which had worked to the Air Force's advantage in recruiting pilots during the war, now turned against it. I recall several naval aviators saying to me of Air Force pilots at the time (the use of the words "aviator" and "pilot" is deliberate; both groups so named themselves): "Have you ever tried to talk to those guys?" The naval aviators, who Air Force planners had believed would join with them to create a super-service, began to shy away from their Air Force brethren. After some soul-searching, they elected to stay in the Navy, believing that they would control the future of that service (as they have), and so better control the country's defense and their own future. It is interesting to speculate what might have happened had fighter pilots, and even nonfliers, had a greater say in the policies of the fledgling Air Force. Would their greater mental flexibility and appreciation of interservice problems and missions have led to more agreement among air-power advocates in both the Air Force and Navy? And so to a more unified Defense Department?

And what of the final military player, the Army, the service that under Marshall's guidance was willingly casting loose the Army Air Corps? Walking down the corridors of the Pentagon, Colonel Fred Young, one of the Army staff at that time responsible for future planning, suddenly turned to me and remarked, "You know where the Army is today? The Navy has come out of this war with the concept of control of the seas and worldwide projection of power through the fast carrier task force. The Air Force has come out with the nuclear weapon and strategic bombing of the enemy heartland. And the Army? What have we done? We have this week, after two years of deliberation, added a laundry and bath company to the infantry division."

Unlike the Navy and Air Force, the postwar Army had no completely dominant faction to insist on a given future role. The prewar Army had been a tight club that existed to be the cadre around which would be built the mass wartime Army. In World Wars I and II, the old Army had performed this role with excellence. Was this still the Army's peacetime mission? Or should that mission now become, as some officers, mostly airborne, advocated, the maintenance of a permanent standing Army of sufficient size to both deter and overcome threats that called for less than the strategic nuclear response? With the draft halted and Congress in an economy mood, there were great pressures to become merely a small cadre. After the war, the Army, led by a conservative infantry faction, cut back both its airborne and mechanized forces and returned to thinking of itself primarily as a cadre from which emergency forces could spring.

Historically, the Army had been the service with the most constrained peacetime budget. At war's end the Army had already taken the most drastic cutbacks in size and equipment. By 1946 Marshall was privately warning President Truman and Congress that he doubted the Army could even defend the overseas air bases from which the Air Force planned to launch its strategic nuclear attack. The Army believed in as much unification as possible, in the hope that with the defense of the United States seen as an entity, the importance of ground forces would be recognized and the Army would be given, if not the lion's share, a better portion of the funds.

Continuing Army fears, one could almost say paranoia, about being the service most damaged by budget cuts, bears brief examination as it remains an important part of the Tooth-to-Tail/Readiness problem. Quick military savings, the kind usually made to trim the budget, most often fall on the Army. For example, in Boston on 20 August 1980, candidate Reagan promised to "implement a program of compensation and benefits for valued military personnel comparable to what is available in the private sector." Then in May 1981 the Reagan administration cut back the military pay increase from 8 percent to 4 percent. Since the Army has the most people, this traditional method of budgetary pruning falls most heavily on that service.

Further, Army equipment is also the most vulnerable to the budget knife. The so-called big-ticket items, such as bombers, carriers, and air bases, are politically harder to cancel than small items like rifles, tanks, and helicopters, while pruning the smaller items produces quicker savings. In May 1982, when the Senate had to choose between two supercarriers, cost $3.4 billion each, and fifty AH64 attack helicopters at $15 million apiece, the choppers were chopped. This happened even though the carriers were controversial and there was general military agreement that the helicopters were necessary, both to counter Soviet tank superiority and as antiterrorist weapons in the Middle East.

In 1947, the Army neither burned with the Air Force's desire for independence nor felt the Navy's anxiety over its very existence. The Army largely left the field to others during the debates on future military organization. This was surprising, as the Army's commitment to a single command went deeper than the hope for a more just (as Army officers saw it) distribution of promotions and dollars. The psychological attitudes in favor of teamwork, fostered by early Army experience, had been reinforced during the war by the cooperation with the Air Force and Navy necessary for victory on the ground.

Then there was Army loyalty to General Marshall. Marshall favored complete unification, and where Marshall marched the Army followed. The Army alone during World War II had fought major battles in both the Pacific and the European theaters. By and large the Navy had fought in the Pacific and the Air Force in Europe. Having fought in both theaters, the Army could contrast the way it had been able to fight in Europe, where it had a strong voice in planning operations, with how it had had to proceed in the Pacific (outside of Douglas MacArthur's area of command), where it had little voice in command or operations. The European experience, the Army was convinced, had produced victory with fewer casualties.

Largely to its own detriment, there simmered in the Army position a large dollop of self-righteousness. The President and the civilian leaders in the Army and Air Force wanted service unification. Senior Army officers and former Army Air Corps officers were in the forefront of the unification battle. The Army had let the Air Force go without protest, even encouraged the growth of that service. Now the Army should be rewarded with the gift of complete service unification because it had "played on the team." Perhaps this was the doctrine with which the Army had exited World War II: "We play on the team." If so, it was not a potent enough program, viewpoint, or slogan to prevail against the Navy fighting for its life or the Air Force intent on exploring the limits of the air-power envelope.

The shape of America's future defenses would be determined by legislation, so it was before and inside Congress that the organizational battle was fought. In fairness to the legislators, they were called upon to make some difficult political and intellectual choices, with the historical precedents unclear at best, misleading at worst.

Admiral Alfred T. Mahan, a pioneering American military thinker, had held that no country could become dominant on land and sea simultaneously. Successful nations had kept the peace by emulating the hedgehog of the Greek proverb "The fox knows many things, but the hedgehog knows one great thing." Traditionally, the British had navies, the French armies. Neither nation in peacetime had both; this had been true since before Napoleon. Athens, the mother of democracies, had been the sea power, Sparta and Rome, land powers. Nations had never been, did not have to be, both. Air power was seen by most as decisive in the recent war. Was not the proper course of action to create a separate Air Force and also assure that naval air could make its contribution as before?

American tradition and the immediate past reinforced such beliefs. The United States had always been a sea power, never a land power. World War II had been fought on land, air, and sea at great cost in dollars and men. Should America now turn her back on her history and begin a new and expensive policy to maintain three military forces inside some untested and powerful unified structure? Would this not bankrupt the nation and cause another fearful Great Depression, like that which had existed before the war? It certainly meant reviving the politically explosive draft.

The attitude of those in Congress was particularly decisive because President Truman, elevated from the Vice Presidency by Roosevelt's death and not yet elected in his own right, remained unsure and hesitant in his use of presidential power. His correspondence, memoranda, and recorded conversations make clear that Truman wanted a strongly unified Defense Department. "What I don't want is three separate services," he told Marshall. But while Truman argued and cajoled for this principle, he was not as effective politically as he would become in his second term.

General Marshall believed that he and General Eisenhower together could convince the Congress of the need for complete unification. At the close of World War I, Marshall, then a major, had written: "Immediately following the termination of war, the public mind centers on the tragedies involved. All are thinking of the recent sacrifices of life which always have been due in a serious measure to a lack of methodical preparation. Therefore, the legislators are in a frame of mind to recognize our military necessities and they draft their laws accordingly."

For once, Marshall overestimated his power and underestimated the antimilitary mood of the country in those years before the Communist coup in Czechoslovakia and the Berlin blockade. He failed to realize how quickly and completely America had lost interest in defense and turned to former ways of thought. Marshall was respected, he was listened to, he could usually persuade a majority; but he could not command the broad support for necessary programs, as he had in the past and would again in the future as Secretary of Defense during the Korean War.

One time during that war, at the end of his testimony before the House Appropriations Committee, some smarmy placeman on the committee unctuously asked, "Is there anything more we can do for you, General Marshall?"

Marshall was gathering his papers together and icily replied, "Yes, give me the same considerate attention when I next come before you in time of peace to ask for far less." During the Defense Department's creation, not even the combined wisdom and prestige of Marshall and Eisenhower could override considerations of domestic politics.

The Air Force, while favoring complete unification, was not as effective an advocate as it might have been. With its attractive strategic doctrines, the prestige and glamour of its generals, and the lobbying clout of the aircraft industry, the Air Force could deploy potent political power. But once the Air Force had won its independence, the aircraft industry had no real interest in what type of organization would knit the three services together. Indeed, as the aircraft companies also wanted Navy contracts, they usually stayed neutral in the unification fight. In addition, as we have seen, General Kuter, in his distrust of the Army, had prepared the wrong arguments and lined up the wrong allies for the legislative battle. He had believed the Army would fight Air Force independence. When the Army willingly let the Air Force go while the Navy moved to block unification, Kuter found himself with his legislative troops facing the wrong way.

The most important player in the congressional battle was the House patriarch, "Uncle Carl" Vinson of Georgia, Chairman of the House Armed Services Committee. In those days House committee chairmen wielded close to absolute power; and Uncle Carl was regarded as the most powerful of all these. Ever since the early thirties the Navy had assiduously and brilliantly courted this crusty gentleman. He and Roosevelt had on occasion used relief agency funds for naval construction. In 1934 Vinson sponsored the Vinson-Trammel Act, which began the rebuilding of the prewar Navy.

By the war's end it was said, with some truth, that the Navy had built so many bases and poured so much concrete in Georgia that the whole state was in danger of tipping into the Atlantic. Minor service secretaries and junior admirals and generals were terrified of Uncle Carl. Newsmen both respected and feared him, for he could be of great benefit to their careers through his use of one or another of them as conduits for inside defense information. Few of his colleagues would cross him, because of the enormous defense funds he could give to or withhold from their districts and the political alliances he had forged as a result.

Yet in many ways Vinson, like most successful politicians, reflected as much as led the feelings and concerns of Congress. The Navy had certainly done a superb job of lobbying Congress in favor of its position; however, in addition, a series of intangibles favored an organization that left each service free to pursue its own policies relatively unhindered. Congress has always seemed to feel less threat from the Navy than from the other services. No regular naval officer has ever been President or seriously sought that office, so Congress does not see admirals as political threats the way they do generals, remembering Presidents and presidential candidates Dwight Eisenhower, Curtis LeMay, Douglas MacArthur, Ulysses Grant, even George Washington. Naval battles take place far away, on an ocean. They are deadly but produce less horrendous American casualties than ground battles or the bombing of cities. This makes naval force the cleanest and most acceptable form of military power.

There is a romantic aura about great ships of the line, battleships or aircraft carriers, that the other services cannot match. The Air Force can fly one round the world on a junket; but the Navy also can do that and throw in a Caribbean cruise. (You don't hear much talk about submarines in Congress. Or committee members and hotshot staffers spending two weeks under the ice cap to check out the Polaris system.) Finally, the Navy is a volunteer service and admirals tend to feel the draft unnecessary, an attitude shared by most of Congress. Over and over Capitol Hill old-timers tell newcomers, "There are two issues that will kill you: the draft, and gas rationing."

Congress, like all political bodies, is loath to share power. A truly unified defense posture might dilute the ability of politicians to press forward with their favored programs, get funds for their own districts, or champion their preferred weapons systems. Those who felt this way fought under a dubious standard which had emblazoned on it, "Beware a sinister German General Staff type of organization."

This was a popular, budget-cutting antimilitary stance to adopt, and parts of the press, most notably the influential Chicago *Tribune*, joined the cry. Navy lobbyists exploited this pseudo fear brilliantly. As finally written, an appendix to the National Security Act of 1947 stated, "The Joint Staff shall not operate or be organized as an overall Armed Forces General Staff and shall have no executive authority." The German General Staff had not been organized that way since the middle of World War I, and no one had the slightest intention of creating such a discredited form of organization. Yet the slogan carried the day and the Joint Chiefs and their staffs were created—and remain—militarily impotent.

Two different plans for armed force organization came before Congress. The Secretary of the Navy, James Forrestal, was a strange, able, and lonely man, and an extreme partisan of the naval view. Within two years he would change his mind, feel he had been "sold a bill of goods" by senior admirals, and destroy his health trying to create a stronger Defense Department. But in late 1945 Forrestal, convinced that the Navy had lost its case before both the Congress and the public, turned to his friend and business associate, Ferdinand Eberstadt, to devise a plan that would lend intellectual credibility to the Navy's position. What Eberstadt did in effect was broaden the discussion about military reorganization to include all foreign policy. In his plan, the Air Force joined the Army and Navy as an independent service, and all three services were coordinated by some committees at the top. This Navy plan, known as the Eberstadt plan, went before Congress along with the Army/Air Force plan for full unification. This latter was known as the Collins plan, after its author, J. Lawton Collins. He was the Army general who during the Battle of the Bulge had found the two small towns that permitted him to roll forward with the punch.

Congress debated the two plans, though debate may be too

polite a word for the year and a half in which the partisans of each view hurled charges at one another and leaked loaded figures and reports to their allies. The *New York Times* was then, as it is now, quite properly enormously influential—perhaps more so then, since there was no television news to speak of, and the *Washington Post* and *Wall Street Journal* had not risen to their present national eminence.

The *New York Times* alone among the press had a full-time military affairs correspondent in addition to its Pentagon correspondent. That able man was Hanson Baldwin, a 1924 graduate of the Naval Academy. Other reporters with less knowledge looked to him for guidance. His paper more than any other set the public stage for the defense debate. I am certain (I am not just being polite; having known him and admired his integrity and craft, I am *certain*) that he never consciously distorted the news. However, the unfortunate extent of his unconscious pro-Navy bias time and again had a chilling effect on efforts of President Truman, Secretaries Stimson, Lovett, and Patterson and Generals Marshall, Eisenhower, Bradley, Spaatz, Vandenberg, and Norstad to unify the armed forces efficiently.

On 25 July 1947, Congress legislated what almost no one had wanted, three separate services barely linked together by coordinating committees at the top. The Navy had won the day. People who believe they are fighting for their lives fight with more vigor. At the time, few outside the greatly reduced armed services cared about the legislative outcome.

The act of 1947, which controls today's American armed forces, created the National Military Establishment, with a Secretary of Defense at the top who had practically no authority over the three services, budgetary or otherwise. The Secretary was allowed several personal assistants but not even given a deputy secretary or any assistant secretaries. He was specifically forbidden to interfere with the services in their major roles and missions. A Joint Staff was created but limited to one hundred men. (It is now four hundred.) The chiefs of the three services sat as coequals at the head of this staff, over which they had no command. They did not even have a chairman, so thoroughly had Congress bought the Navy view that centralization was to be feared. In addition to creating the Air Force as an independent service, coequal with the Navy and the Army, the act created the National Security Council to coordinate military and diplomatic policy. Also given life at this time was the Central Intelligence Agency, to supply and oversee intelligence. A Munitions Board, before which the three services could haggle over supplies, was also created (it has since disappeared).

In addition to these main features, many special fiefdoms and restrictions were incorporated into the act. Most of these were legislative fiats in favor of the Navy's retaining a cherished function.

These deals were arrived at in a small, tightly controlled committee where General "Laury" Norstad negotiated for the Air Force, General Collins for the Army, and Admiral Forrest Sherman for the Navy. For example, the emergent Air Force was given control of all military logistical air transport with the creation of the Military Air Transport service. In return for losing its air transport arm, the Navy was given control over all sea transport, some of which had previously belonged to the Army. (By 1985 the Navy had gotten most of its air transport arm back.)

A bitter battle was fought over the antiaircraft mission. Initially the Air Force insisted that this should be its job. The Army argued that antiaircraft was an extension of artillery and should remain its responsibility. Here the Army won. Many of the antiaircraft officers were quite senior and were not pilots. To place them in the Air Force would have created problems for that service. Pilots would have had to be demoted to accommodate the nonflying antiaircraft officers. (Interestingly, after studying the United States and British experiences where the Army has the antiaircraft responsibility, the Germans, in recreating their armed forces, went the other way, giving antiaircraft to their Air Force.) In the beginning the Army was enthusiastic about the antiaircraft mission, seeing it as an entry card into the world of missiles and strategic missions. More recently this enthusiasm has waned, and antiaircraft is an underfunded and underdeveloped area.

Writing in his diary about such battles, General Eisenhower recorded, "Some services [he meant the Navy] were apparently so unsure of their value to the country that they insisted upon writing into law a complete set of rules and specifications for their future organization and duties. Such freezing of detail in an age that is witnessing the most rapid and significant scientific advances of all history is silly, even vicious. The writers of such provisions would probably have done the same with respect to horse cavalry . . . and towed field guns." Even Admiral King, whose steadfast opposition to unification had done as much as anything else to ensure a weak Defense Department, did not like the legislation finally passed by Congress. "Now look at the damn thing!" he remarked to friends.

Almost from the beginning it was obvious to all but the most violent Navy partisans that "the damn thing" was not working. One of the first to change his mind was the former Navy supporter James Forrestal, who became Secretary of Defense on 17 September 1947, after Truman's first choice, Assistant Secretary for War Robert Patterson, who favored a unified department, had refused the position. Less than a year and a half later Forrestal and his small band of assistants had become completely discouraged trying to manage the new department without the necessary authority. Even with the best of organizations, the job, with Congress insisting on severe military austerity, would have been difficult and politically treacherous. The military budget was around $11 billion, with 1.6 million military personnel on active duty. As always, as funds decreased, interservice squabbling increased.

Powerless to enforce order himself and with the Joint Chiefs equally impotent, a now-desperate Forrestal took the three chiefs into seclusion at Key West, Florida, in March 1948 and at Newport in August of the same year in an effort to stop the departmental infighting over missions. He made some progress, largely because, with the Czechoslovakian coup and the Berlin blockade, $3 billion had been added to the military budget and nuclear explosives were becoming more plentiful. However, in the main one could quote Othello: "Chaos is come again." These Key West agreements were made before the days of intercontinental missiles, smart weapons, nuclear plenty, Korea, NATO, Vietnam, terrorism, satellites, and nuclear submarines. Yet they remain the vaguely defined guidelines for today's defense actions.

The inflexible dominance of the bomber generals now had a number of unfortunate consequences for the newly created Defense Department; and these began inside the Air Force. As in any organization that imposes a doctrinal rigidity upon its members, thought began to suffer. The Air Force was the newest service, a pioneer, closely involved with new weapons and tech-nology; air officers should have been pioneering new doctrines and showing great flexibility of thought. The opposite happened—a trend that unfortunately continues.

Tactical weapons such as fighters, fighter bombers, tanks, or more recently, the smaller precision guided missiles are not in themselves decisive, war-winning breakthroughs. To be effective, these weapons must be correctly integrated into the overall battle. The example usually cited is the first use of tanks in World War I, by the British at Cambrai. The tanks broke through the German trench lines; but because tactics had not been changed, there was no follow-up advance and so no decisive victory. Officers who excel at the use of tactical weapons must show mental flexibility, inventiveness, and broad teamwork. Fighter pilot officers there-fore tended to be more at home with complexity than their bomber brethren. By denying fighter officers an appropriate voice in positions of power, the Air Force found itself often backing rather simplistic defense policies that alienated the other services.

Strategic weapons, on the other hand, whether they are bomb-ers, missiles, or satellites, while technically complex, tend to be simple to employ. In strategic warfare technology is paramount. A breakthrough, such as multiple independently targeted war-heads on a single missile, or effective lasers in space, or the atomic bomb, can be decisive. But such breakthroughs require little change in tactics, nor are new methods of cooperation with other services made necessary. The challenging, close interweaving of many separate parts that is vital in tactical warfare is absent. The simpler nature of strategic warfare and its general destructiveness meant that bomber generals tended to be tough, inflexible, and oriented toward hardware.

For example, General "Hap" Arnold, a bomber general and the Air Force Chief of Staff during and immediately following the war, when planning the Air Force future, used a Mercator projection map until mid-1945. Then, even when familiar with more accurate maps, he failed to grasp that the shortest way be-tween the Soviet Union and the United States was over the North Pole. He continued to treat the North and South Poles as areas of equal threat. A civilian aide who came into the office of James Forrestal, the first Secretary of Defense, at a late hour and found him hard at work remarked on the difficulties of defending against the Russians; Forrestal blurted out, "It's not the Russians, it's not the Russians. It's the weakness of the Air Staff."

The Air Force became further divided as the dominant bomber faction pushed for the development of the hydrogen, or thermonuclear, bomb at the expense of other Air Force weapons systems. The Navy distrusted this effort because the hydrogen weapon would be even heavier than the atomic weapon and so would not be "carrier deliverable." The Navy tended to see the hydrogen bomb as part of a plot to keep it from taking part in strategic warfare. The Tactical Air Command wasn't too enthusiastic about the hydrogen bomb either. TAC, like the Navy and to a lesser extent the Army, wanted scientific research concentrated on making nuclear weapons smaller and lighter, that is, capable of being hung on fighters or put into artillery pieces.

The first hydrogen bombs, before Edward Teller's breakthrough made it possible to construct them from materials such as lithium deuteride, were made from liquid hydrogen and had to be flown to the Soviet Union and dropped at extremely low temperatures. The B-36s modified to carry these bombs, refrigerated to many degrees below zero, looked inside like flying honeycombs of pressure pumps and tubes. A friend in the Tactical Air Command slipped me into one during a refueling stop at Pope Air Force Base. The bomber was at a fighter base and a fighter general wanted to show me how the bomber generals in his own service were "lying."

"Christ, Hadley, look at that! A peashooter will stop that s.o.b. from getting to Moscow." If Air Force fighter generals were saying that about their own, imagine how senior naval officers felt about coming under control of the bomber mafia.

During early 1949, Forrestal further reversed himself. Again with the help of Eberstadt, now also a convert to a unified Defense Department, he presented a new set of legislative proposals to Congress. These changes, while still not going as far as the original Collins proposal, were designed to greatly increase the authority of both the Secretary of Defense and the Joint Staff. Among other items Forrestal asked Congress for were (1) a legal increase in his authority over the services; (2) an increase in his staff and the creation of a deputy secretary of defense along with three assistant secretaries; (3) the transfer to the office of Defense Secretary of the power to appoint the chairmen of the statutory boards, the director of the Joint Staff, and other key civilian personnel; (4) the transfer to his office of the functions of the Munitions Board, the Research and Development Board, and the Joint Chiefs of Staff; and (5) the grant to the Defense Secretary of effective control over the budgets of all three services. Later these proposals were expanded to include the creation of a chairman of the Joint Chiefs of Staff.

While these proposals were being debated Forrestal's health deteriorated and he began the drift into the depression that would lead to his suicide. Meeting him at this time, Eisenhower wrote in his diary, "Jim F. is apparently highly discouraged. . . . He blames himself far too much for the unconscionable situation now existing. He is obviously most unhappy. At one time he accepted unequivocally and supported vigorously the navy 'party line,' given him by the admirals. Only today he said to me, 'In the Army there are many that I trust—Bradley, Collins, Gruenther, Wedemeyer, and Lemnitzer and Lutes, to name only a few. In the Navy I think of only Sherman and Blandy among the higher ones. Possibly Conolly, also.' It must have cost him a lot to come to such a conclusion."

As the Pentagon slid further into anarchy and Forrestal's health grew steadily worse, President Truman, now President in his own right, appointed as Defense Secretary the rough and abrasive Louis Johnson. Johnson had been the chief fund-raiser of Truman's 1948 come-from-behind victory; and the President hoped that Johnson, famed as a tough administrator, would be able to force harmony on the Pentagon. In April 1949, without warning and almost without consultation, Johnson personally canceled work on the $188-million supercarrier the *United States*, which the Navy regarded as its sole hope to get back into the strategic nuclear mission. "The Navy has built its last big carrier," Johnson told associates. (If the Defense Department didn't cost so much you could put its history on Broadway and play it as farce.)

The Navy struck back in the infamous "Revolt of the Admirals." The admirals were sincere in their desire for a supercarrier and correct in their belief that naval air had a place in the United States' arsenal. However, they adopted an indefensible course of action. In a series of leaked reports they charged that the mainstay of America's defense, the B-36 bomber, was worthless and had been built solely to enrich certain senators, Air

Force officers, contractors, and senior defense officials, including Secretary of the Air Force W. Stuart Symington and Defense Secretary Johnson. Here the admirals reverted to an unfortunate pattern of the prewar world, one that repeats itself today: Leaders of a service who fear that they will lose a strategic argument, instead of stating the merits of their case, attack the chosen weapons system of a rival service. At that time the admirals making the charges would tell you privately they knew the charges were false; but they felt there was no other way to stop the runaway self-aggrandizement of the newly independent Air Force.

The charges of fraud in the bomber purchase alarmed the country sufficiently that Congress called an investigation. This time the Navy was routed; its Chief of Operations, Admiral Louis Denfeld, an oleaginous timeserver whose rise to the top baffled even his fellow admirals, was forced to resign. Its farcical Secretary, Francis P. ("Rowboat") Matthews, who once sent parts of the nation's top secret war plans out to the cleaners in his jacket pocket, became a cartoon character of fun. The mild-mannered General Omar Bradley, just appointed the first Chairman of the Joint Chiefs, carried the day with his stinging testimony before the House, castigating the revolting admirals as "Fancy Dans who won't hit the line with all they have on every play, unless they can call the signals . . . Many in the Navy are completely against unity of command and planning as established in the laws. . . . the Navy has opposed unification from the beginning, and they have not, in spirit as well as deed, accepted it completely to date."

The investigation closed with the Congress now supporting the Army/Air Force view; and the B-36 got a clean bill of health. The supercarrier stayed canceled for a few years. But in the ruckus, vital parts of Forrestal's proposals got lost. The Secretary of Defense got more control over supplies but failed to achieve unification in weapons design and production, a failure that still handicaps the country.

The admirals' revolt raised a serious question that still troubles the country: When should military professionals speak out? There is an easy answer to this, one unfortunately too often advocated by Congress and the Executive: They should speak when they agree with you; otherwise they should "get on the team and keep quiet."

The problems of discipline, security, leadership, and freedom involved here are difficult. But how can you promote someone to admiral or general, give him life-and-death responsibility over thousands, ask him to be honest with his subordinates, and then not allow him to speak out publicly? Undoubtedly my press bias is at work here, but I cannot see the impropriety of allowing officers to respond on selected occasions: "I've been given an order I don't agree with for such and such reasons. But then, I've been wrong in the past, and I'm trying to make this work."

Further, permitting those in authority to speak out is a partial solution to the grave problems of leaks. If a service viewpoint is being publicly stated by those in command, juniors are far less likely to incontinently spray secret information over the body politic. Just after the Korean War the Eisenhower administration severely cut back the military budget. General Vandenberg, the Air Force Chief of Staff, felt that the cuts were falling too heavily on strategic bombing. He stated this opinion forcefully before Congress. At the time I thought he was wrong on the issue, and I still do. But I believe he was absolutely right to take his doubts to Congress. Interestingly, with Vandenberg speaking out publicly and then following orders, there was no Air Force revolt. And today Air Force officers can discuss Vandenberg's objections rationally, some agreeing with him, others not. Naval officers still tend to be uptight about the admirals' revolt.

In the eight months between the Revolt of the Admirals and the onslaught of the Korean War, the Defense Department, disorganized, demoralized, and without strategic guidance, continued to prepare for the wrong war with insufficient funds. Intent on cutting the budget, Congress and much of the civilian executive leadership remained certain that the *only* weapons system necessary to preserve peace was strategic nuclear air power. All three services at least tipped their hats to the possibility of limited nonnuclear war; but all three services funded first, and often second and third, those parts of themselves that would maximize their participation in the strategic nuclear mission (though the Army, with less claim on any strategic mission, had fewer dollars to spend).

There was nothing wrong with emphasizing strategic nuclear warfare. Intelligence had revealed a concerted drive by the Soviet Union to manufacture hydrogen bombs and bombers, and letting this go unchallenged would have been highly dangerous. It was the exclusion fixation on one particular form of warfare, one particular military mission, that was about to raise doubts over the Giant's strength.

I happened to be alone on duty at *Newsweek* in Washington that Sunday in June 1950 when the first reports that North Korean troops had invaded South Korea came in. The *Newsweek* Washington office closed on Sundays and Mondays with only the junior member, myself, on duty. I was glum at having to spend both my birthday and the day after at work. That sunlit morning after the ticker had chattered out the first tentative reports that an invasion of South Korea might be in progress, I cabbed over to the Pentagon to contact my friends and see what was going on. In those simple days you didn't even need passes to get into the Pentagon on a weekend. Officers slowly began to drift in to work, as puzzled and confused as I. The fact that "Pearl Harbor happened on a Sunday" received much comment.

Some of the colonels down at International Branch had been at the Yale Graduate School with me, and in the Operations Branch were a couple more with whom I had fought the war in Europe. We all got together and began talking the situation over. What I mainly remember, looking back, though my notes don't reflect that feeling, is our complete innocence. We sat there or stared out the window at the lawns, drinking coffee and asking each other what was happening. Was this the start of World War III? Would the United States resist? Would we use the atom bomb? Were the reports even true? How good was the South Korean Army? The North Korean Army? From time to time some wag would stick his head in the door to ask if we had called the National Guard to duty and federalized it yet.

It soon became obvious that the Associated Press and United Press reports out of Korea were more up-to-date than anything official reaching the Pentagon from the Far East. I asked if the CIA was reporting anything that might help my editors, now holding the magazine for late developments. No one in the Pentagon had heard from the CIA. Sitting in the Army's International Branch office I called Admiral Roscoe H. Hillenkoetter, the director of the CIA. I reached an aide, explained my plight, and Hillenkoetter came on the phone. I am recounting this not to prove myself a hotshot but to stress the difference between then and today. What was the AP saying, Hillenkoetter wanted to know. He hadn't been able to get hold of the AP wire.

I read him the Associated Press reports. He indicated his people were as much in the dark as everyone else about the size and intent of the invasion. I called up *Newsweek* in New York. They didn't think much of my noninformation. I didn't either, though this lack of knowledge about what was actually happening foreshadowed many of the fiascoes to follow. The colonels and I got out some yellow legal-size pads and began making notes to try to figure out what forces we had, if we decided to fight in Korea, and did so by some method other than dropping our few atom bombs.

There were three occupation divisions in Japan, each at about one-third strength. That would make one division, particularly if you added the understrength regiment in the Philippines. Then in the United States there were the 82nd Airborne and 3rd Infantry divisions and two Marine divisions at half strength. But those divisions were the strategic reserve for all of Europe and the Mediterranean. The draft had been officially stopped two weeks before. Would the politicians allow that to start up again?

In the Air Force, the F-84s, the best ground-support aircraft, were grounded with engine bearing problems. We could probably get about twenty F-80s out of Japan over Korea in the next week but they'd have about ten minutes over target at that range. And who the hell would find the targets? What about the Navy? There was a carrier in Japan. But she was part of the strategic force. Could she be used? That was the total of military power available from the superpower of the free world. After the double warning of the Czechoslovakian coup and the Berlin blockade, the stark choices facing America were to acquiesce in the invasion, commit that pitifully small force, and hope; or go to nuclear war. Unfortunately, on an expanded scale, these are much the same choices we would face today.

FOUR

Korea and NATO: Successes and Failures

Soldiers refusing to fight; pilots refusing to fly; supplies that never arrive, units that simply melt away. Today to most Americans this conjures up Vietnam. Yet all that happened in Vietnam had occurred a decade before in Korea, a war we forgot almost at the instant of battle. Indeed, until 1969, for the majority of the professionals who had fought in both Korea and Vietnam, the Korean experience left the more bitter taste. Only after 1969, when the returned warrior was reviled as a butcher or worse, when the breakdown of discipline left the American armed forces divided, maiming each other and incapable of sustained combat, did the Vietnam experience become the more enraging and painful.

Nineteen years after the Korean war, I sat in a Vietnamese bunker about an hour's chopper-ride northeast of Hue, commiserating with a dedicated and able officer, then Lieutenant Colonel "Chuck" Shea, about his problems commanding a battalion in Vietnam during 1969. Shea politely disagreed with my gloomy assessment of his problem's extent and uniqueness. Even now, he felt, with the war winding down, much of the country back home turning antiwar, and the draft sending Vietnam a skewed segment of American society, his life was easier than it had been in the early days of the Korean War.

In Korea he had been an unfledged lieutenant going forward as an infantry replacement. He joined his company at night. The company was at less than half strength, partially dug in on the forward slope of a hill and in contact with the enemy. He and the captain commanding were the only two officers. Shortly after shaking Shea's hand the captain wandered off the hill into the wet, stinking dark and was never seen again. The first sergeant declared himself sick and took off for the rear. When Shea crawled out to inspect his five outposts, he found all the soldiers at four of them asleep. Which, as he remarked, could have been for the best; because they were green and nervous and might well have shot him by mistake. Making the corporal in charge of his only awake outpost his new first sergeant, the lone officer and his exhausted and indifferent company settled down to await the dawn attack.

Korea, a war far more intense than Vietnam, is our neglected war. No histories or biographies have emerged from it comparable to those of World War II or Vietnam. Nor have novels appeared to march alongside such classics from Vietnam as *The Centurions, Parthian Shot,* or *Fields of Fire.* Nor did the reporters who covered Korea produce such reflective books as those on Vietnam by Braestrup, Fall, Halberstam, Herr, Just, Oberdorfer, Sheehan, to single out a few arbitrarily. For those inside the Other America of Defense today, the frustrations and limits of Korea and Vietnam, rather than the triumphs of World War II, color their perceptions of military power. Korea was the first test of the newly created Defense Department. All of the old faults, from Interservice Rivalry through the Great Divorce, that had handicapped the war effort in World War II remained. Indeed, in many areas, thanks to the Flawed Organization created in 1947, and faulty strategic perceptions by the nation's leaders, the situation was initially worse.

The United States had not intended to fight in Korea, nor had it planned to wage the type of warfare fought there. The defense of the United States relied at that time almost exclusively on strategic nuclear war and was based on a secret war plan called Off Tackle. Off Tackle called for holding the line of the Rhine in Europe and in the Far East fighting only for Japan, Okinawa, and the Philippines. The offensive punch of the United States would be a massive bomber-launched nuclear attack against the Soviet Union. Two hundred and ninety-two atomic bombs were to be delivered in ninety days on Russian targets from bases in Great Britain, the United States, Okinawa, and Morocco.

Korea had been specifically and publicly excluded from those areas to be defended. In March 1949 the Far Eastern Commander, General Douglas MacArthur, stated: "Our line of defense runs through the chain of islands fringing the coast of Asia. It starts in the Philippines and continues through the Ryukyu Archipelago, which includes its main bastion, Okinawa. Then it bends back through Japan and the Aleutian Island chain to Alaska." Dean Acheson, the Secretary of State, had said in January 1950, "[Our] defensive perimeter runs along the Aleutians to Japan and then goes to the Ryukyus . . . [then] from the Ryukyus to the Philippine Islands."

These almost identical statements by leaders of the civil and military puissance of the United States left no doubt that Korea was outside any U.S. defensive line. Given the limited conventional power the United States possessed after demobilizing itself, such strategy was perfectly logical. Frederick the Great had written, "He who defends everything, defends nothing." Choices had to be made. Even the veterans' organizations wanted fewer men in uniform, American prosperity defended by nuclear weapons almost exclusively, and the country returned to business as usual. The nonnuclear (conventional) forces possessed by the West in 1950 were inadequate to hold the line of the Rhine. The Russians could have overrun Western Europe; we could have destroyed the Soviet heartland.

A few paragraphs of theory must intrude here. In military affairs, strategic doctrine comes first. The nation's strategic assumptions then determine what weapons are purchased. Those weapons then dictate the nature of a war the nation must fight. If all a nation has is nuclear weapons, then the only type of war that nation can fight is a nuclear war. If all a nation has is ships, it will be forced to fight a naval war. If the war lasts long enough a nation can, if lucky, build up other types of forces; but the initial shock will either be resisted with the weapons in being or not be resisted at all. In the abstract this sounds like a simple, easily understood idea. In the world of political and economic pressures and the claims of conflicting doctrines, this reality too often falls by the wayside.

For example, before the start of World War II, French military doctrine called for tanks to be used in small packages in support of infantry. During the war the French had more tanks than the Germans; but since these tanks were to be used only in little, easily controlled units, there were no radios in them. German strategy called for their tanks to be massed and used in large formations. To control such large organizations the Germans had equipped their tanks with radios. The French had the tanks to meet this mass but could not fight them effectively in large numbers because they had no radios to direct them.

At the time America attempted to rescue our hostages in Iran, the country had a great many B-52 bombers but only four helicopters that could be refueled in the air. As the Southern cavalryman remarks in Stephen Benet's "John Brown's Body": "I could whip three Yankee Squadrons with my fine cocked hat./Only the Yanks won't fight like that."

In 1952 I was making this point about weapons determining warfare to a group of international-relations students from the West and Southwest gathered at Texas A&M. I was followed by a Strategic Air Command general who eloquently made the case for pursuing the single, cheap, effective policy of strategic nuclear deterrence. I wasn't sure I'd made my point, till a small fire broke out in an ashtray in the auditorium. "For God's sake, get rid of that ashtray," someone yelled, "before the general drops an H-bomb on it to put it out."

To leave theory and return to the Korean War: What of the land itself, the place where the new defense organization and policies would first be tested? At the end of World War II, six days after V-J day, 8 September 1945, American troops landed in Pusan, the port on the extreme southern tip of Korea, and drove to the capital, Seoul, through wildly cheering crowds. The troops were there to garrison Korea south of the 38th parallel. The country north of the 38th parallel had been assigned to the Soviets at the Yalta Conference between Roosevelt, Stalin, and Churchill in February 1945, as an additional incentive for the Russians to enter the war against Japan. The American troops were under command of General John P. Hodge, a tough regular soldier. He was one of those commanders whom fellow officers, when talking to outsiders, call "a soldiers' soldier." Which is code for "He fights like hell, but unwatched, he will foul it up." He did. He announced he considered the Koreans "breeds of the same cat" as the Japanese, and until he was ordered to stop by Marshall, he left the Japanese police in place to control the Koreans. Hodge stayed in Korea four years.

When the United States military forces left in 1948, a Korean Military Assistance Group (KMAG) was created; known as "kaymag," it was a forerunner, unfortunately in more ways than one, of MAACV (Military Advisory Assistance Command Vietnam). The KMAG, whose duty it was to train the South Korean Army, was under the command of Brigadier General William L. Roberts (West Point 1913), a decent, average tank officer from Europe serving his last tour before retirement. Roberts hated the job, didn't like Korea, and, naturally, spoke no Korean. He was there because he hadn't been outstanding enough to land a better billet. The officers serving with him, most of them fellow outcasts from rapid promotion and the chain of important assignments, felt the same way.

A week before the Korean invasion, in June 1950, General Omar Bradley, then Chairman of the Joint Chiefs, was in the Far East. He states in his autobiography that General Roberts assured him that the South Korean Army would be able to impose its will on the North Koreans. There is no reason to doubt Bradley's account. He was, bless him, a man who believed truth important and acted on that belief. Also, high Pentagon staff officers were telling Congress the same thing. Interestingly enough, the assessment given by the State Department was not so sanguine. Three weeks before war's outbreak the American ambassador to Korea, John J. Muccio, told Congress, "[The] material superiority of the North Korean forces would provide North Korea with a margin of victory in the event of a full-scale invasion." Those familiar with Vietnam will immediately recognize the pattern: the military being far more optimistic about the progress of indigenous forces than the diplomats, and the diplomats unfortunately being proved right.

As the South Korean forces retreated and the situation in Korea worsened, Truman and his cabinet held a series of hastily called meetings and decided to aid the South Koreans, even though South Korea was outside the U.S. defense area. Initially, the U.S.

leaders believed that air and naval power alone would halt the North Korean advance. The Air Force Chief of Staff, General Hoyt Vandenberg, and the Chief of Naval Operations, the able naval aviator Admiral Forrest Sherman, both advised the President that air and naval power would be sufficient for victory. General Douglas MacArthur, the Far East Commander, cabled that the Far Eastern Air Force pounding the North Koreans with "every resource at its disposal" would "drive the North Koreans back into their own territory in disorder." That MacArthur, a hero of World Wars I and II, the *ground* commander and a previous air-power skeptic, believed the air attack alone would be sufficient to defeat the North Koreans indicates how completely the country had accepted the doctrines of air power.

Air and naval power didn't defeat the enemy, any more than air and naval power alone would later bring success in Vietnam, Iran, or the Falkland Islands. Only four planes, obsolescent B-26 bombers, made it to Korea in the first two days, and these couldn't find the battle area because of bad weather. The F-80 jet fighters, the first generation of jets, were not designed to operate at low altitudes and their fuel capacity allowed them fifteen minutes at best over the battle area. Later in the war the B-29s and their crews, reconfigured and retrained for nonnuclear bombing, tore up a lot of hills in North Korea. (Twenty years afterward their replacements, the B-52s, were tearing up the jungle of Vietnam.) The North Korean tank columns rolled on, pushing the South Koreans toward annihilation at the southern tip of the Korean peninsula.

There were no decisive nuclear targets in Korea: and the invasion, while serious, did not threaten the United States in a way that called for nuclear weapons. Also, the few nuclear weapons available had to be held for the strategic defense of America. Finally, on 30 June 1950, faced with the loss of Korea, President Truman authorized General MacArthur to send one regimental combat team from occupation duty in Japan to Korea. A ground war had begun, of the exact type we had expected never again to fight.

One regimental combat team, 6,000 men. (That is like Lincoln's initial call-up of 75,000 volunteers to fight the Civil War; four years later the Union dead alone were four and a half times that number.) A year later the number of U.S. ground troops in Korea was 253,000. Wars have a nasty habit of escalating, particularly when the nature of the conflict is not understood and its consequences are not foreseen.

Instead of 6,000 trained infantry men usual in a regimental combat team, 440 soldiers loaded in Japan for Korea. These were mainly cooks, clerks, military police, and bakers hastily thrown together and called a regiment. Of these 440 going into action five years after the close of World War II, some 75 had seen combat. One with combat experience was the task force leader, Lieutenant Colonel Charles Bradford Smith, who had been routed out of bed to lead the makeshift force. On 7 December 1941, then Lieutenant Smith had been ordered to find what he could of his company at the burning Schofield Barracks outside of Pearl Harbor and proceed to Barbers Point to repel a Japanese invasion.

As in World War II, lack of strategic control over manpower now produced infantry unconscionable for a great power. (That's not true; the caliber of infantry initially produced in Korea was unconscionable for a tenth-rate power.) At the war's beginning, 43 percent of the ground troops in the Far East tested in the lowest two categories on the Army intelligence tests, those at the bottom being just marginally able to read and write. They had been living the soft life in Japan, often with servants, and no large-scale training exercises had been held. The ablest of the Army's soldiers were back in the United States in the airborne units that formed the United States Strategic Reserves.

These Strategic Reserve units were stripped of their skilled personnel, who were rushed to Korea; but in the meantime much deadly damage had been done. With untested officers, with weapons they had never fired, with radios that would not work, without promised air support, manned by the least intelligent, the least trained, and the least motivated, certain Army units simply fell apart. America's early battles were disasters. On the vital northwest flank, the 34th Infantry Regiment turned and "bugged out," abandoning its equipment. The 29th Infantry Regiment, entering combat similarly untrained and with much of its equipment still coated with protective grease, had one of its battalions break and run during an ambush. Four hundred of its 757 men were lost in two terrifying hours as they threw away their weapons and fled over the Korean hills and streams.

Later, at Kunri Pass, the 2nd Infantry Division, of ancient lineage and World War I and II glory, was so badly shattered it had to be withdrawn from the lines. Even at its worst, the Vietnam War produced no disasters of such magnitude.

Nor were there American replacements immediately available to refill the decimated ranks. Instead, thousands of Koreans were scarfed up off the streets of their cities, sent to Japan for two weeks of training, and then "integrated" into the American infantry divisions, each with a U.S. "buddy" beside him.

Drinking deep of Victory's horn of oblivion at war's end, most Americans forgot such things. Those inside the Other America of Defense did not forget. Only one-fifth of the officers fighting in Korea were regulars; but by war's end this fifth had suffered one-third of the officer casualties.

The initial Washington response to the invasion had been slow and tentative. Eisenhower, visiting Washington during the first week of the war, noted in his diary: "I went in expecting to find them [the war leaders] all in a dither of effort, engaged in the positive business of getting the troops, supplies, etc., that will be needed. . . . They seemed indecisive . . . at lunch both George Marshall and I told the President that . . . speed and strength both are needed. We encountered good intentions but I'm not so sure that we met full comprehension. . . . There seems no disposition to begin serious mobilizing. I think that it is possible that military advisers are too complacent when talking to HST."

President Truman soon recognized the limits of good intentions and moved with political courage and speed to repair the damage of military neglect and warped doctrine. Within three weeks, at Truman's insistence, $10 billion had been added to the $16-billion defense budget. The draft had already been greatly increased. To call up the National Guard and the Reserves meant marching into a political minefield. However, unlike President Johnson, who during Vietnam falsely claimed he did not need such forces, Truman courageously called up four National Guard divisions, two Guard combat teams, and numerous individual Reservists. (The Reserve Officers Association mounted a strong enough lobby to prevent the calling up of larger Reserve units.) In this way, while grave inequities continued to exist as to who served where, the pool of skilled military manpower was effectively tapped. This was a major difference between Korea and Vietnam. The caliber of troops serving in Vietnam declined as that war progressed, while the caliber of troops serving in Korea increased as that war progressed.

By the end of August the early defeats had ripped to shreds both the morale of the troops in Korea and the faith of the country in its military. Truman wisely, if a bit belatedly, changed his civilian high command. Louis Johnson and Stephen T. Early departed as Secretary and Under Secretary of Defense; and General George C. Marshall came in, with Robert Lovett as his deputy. Admiral Hillenkoetter, the CIA director, was replaced by Eisenhower's World War II Chief of Staff, General Walter B. ("Beedle") Smith. Dean Acheson remained Secretary of State, with Averell Harriman arriving to run congressional interference. These seasoned men, many of whom, like the President, had been tempered in actual battle, constituted a war cabinet of exceptional strength. Taking over as Secretary of Defense, George Marshall sat down with General Omar Bradley, Chairman of the Joint Chiefs of Staff, and said, "The two of us know this organization was designed not to work. We will make it work."

The call-up of Guard and Reserves and the increased draft calls, plus the arrival of Marshall and Lovett, solved many problems, but Interservice/Intraservice Rivalry continued seriously to impede the war. There was less unity among the armed services, now officially three, during the Korean War than in World War II. Though Marshall, Lovett, and General Bradley were men of ability and prestige, respected by both the public and Congress, control over the war was continually frustrated by the Flawed Organization.

Secretary of Defense Marshall now held a supposedly more powerful job than his World War II position as Army Chief of Staff; however, his real power had been reduced. While Chief of Staff, Marshall had made the key Operations and Policy Division, where matters between the Army Air Corps and the Army were thrashed out, into a truly joint ground and air operation. He assigned the best officers to that division and promoted them only if they cooperated with each other. Further, Marshall sent bright officers from that division over to deal with the Navy on questions requiring joint action. Again, promotions were based on how well officers had handled these Interservice/Intraservice assignments. Under this policy the ablest Army and Air Force officers sought joint duty to further their future careers. During Korea, able officers began avoiding joint duty as a threat to their careers. Their services would punish them by denying them choice assignments and promotions if, in the name of national good, they took an action contrary to parochial service interest.

As Secretary of Defense, Marshall could reason, cajole, use his prestige and authority, occasionally and carefully display his temper; but he lacked command. Nor was the World War II authority he had exercised now invested in JCS Chairman General Omar Bradley. Bradley could neither promote nor remove a single officer. Paraphrasing Shakespeare's Ulysses, one could indeed say: "Take but 'command' away, untune that string, and, hark, what discord follows."

I recall Marshall's rage when one of the Army's ablest engineer officers, Charles H. ("Tic") Bonesteel, had his promotion held up for siding with the Air Force in a Joint Staff committee. In this instance Marshall still had the prestige to have his way. But such successful and precise secretarial intervention occurred less and less as the caliber of the Defense and service secretaries declined after Marshall and Lovett. By the time of Robert McNamara, who often vengefully hectored those in uniform who crossed him, all three services had hunkered down to protect their own. Joint service assignments had gone from being the career route to the top to what they too often are today—a stigma to avoid.

In the nation at large, while the majority of the population supported the Korean War, there was no rush to the colors. As General Lewis B. Hershey, the director of Selective Service during both World War II and the Korean War, succinctly put it, "Everyone wants out; no one wants in."

Even the Air Force had trouble finding volunteers to be pilots, though the prerequisite for pilot training had been lowered from two years of college to high school graduation. By late 1952 the Aviation Cadet program was running at only 50 percent of capacity. At the same time only a third of the 7,500 college seniors who graduated from the Air Force ROTC program volunteered for flight service; and many of these were found to be unqualified physically. At West Point the Air Force failed to achieve its quota of 25 percent of the graduating class.

This inability of the Air Force to obtain pilots came as a shock to the nation, still under the impact of the World War II myths that we were a nation of volunteers. For the Air Force the problem was worse in the Korean conflict than in the Vietnam War. Not only was there a pilot shortage, but some 200 fliers scheduled for

Korea refused to fly. No such mass refusal of combat flight duty occurred in Vietnam.

With the shortage of pilots, the Air Force faced the questions of where to put the best fliers it had, and on whom to unload the not-so-good. Predictably, the Air Staff, bomber-dominated, put its best fliers into that part of itself in which it most believed, the Strategic Air Command (SAC). After SAC had skimmed the cream, the next call on the best was given to the fighters of the continental Air Defense Command. This was happening at a time when the Russians had practically no long-range bombers or nuclear weapons and when the ground troops in Korea were literally fighting for their lives.

After SAC and Air Defense, the Tactical Air Command (TAC), whose mission was to give close air support and battlefield interdiction to the Army, picked next. Finally, the residue was culled by Military Air Transport Systems (MATS), whose mission was support of the Army and Navy. The last gleanings went to the Troop Carrier Command, whose main mission was aiding the airborne units of the Army. Ill feelings created by this maldistribution were further embittered because the pilots of SAC and the Air Defense Force were living in the United States and not taking casualties, while those in TAC and occasionally Troop Carrier were stationed overseas and often getting shot down. The Joint Chiefs of Staff and the Pentagon civilian leadership realized what was going on, but the organization created by Congress was powerless to enforce war-winning decisions.

So if we are to apportion blame—and in the harsh light of history, since many Americans died unnecessarily, we cannot merely avert our eyes—those who had crafted an impotent Defense Department bear a heavier burden than does the Air Staff, which was at least following its own doctrine. Nor should we be surprised to learn that the same organization did not assign the best helicopter pilots available to the Iranian rescue mission.

I first began to suspect a maldistribution of pilot abilities when several MATS planes ferrying troops to the Far East crashed. The pattern of these accidents suggested pilot deficiencies, though the Air Force strongly denied this. Then, during a Texas maneuver called Long Horn, a whole flight of paratroop-carrying planes came in too slow over the drop zone, began to stall, and mushed down among the paratroopers who had already jumped in the echelons ahead. One man was killed, twenty-five seriously injured.

At my suggestion, some concerned officers on the Air Staff investigated the number of flying hours officers piloting identical planes had in SAC, TAC, MATS, and Troop Carrier. The results showed those flying the same fighters for SAC had over 500 more hours than those actually fighting the Korean War in TAC. Troop Carrier, the 18th Air Force, had pilots in command of four-engine transports with only 5 hours in such planes, as against close to 1000 in SAC. "Christ, Hadley," the friendly colonel who had ordered up the study told me, "you really put us on to something. We didn't believe it ourselves. Listen, the Secretary himself wants to put you in the pattern on this."

I never did get the figures officially. The Air Force Secretary, Thomas K. Finletter, a New York lawyer active in liberal Democratic politics, decided to make them secret instead. I never wrote the story. The colonel had been a friend for several years and the information would have been traced to him immediately, ruining his chances for promotion.

In addition to major disputes over strategy, organization, and manpower, there grew up a series of petty actions and frustrations that made interservice cooperation and trust difficult. General Collins, the Army Chief of Staff, wanted to fly from Washington to Fort Knox to address the Armor (tank) Association. The only plane the Air Force could find to fly the chief of their "rival" service, a man who had supported all their efforts to become independent, was a partially converted, unpressurized, ancient B-17 bomber. Collins, a couple of other officers, and I were sitting on cushions on the floor shouting at each other when the pilot came back to see us. "Jesus Christ, General Collins," he said. "I am about to leave the service. And I guess you are the biggest noise I'll ever fly with. Would you give me your autograph?" Taking off his gloves and blowing on his chilled fingers, General Collins obliged.

Another time, when Collins wanted to fly out to Los Angeles to inspect one of the Army divisions leaving for Korea, the Air Force could not find him any plane at all—and this at a time when most Air Force generals had their individual, luxury-equipped aircraft. Admiral William M. Fechteler, by then Chief of Naval Operations, lent Collins his personal plane.

The day of the Inchon landing, a risky amphibious invasion behind North Korean lines and the critical operation of the Korean War, Robert Lovett was acting Secretary of Defense. The first item on his agenda was to settle a split decision of the Joint Chiefs that had reached him because the Chiefs could not agree. The issue was the number of parking spaces to be allocated to Marine officers at the Mall entrance to the Pentagon.

With grown men behaving in such a ridiculous and petty fashion over the minor details, you can imagine with what bureaucratic tenacity they battled when they felt basic service policy was at stake. Roswell L. Gilpatric, then Under Secretary of the Air Force, revealed that the Joint Chiefs had been in such bitter disagreement over several major weapons systems that they had finally allocated the funds for them by flipping a dime.

On the battlefield itself Interservice Rivalry flourished. Communications between air and ground had deteriorated since World War II. As late as the second year of the Korean War, infantry and airplane radios often could not talk to each other. The problem was compounded because the Navy planes off the carriers not only were unable to talk to the ground troops, they could not communicate with Air Force target spotter planes, or Air Force fighter operations centers. "My kids just wander round, their racks loaded with bombs and rockets and no place to put them," Admiral Edward C. Ewen, a naval air commander off Korea, reported bluntly. The marines, with their own separate air force, fared far better. With Marine ground officers guiding them in, they provided exemplary close air support for their infantry. However, the marines were extremely reluctant to share—one could say almost would not share—their aircraft with anyone else.

Time and again after-action reports from Korea record the dire travail of American ground units while planes circled overhead unable to respond. Nor can these failures be excused by pleading "the fog of battle." In the second year of the Korean War NATO held its first large maneuver, called Main Brace, part of which took place in, over, and around northern Norway. I sat in a fox-hole slightly north of the Arctic Circle with several young Norwegian infantry and artillery officers, a British observer, and an American Air Force forward air control party. The maneuver, meticulously planned for over a year, was to be a showpiece that demonstrated how American firepower could support European ground forces anywhere in Western Europe.

In front of us on the icy mountain slope some 1,000 Norwegian paratroopers were fighting the usual mythical enemy. U.S. Navy planes off carriers in the North Sea, vectored in by U.S. Air Force Forward Air Controllers (FACs) and Tactical Operations Center (TOC), were to give the Norwegians much-needed fire support. Dawn broke with a tinkling of cow bells and the weather wonderfully clear. The planes arrived on time. Then for an hour and a half they orbited overhead. The Air Force officers worked their radios frantically. Then the Navy planes flew away. No contact.

"This is a bloody long way to come to sit around in this flipping cold snow just to learn your bloody Air Force and Navy still don't speak the same flipping language," said the British observer.

The jet fighters of the Korean War, the F-84s and F-86s, had been conceived and constructed for air-to-air battles first and as ground-support aircraft a reluctant second. At lower altitudes they burned so much fuel they had little time over the target. Their guns and rockets, designed for aerial combat, were not highly effective against ground troops. Weapons purchase and design were once again determining the nature of the war fought. The newer planes, the F-86s, were sent to the far north to dogfight with the Communist Chinese MIGs rather than used in support of the ground war. Many TAC generals privately questioned this policy. In one week in March 1951 no F-86 was lost dogfighting the MIGs; but nine F-84s were lost in close support and battlefield interdiction. Should not the newer plane have been placed in the more intense action? And what of the F-84 pilots who were taking casualties while those in the interceptors got the publicity and the promotions?

Interservice rivalry crippled secret warfare and intelligence. Here not only were the three armed services involved, but, as on the Iranian hostage rescue mission, the presence of the CIA splintered cooperation further. The Korean lessons regarding intelligence are especially apropos today because the arrival of more accurate, or "smart," weapons (covered in chapter 7) and the growth of terrorism increase the importance of precise, timely information about the enemy. The cruisers and carriers of the Navy ranged along both coasts of the Korean peninsula with impunity; the Air Force commanded the air. The country was wild and mountainous and much of the population friendly. These two services should have had a field day destroying targets in enemy areas located by teams of secret agents. They did not.

During World War II General Douglas MacArthur, the Far

Eastern Commander, and his staff had been contemptuous of the OSS, the forerunner of the CIA, and had severely restricted the operations of its personnel and agents. In the interim between World War II and the Korean War their hostile attitude toward strategic and secret intelligence continued, and it did not change with the coming of hostilities. The result was a dismal series of missed opportunities and disasters. In the worst of these, during the war's second year, several Chinese Communist armies secretly crossed the boundary between China and Korea, the Yalu River, and bloodily defeated unwarned American forces.

The CIA had active agent teams in North Korea at the time. However, MacArthur had not been willing to support and supply in-place agents along the Yalu River. Indeed MacArthur's distrust of the CIA reached such heights that shortly before his relief in the middle of the war, CIA agents discovered that his G-2 (intelligence officer), General Charles A. Willoughby, had put the senior CIA agents in the Far East under surveillance by the Japanese secret police, who were commanded by Willoughby.

Such an atmosphere helps to explain why the CIA six-man Korean country team was as surprised by the invasion as the rest of America. The day after the invasion the secret-intelligence-gathering side of CIA, then called OSO (Office of Special Operations), flew a special secure radio and trained operator into Kimpo airport outside of the Korean capital, Seoul. The South Korean Army the next day blew the bridges over several rivers too early during their retreat, and the American Air Force plane carrying extra radio equipment to Korea crashed into Japan's Mount Fuji. These twin disasters left the CIA radio, which managed to get ferried across the Han River, as almost the only secure link between noncommunist Korea and the rest of the world for the first weeks of the war. With such limited communication facilities as the headlong retreat of the South Koreans continued, the CIA team lost touch with what few agents they had in place.

Recovering from the first disasters, the CIA began to train teams of agents who could be inserted into the rear of the North Korean Army. In theory these agents would commit acts of sabotage and locate targets for the Air Force and Navy. Almost immediately Interservice Rivalry crippled this promising operation. Not believing in secret agents, the Navy was unwilling to risk its ships in the hazardous in-shore work of agent insertion. The CIA and

Army developed a little Navy of their own, built up out of small coastal steamers and barges that had been used by the Japanese in the Pacific Island campaigns of World War II. These ships were manned by our recent enemies the Japanese and were often commanded by Koreans. As for those agents dropped by air, the Air Force assigned such a low priority to this work that they were often parachuted far off-target and were easily rounded up.

The after-action report from the island of Yodo off the east coast of North Korea typifies the intelligence agents' problems. "From its inception in early June, things went satisfactorily except for three harsh buffets of fate. We suffered several fatalities when shelled by a U.S. cruiser which had not gotten the word that the islands were in friendly hands; an American carrier plane strafed one of our sampans, killing two men and a woman agent; and Lt. Cochran and two Marines were captured." In other words, more of the team was lost to friendly fire than to enemy action.

The Yodo report further details how numerous Navy destroyer captains refused to fire on the targets found by the CIA team since they regarded the coastal waters as Navy territory and would not accept targets from a non-Navy unit, particularly one commanded by an Army officer. Finally, after the dispute was carried all the way to the commander of the Pacific Fleet, who steamed by in the battleship *New Jersey*, relations improved. A working arrangement developed which resembled that established by the British Navy on the west coast. British vessels had never had any difficulty in accepting targets found by other services.

Unfortunately, cooperation between the Navy and the agents on Yodo lasted only a few months. Then a new naval officer took command and stopped the operation! In the meantime, the Air Force landed a huge searchlight, with a three-man Navy maintenance crew, to serve as a beacon for the Okinawa-based B-29 bombers on their runs over North Korea. As the bombers got close to the island the planes would radio for the beacon to be turned on. Naturally, the agents staging off the island could never know, because of security, when the light would turn night into day. This made close to impossible the secret movement of the sampans delivering and retrieving agents along the coast. It would appear the Green Door problem had surfaced again. The agents were not cleared to know about the bombers. Those who placed the searchlight were not cleared to know about the agents.

If agent or Ranger teams guiding in precision weapons are an important part of our military future, as I and others believe they are, our past does not augur well for our future. During the Cuban missile crisis in the early Kennedy days, there were no spy flights sent over Cuba for five days. The Air Force and the CIA could not agree which of them would fly the planes.

In spite of all the problems, by the last month of the Korean War the CIA had some 3,000 allied secret agents established in North Korea. To record the fate of these agents is to say, as Edgar of aged Lear, "The worst is not, so long as we can say, 'This is the worst.' " The CIA's secret after-action report on Korea states: "The cease-fire talks enabled the enemy to concentrate fully on eliminating the [U.S.] guerrilla threat . . . eventually most of the [U.S.] guerrillas were killed, captured or neutralized by North Korean or Red Chinese action. . . . The surviving guerrillas were declared expendable, told to go underground and shift for themselves, and were left stranded a hundred miles behind enemy lines." The same fate fell upon our Vietnamese allies and agents twenty-five years later.

In Washington President Truman and his most intimate advisors understood the possibilities and limits of secret intelligence. When faced with the opportunity for political assassination, they looked that tiger in the face and then wisely and successfully leashed the animal. In the winter of 1951 the United States, acting for the United Nations Command, was holding peace talks with the North Korean and Chinese Communists. The talks' objective was an armistice agreement that would divide Korea, north from south, along its narrow waist, an agreement finally achieved a year later. The aged president of South Korea, Syngman Rhee, grown slightly senile and dominated by a young wife, still dreamed of a unified Korea ruled by himself. Beguiled by such dreams, he tried to sabotage the truce talks and engineer a coup de main to force the United Nations to restart the war and drive north. By late November 1951, informed circles in both the Korean and United States governments knew that serious friction existed between President Rhee and the senior American military and political leaders in Korea.

In such an atmosphere, one day during a walk through the streets of Seoul, the Assistant Chief of Staff for Operations of the Korean Army, General Lee, asked a CIA agent with whom he was on intimate terms if he could talk to the CIA station chief, the legendary John Carlton ("Teddy Bear") Root. Lee gave as his reason, according to the case file, a wish to discuss "problems between our countries."

With the consent of Ambassador John J. Muccio, a pheasant hunt was arranged for General Lee, the agent, and Root. On that hunt, after bagging a few birds and making sure that there was no chance of their being observed, the Korean general outlined for Root a plan to overthrow President Rhee, exile him, and replace his government with a military junta. Both the Korean Army Chief of Staff, Song Yoschan, and the commander of the Korean Navy, Admiral Sohn Won Il, were part of the plot, as were several key civilian officials. There seemed scant doubt but that the coup would succeed. General Lee wanted to know what the United States reaction would be if the plotters succeeded.

Returning from the hunt, Root contacted Ambassador Muccio and informed him of the proposed coup. The ambassador and the CIA station chief then met with General James Van Fleet, who was the United Nations commander in Korea. The three men on the spot, the general, the ambassador, and the CIA station chief, approved the proposal of the Korean generals. They believed the participating officers and officials to be loyal Koreans who had the best interests of both their country and the United Nations at heart. Two copies of the Korean cabal's proposals were sent forward to Washington. Military channels of communications were not used, since there had been leaks from these when President Truman had relieved General Douglas MacArthur for insubordination. One copy of the proposal and the request for official U.S. reaction went to Washington through diplomatic channels, the other through CIA channels. Both copies carried the same recommendation, that the United States support the planned coup.

Tightly controlled in Washington, no word of the proposal leaked to Congress or the press. After consultation between Acheson and Smith, the President was informed. Truman and his advisors all agreed that though Rhee was, to say the least, difficult, the United States should not support a military coup. The risks were judged to far outweigh the gains, and the project was killed. In Korea, the CIA arranged a clandestine meeting with General Lee and the plotters were told that the United States would not support their revolt. America had wisely avoided those complications and commitments that President Kennedy and later President Johnson were forced to assume in Vietnam after they and their advisors supported the coup in which Vietnamese President Ngo Dinh Diem was murdered.

Unfortunately for the Korean plotters, "Tiger" Kim, head of Rhee's secret police, in some way became aware of the projected revolt. Over the next two years a series of airplane crashes and "deaths in battle" mysteriously carried away many of the plotters, including the Korean Army Chief of Staff and Admiral Song. General Lee, who had initiated the contacts with the CIA, was flying south to meet with President Rhee in the president's personal plane when that plane developed engine trouble. The pilot and copilot, who happened to be wearing parachutes, were able to leap to safety. There were no other parachutes on the plane.

By its third year the Korean War had become intensely unpopular in the United States. Casualties mounted, the war seemed to have no end, and President Truman was attacked vociferously, both by critics who wanted a "victory," and by those who wanted to "get out." The meaning of these two alternatives was seldom defined, nor were their consequences examined. During the war, President Truman, with the full support of his Defense Secretary, George Marshall, and the Joint Chiefs of Staff, had been forced to fire General Douglas MacArthur, the theater commander. MacArthur had lost control of the battle and was attempting on his own to alter the political objectives of the war. The general's removal increased right-wing attacks on Truman's own strategy, which was to force the Chinese Communists and the North Koreans to the truce table by killing the maximum number of them while sustaining a minimum of American casualties. As General Matthew B. Ridgway, by then the United Nations commander in Korea, put it with his usual succinctness, "Steel is cheaper than lives and a good deal easier to obtain." However, this middle-of-the-road strategy was rejected by the majority of the American people.

Finally, the Truman strategy, combined with a secret threat to use nuclear weapons by Eisenhower, who had just been elected President, brought the Korean War to a close. The end came before the tide of antiwar reaction crested. Still, our actions and reactions in Korea, Vietnam, and more recently Beirut pose a question: To what extent can the United States employ its military power in lengthy but limited military situations? We are an impatient people and cry out loudly for quick solutions. And, quite properly, our free press echoes these cries throughout the land.

Impatience is a historical American strategic reality, just as patience is a Russian one. For example, in our Civil War General Ulysses Grant described America's situation shortly before General Sherman took Atlanta as follows: "At this time the North had become very much discouraged. . . . The elections of 1862 had gone against Lincoln. Voluntary enlistments had all but ceased and the draft had been resorted to to fill up our ranks. It was my judgment that [with] any backward movement . . . the draft would be resisted, desertions ensue and the power to capture and punish deserters lost." Is this historic American desire for quick military results another reason behind our recurring belief that nuclear weapons may be all the military power our nation needs?

In the long view of history, the American decision not to employ nuclear weapons in Korea may rank among the most important actions of that war. Praise for the obviously well done is often lavishly donated. Credit for the wisely left alone comes harder. The United States had a nuclear near-monopoly during the Korean conflict. What scant U.S. military doctrine existed maintained that nuclear weapons would settle all future wars. In the beginning of the Korean War there were desperate moments when American forces were almost pushed into the sea and annihilated. Toward the end of the conflict the public, Congress, and the military became generally frustrated with the war's killingly slow course. Yet though the employment of nuclear weapons was considered and even planned, they remained in storage.

As was to be expected, most of the pressure to use nuclear weapons came from the Air Staff, a situation that would continue through the Vietnam War. The Air Staff wished to win the Korean War not by using nuclear weapons in support of the ground troops (they had neither the doctrine, tactics, planes, or electronic equipment to do so) but through strategic attack against the cities of North Korea and Red China. The Army, even though taking the vast majority of the casualties, played its historic role as the service most dubious about the benefits of a nuclear strike.

Suppose we had used nuclear weapons then, when we had the monopolistic power to do so with safety? Precedent would have been set, restraints broken, and the future use of such weapons by anyone—ourselves, our allies, our enemies—immediately made more probable and respectable. Further, the choice of such a violent and extreme solution would have greatly increased the power of the violent and extreme elements in our own society and other societies. Historically, from the Praetorian Guard through Napoleon to Marshal Wojciech Jaruzelski, those who have extraordinary military power soon use it, except in the most orderly of civilian societies. Our nuclear abstinence established in Korea has helped to relegate the threat of a military coup d'etat in America to the outer marches of Hollywood's imagination.

From what little we can learn of Soviet nuclear doctrine, the Soviet leadership, far more fearful of their military establishment than we of ours, have taken elaborate precautions to have the secret police, the military, and a Communist political officer in tripartite control of their nuclear weapons. Our historic restraint with our weapons encourages them to increase their control over their weapons, an action of benefit to us all.

At a time when the Korean War had become divisive and unpopular, the United States undertook to revive the defenses of Western Europe. This initiative led to the creation of forces for the North Atlantic Treaty Organization (NATO), whose deployed strength, nuclear and conventional, still defends Western Europe. Many of the weaknesses that plague NATO today—the separation of the air and ground battle, the weakness of the U.S. ground forces, the irrelevant doctrines for nuclear use—are a direct result of NATO's confused birth during an unpopular war.

The new isolationists who bloomed at the close of World War II felt politically and intellectually threatened by the Korean War. They had halted the draft and drastically cut the military budget, relying on strategic air power alone to defend America and her vital interests. In Korea the very type of war they said would never again occur was being fought. Now, with such a war in progress, these politicians were being asked to provide and fund ground forces to hold Western Europe. They had convinced themselves and told the voters that such a course of action was against American self-interest.

Further, for the Air Force, and the politicians who supported that service, the idea of a multinational NATO under a supreme commander at SHAPE (Supreme Headquarters Allied Powers

Europe) appeared a threat to cherished beliefs. Did "supreme commander" mean that the ultimate weapon, the nuclear bomber, was to go back under the command of some ground general? Was the Army, under the guise of defending Western Europe, in truth seeking to regain control over a portion of the newly independent Air Force? Were we going to ignore air power and fight another lengthy land war in Europe with heavy casualties?

The Air Force felt additionally threatened at this time because during the Korean War, naval aviation, particularly Marine aviation, had turned in the superior performance. Marine doctrine called for close support of ground troops by air power, so the Marine Corps had been ready for precisely the type of action the Korean War required. At the same time the Navy, still largely excluded from the strategic mission because of the weight of the existing atomic bombs, had been much more willing than the Air Force to cooperate closely with the ground forces. Indeed, the Air Force had resisted even World War II–style cooperation out of fear that it would jeopardize its recently won independence and give the Army some control over tactical air power. So the air staff supported efforts by powerful American isolationists to weaken the central authority of NATO and restrict the numbers of U.S. ground troops going to Europe. The British RAF joined the battle against a strong integrated NATO command for the same doctrinal reasons.

Success crowned this effort by the American and British air forces to remain almost totally independent from the NATO ground forces. The headquarters for the various ground and air components of NATO were usually not even located in the same area. The headquarters for the air forces defending the central front of Europe is at Ramstein while that of the ground forces is at Heidelberg, some fifty miles away.

This physical separation is the outward and visible sign of a continuing, though lessening, mental gap. In the beginning, NATO air commanders saw their primary mission as nuclear retaliation and the destruction of enemy air bases with nuclear weapons. Weapons, aircraft, radios, tactics, support organizations were all designed around this nuclear strike concept. The ground forces saw the primary air mission as various types of ground support. Both groups bought weapons according to their divergent strategic perceptions. Today, fears of upsetting these divergent doctrines, now set in the steel and aluminum of thirty years of weapons purchases, prevent both groups from combining into a unified force, though the new weapons and tactics that will arrive in the late eighties make such unification more necessary than before.

Even where the two headquarters have since moved together, as have the Northern Army Group and Second Allied Tactical Air Force (NORTHAG/TWOATAF), there is no unified command, only committees. I quote from NORTHAG/TWOATAF's description of how they intend to fight. "The Commanders Committee is one of many joint committees and agencies at all levels in the two Headquarters by which the essential interface between land and air forces is assured." You don't have to have watched the armed services for over four decades to know that any time they talk about "essential interface," a Pearl Harbor is around the corner.

While feeling no threat from the creation of NATO, the Navy remained rather unenthusiastic. For the dominant carrier admirals, the Navy's most important mission remained strategic nuclear warfare, which they wished to share with the Air Force. The next naval role, given prominence by the Navy's important contribution to combat in Korea, was sea control and the countering of secondary threats about the periphery of the free world.

During World War II the Navy had been the lead service in the Pacific, and not unnaturally its attention was focused there rather than on Europe. Here the Navy was supported by the Marines, who feared the Air Force and saw the Army rather than themselves playing the dominant NATO role. The Army, which was called upon to make large commitments of men and equipment to Europe, gave NATO's creation enthusiastic and unequivocal support.

These attitudes present at NATO's birth now dictate the manner in which the alliances prepare to fight. The dominant bomber faction of the Air Force, along with their strategic missile brethren, continue to orient that service toward strategic warfare and a Fortress America approach. These officers see NATO as an area like Afghanistan or the Middle East, a peripheral challenge that detracts from their primary mission of global strategic warfare. Recently this view has gained support inside the Navy from the submariners, whose promotions, like those of the bomber pilots and missile men, are driven by the strategic warfare budget. On the other hand, pilots of the Tactical Air Command (TAC) now often join the Army in support of the NATO concept of a land battle in which nuclear weapons are not used. However, the TAC airmen also support the Navy and Marine concept of peripheral wars, as they see ways in which their aircraft could intervene decisively about the globe.

The Navy and the Marines, with their lesser role in NATO, continue to stress strategic commitments elsewhere and the need to "protect the flanks of the alliance." A former Navy strategic planner, Admiral George H. Miller, put the naval position succinctly: "The Soviets like to see our forces tied down in NATO so they can pick our pockets every place else in the world. . . . There is no way to do what we're committed to do. Anybody who really thinks we could reinforce NATO in a war is smoking opium." The admiral goes on to conclude that 50,000 troops as "earnest money" is all the United States needs on the line in Europe.

During NATO's infancy in the early 1950s, the United States and Britain enjoyed a nuclear near-monopoly. The few nuclear weapons possessed by the Soviet Union were largely undeliverable. This past monopoly also profoundly affects today's NATO structure. Without nuclear weapons themselves, and overawed by their power, the other countries of the alliance left decisions about their use to the British and ourselves.

The United States and Britain had few troops to give to NATO in 1952. America, which had demobilized at the end of World War II and was now involved in Korea, had, for example, only one tank battalion stationed in Europe. The socialist government of Britain, struggling to bring that country out of wartime hardship, and with Labour's traditional distrust of the military, had drastically curtailed Britain's defenses. The Germans had no military forces at all and the French were reluctant to see German power reappear. When a senator asked JCS Chairman Omar Bradley what the Russians would need to march to the English Channel, he replied, "Shoes."

In such a situation, where one side was a major nuclear power but had few troops and the other had masses of soldiers but few nuclear weapons, it made sense to plan a nuclear defense for

Europe. At the Korean War's end, when the United States stationed veteran combat troops in Europe, the West still enjoyed great nuclear superiority. Even though the situation had changed and NATO had achieved equality with the Soviet non-nuclear forces, there was still some reason to plan a nuclear defense of Europe. NATO's superior strength in all areas enabled the West to determine the type of war that would be fought.

By the mid-sixties the situation had greatly altered again. The French withdrew their forces from NATO and, with the onset of the Vietnam War, the best American forces shipped west. Meanwhile the Russians, recovering from World War II, had modernized and increased their military strength and become a nuclear power. But as we shall see, NATO has not changed and continues to plan and maneuver handicapped both by its divided military structure and by forces and tactics devised in a period of nuclear superiority.

FIVE

Promise and Performance: The Gap Widens

General Eisenhower arrived on the scene as President Eisenhower in January 1953, the Korean War ended that spring, and the armed services braced for further reorganization. Since the close of World War II, Eisenhower had made it clear both publicly and privately that he favored a far more unified Defense Department than the one created. "We will not have unification until the secretary of defense is made very powerful, power to appoint and fire, among other things," he had written in his diary on 17 December 1948.

To bring the Defense Department the efficiencies he had promised while campaigning, Eisenhower appointed as Secretary of Defense Charles E. ("Engine Charlie") Wilson, former president of General Motors. From the beginning Wilson's tenure was stormy. His many gaffs in testimony before Congress led to the legend that he had created the fluid-shift car so that he could drive with one foot in his mouth. And the foot emplaced between his teeth was seldom civil. He also came on board convinced that he knew more about military affairs than the military. "He was," said one of the Joint Chiefs off the record, "the most uninformed man and the most determined to remain so that has ever been secretary." With such a management stance, not surprisingly attitudes within the military began to harden against many of the Eisenhower team almost from the moment they arrived.

When new high-level civilian managers take over at the Pentagon, especially those with little previous military experience, they have to run the gauntlet of what insiders call Operation Pocket. Operation Pocket takes place when the senior military professionals in the department, led by each armed service chief of staff, try to put the new Defense Secretary or Service Secretaries into their pocket. They succeed a great deal of the time. Robert Lovett describes Operation Pocket as "the broom-expert parade." The routine works like this. The new Service or Defense Secretary discovers that there are 126 different lengths of brooms being bought by the Defense Department. To show his expertise and force some economies, he shouts that from now on, by God, there will be just three lengths of brooms: short, medium, and long.

Immediately the roof falls in. Before his desk appear a parade of broom experts from the three services. All other work stops while they explain the ridiculousness of his order and the damage it does to national defense. An admiral explains that you need a special type of hooked broom to get behind the forward turret of a battleship (as any fool who had ever served in a fighting service would know). An Army general recounts the savings the Army patriotically realizes by having special disposable training brooms on which to instruct future broom experts. A Marine general growls that he is going to Congress on this one, since it threatens the future of the Corps. Marines have historically used their own reinforced cast-iron brooms because marines are so strong they break ordinary brooms as they sweep the blood and gore off their boots before shining them to go on parade. And what is more it just so happens that these brooms are built in the district of the chairman of the House Appropriations Committee. After checking the room for bugs, an Air Force general in hushed tones tells of a highly classified broom to sweep up radioactive leaks that may occur in nuclear-weapons-storage bunkers. And each one of these men is backed by at least twenty highly decorated colonels flipping charts and showing slides.

I watched Operation Pocket pick up and pouch an assistant secretary of the Air Force, whom, since he is a successful industrial executive, I shall call X. Shortly after Eisenhower had replaced Truman, I called on X while trying to track down some now-forgotten story. For a newly appointed and confirmed official in a rather important job, he seemed to me strangely quiet, pensive, and replete with spare time. He confided in me (another reason I'm calling him X is that I don't want it to seem always an error to confide in a reporter) that he was having trouble not just in finding things to do, but in learning what was going on within the Pentagon. "That's not hard," I said. "The Joint Chiefs by law are required to keep a status sheet indicating what they are considering. You get a weekly copy of that status sheet." He shook my hand gratefully. I looked forward to a source in high places, perhaps even a peek at the status sheet. On the way out I paused to look at his secretary and suddenly something clicked.

"Weren't you one of General LeMay's personal secretaries when I was out at SAC headquarters in Omaha, last summer?"

"How nice of you to remember. Yes, I was."

I went back into X's office. "Another thing," I added. "You'd better get rid of that secretary. She used to work for LeMay. Anything you do, he'll know within twenty-four hours."

"You don't think she'd do a thing like that?"

What is this management expertise that businessmen are meant to bring to Washington?

Three weeks later I called on X again. The same secretary was guarding his outer door. He still had not gotten to see a JCS status sheet. "They tell me I don't have any right to see it," he said.

A Classic Operation Pocket. They should study it in the War Colleges.

To draw up their plans for reorganization, President Eisenhower and Defense Secretary Wilson selected H. Struve Hensel, who had helped draft the original faulty legislation for James Forrestal. Hensel had since become convinced that a stronger Defense Secretary was necessary. Writing about the performance of his own creation during the Korean War, Hensel said, "The marvel is not that the structure failed, but rather that it was able to continue at all." Hensel now favored strengthening the power of the Secretary of Defense. However, his proposals for changes in the Joint Chiefs were far milder and mostly technical, dealing with how overseas theater commanders would report.

Further, Hensel exacerbated the Great Divorce, already widening as a result of Korea, by advocating his changes in rather arrogant prose. "Strategic overall decisions, the development of new weapons, industrial mobilization, relations with allies, arousing the moral support of the allied peoples, support of the civilian populations, extension of supply lines and materiel distribution—to name a few important problem areas—involve a spectrum of knowledge and experience not usually available in any single profession, particularly in the military profession. . . . [M]odern warfare requires a weighing of factors and a bundle of skills not solely, and perhaps not normally, within the experience and knowledge of the professional military man." Readers will know how they would feel were such a charge leveled at them about their ability to practice their profession.

As passed by Congress and enacted into law on 30 June 1953, Hensel's recommendations abolished most of the unwieldy debating societies, such as the Munitions Board, that had plagued procurement and research. Their functions were transferred to eleven newly created or strengthened assistant Defense secretaries and assistants to the Secretary. These reforms stopped far short of the fuller unification envisioned by Truman, Marshall, the Army, and the Air Force at the Defense Department's creation. The equally flawed structure of the Joint Chiefs and Joint Staff was left alone. So a pattern began—though at that time no one, including me, noticed the development—that military "reform" would focus almost exclusively on the civilian side of the Pentagon, the Office of the Secretary of Defense and his assistants. But the military side, the Joint Chiefs and Joint Staff, would be left unchanged.

This pattern of augmenting and reorganizing only the civilian side of the Pentagon while avoiding reform of the military was continued and expanded under Secretary Robert S. McNamara in the 1960s. The civilian Office of the Secretary of Defense now consists of some seventy-five assistant secretaries with their assistants and deputies. The military professionals, who remain trapped in their own unmanageable bureaucracy, have less and less influence over policy. This in turn discourages the more able professionals and they quit the service early. So the Great Divorce becomes part of a self-fulfilling prophecy.

The frustrations of those inside the armed services are increased by the inexperience of many top defense civilian officials and the speed with which important positions turn over. By 1967, twenty years after the Defense Department's creation, there had been fourteen Defense Secretaries, fifteen Navy Secretaries, thirteen Army Secretaries, and twelve Air Force Secretaries. The merry-go-round continues. By 1982 the average tenure for top defense officials was two years and five months. Even a genius has a problem learning a complex job in two plus years, and some who occupied the musical chairs were closer to clown than genius.

Those in the Other America of Defense contributed, in part, to their own downgrading. In the years after the Korean War, military advice was not at its best. The Joint Chiefs no longer "split"—there were only 23 splits in 2,977 actions between 1955 and 1959—but they began to "waffle," a practice that continues into today. A "waffle" is when a recommendation is so written that all parties can find in it what they wish. The guidance on a Defense matter from the Joint Chiefs to the Secretary of Defense and the President by law must be unanimous. To obtain this unanimity the advice is usually so hedged with *if*s, *and*s, and *but*s that it is worthless. Or, to use the jargon of the trade, "When the green comes up from the tank with a red stripe, it's been waffled out of existence." (The Chiefs work in "the tank," their advice to the Secretary is on green paper, and final decisions have a red stripe.)

Many of the Chiefs and former Chiefs, along with the abler members of the Joint Staff, know they have not done their job of providing military advice. Privately, they talk all the time about the Straw Giant's condition. The Chairman of the Joint Chiefs in the early 1980s, Air Force General David C. Jones, publicly aired the problem at the end of his term:

> The Joint Chiefs of Staff, if viewed as the military board of a government corporation, would provide some striking contrasts to organization and management principles followed in the private sector: . . . [the] Board consists of five directors, all insiders, four of whom simultaneously head line divisions . . . [it] reports to the chief executive and a cabinet member . . . [It is] supported by a corporate staff which draws all its officers from line divisions and turns over about every two years . . . line divisions control officer assignments and advancement; there is no transfer of officers among line divisions . . . Board meets three times a week to address operational as well as policy matters,

which normally are first reviewed by a four-layered committee system [with] full participation of division staffs from the start . . . at seventy-five percent of the Board meetings, one or more of the directors are represented by substitutes . . . if the Board can't reach unanimous agreement on an issue, it must—by law— inform its superiors . . . at least the four top leadership and management levels within the corporation receive the same basic compensation, set by two committees consisting of a total of 535 members . . . and any personnel changes in the top three levels [about 150 positions] must be approved in advance by one of the committees.

After the Hensel reforms of 1953, the next opportunity to reorganize the Defense Department occurred in 1957, during Eisenhower's second term. A series of nuclear breakthroughs and tests beginning in 1950, called Sandstone, had made the manufacture of atomic weapons more efficient. By 1957, there was enough nuclear explosive to go around, and the size and weight of individual nuclear weapons had dramatically shrunk. SAC had initially tried to keep the nuclear plenty to itself, denying the new weapons even to the Tactical Air Command, as the old fighter pilot versus bomber pilot feud continued. When I broke the story that fighters were now able to deliver atomic bombs, the Secretary of the Air Force vowed to send me to jail, the FBI launched a full field investigation of the leak, my phones were tapped, and *Newsweek*'s editors received letters intimating I was a Red.

However, as more and more nuclear explosive became available, not only did TAC receive nuclear weapons but the Air Force became more willing to share parts of the nuclear mission with the Navy. With the hydrogen bomb now light enough to fit in carrier-based aircraft, the Navy felt its strategic role was secure. In this more relaxed atmosphere a remarkable Chief of Naval Operations, Admiral Forrest Sherman, had, before his untimely death, brought an unusual degree of peace and harmony to the Navy.

The Chairman of the Joint Chiefs of Staff in 1957 was General Nathan ("Nate") Twining, a doughty, totally honest if somewhat parochial Air Force general. (I always liked his dictum about testifying before Congress: "Don't ever lie to them. But don't blab the truth either.") The real power on the Joint Chiefs, however, was the Chief of the Air Staff, General Thomas D. White.

"Tommy" White, like Admiral Sherman, was a thoughtful officer who had become convinced that the Joint Chiefs, the Joint Staff, and the armed services as then organized were unworkable. But unlike many others, he took personal risks to accomplish change. A man of political skill as well as strategic foresight, he put the Air Force Association out in front to block for him by having them propose "a single service, true unification, with military organizations based on missions." With that radical proposal drawing the flack, White himself promulgated what was essentially the Collins or Army plan of 1947. White fought for this proposal in the Pentagon, while Twining, inspired by White, used his prestige with the Congress. In the Senate, in particular, there was bipartisan support for such unification, led by Republican Prescott Bush of Connecticut and Democrat Stuart Symington of Missouri, a former Air Force Secretary.

The Navy, remaining fearful that further unification might force changes that would lessen its strategic role, opposed the reforms. But with a nuclear mission and Sherman's remembered example, naval opposition was not as violent as in 1947. The Air Force position had also substantially changed. In 1947, as we have seen, the Air Force, having achieved independence, was somewhat indifferent to Pentagon organization and still regarded the Army as its most serious bureaucratic rival. Under White in 1957 that service was, in effect, fighting for the Army proposals of ten years before.

Unfortunately, the Army itself, feeling it had been forced to fight the Korean War on the cheap and was being denied funds and weapons it needed for modernization, was now fearful of further unification. That service had just suffered through its own internal bloodletting in the "revolt of the colonels," when a group of younger colonels had leaked to the press secret information critical of the strategic bomber program. Further, Army Chief of Staff Matthew B. Ridgway, and other powerful Army generals, believed that they had only just been able to prevent Admiral Arthur Radford, then Chairman of the JCS, from entering the Vietnamese War on the side of the French at the time of Dien Bien Phu. (Radford had pressed hard for a carrier air strike to prevent French loss of the fort.) The Army wanted no further strengthening of the JCS Chairman's power, and its generals joined admirals to fight White's proposals.

Another factor working against White's reorganization was that he had, without knowing it, incurred President Eisenhower's displeasure. The President felt White had been too critical of the other armed services in one of his speeches. Secretary Wilson was persuaded that the proposal was an attempt to curtail civilian control. Blocked inside the Department of Defense and with crucial administration support lacking, this last service-initiated attempt (until 1983) at self-reorganization died. Four years later White was dead, one of "the choice and master spirits of this age," exhausted by excessive care for the Republic.

At the end of the Korean War, the Eisenhower administration adopted as its major strategic policy the principle of "massive retaliation." This doctrine was known as "the new look" or "more bang for a buck." Massive retaliation in essence was a more elegant formalization of the pre–Korean War reliance on nuclear power alone to secure the defense of the United States. Eisenhower's Secretary of State, John Foster Dulles, enunciated the policy: "In the face of [Soviet] strategy . . . it is not sound to become permanently committed to military expenditures so vast that they lead to 'practical bankruptcy'. . . . We want . . . a maximum deterrent at a bearable cost." Any hostile move by the Soviets would be met by the United States with massive force, "strik[ing] back where it hurts, by means of our own choosing."

Since massive retaliation committed the United States to respond with nuclear weapons to any type of armed provocation, the nonnuclear parts of defense were once again allowed to wither. The Army, the Marines, Tactical Airpower, and parts of the Navy were restricted in mission and reduced in size. The few bucks available (this was another time of military famine) went to build up the Strategic Air Command and the atomic bombers on the Navy's two supercarriers. Later, Intercontinental Ballistic Missiles (ICBMs) and the Navy's missile-carrying submarines were added to this priority list. I do not wish to imply that such policy was all bad, only that it was extremely limited. Among the doctrine's many benefits was the rapid construction and deployment of the country's first ICBMs, Titans, Atlases, and, most important, Minutemen, and missile-launching submarines, weapons systems that today remain the country's principal nuclear deterrent.

The response to the Eisenhower doctrine of massive retaliation varied by service. The Air Force, with the exception of the Tactical Air Command, wholeheartedly supported a doctrine that gave it the largest portion of the available funds; and the bomber-dominated Air Staff successfully kept the officers of Tac Air under control. The Navy, while more skeptical, "stayed on board," as they put it, because the concept contained money for carriers and later for missile-carrying submarines. But "more bang for the buck" threw the Army into genuine revolt. The power structure in the Pentagon had reversed itself. An Air Force/Navy alliance to emphasize strategic warfare replaced the Army/Air Force alliance favoring stronger unification of the Defense Department.

Politically, the new Air Force/Navy axis was much more potent than the old Army/Air Force axis. Not only did the Air Force and the Navy employ the major weapons systems that meant large contracts for the industries in the home states of congressmen and senators, they also appeared, with their more modern hardware, to be the forces of the future. The Army, talking about large ground forces, maintenance of the draft, and less-than-nuclear warfare, by contrast seemed mired in the past.

In this atmosphere the Great Divorce and Interservice Rivalry produced some incredible disasters. One of these led to the Russians, not the Americans, being the first to launch a space satellite.

The Soviet space victory had its roots in the Army/Air Force squabble at the time of unification over control of antiaircraft artillery. The Air Force had originally sought control of all antiaircraft weapons, on the logical ground that they killed in the air. However, for bureaucratic reasons, it was finally agreed that antiaircraft weapons, missiles as well as guns, should remain with the Army.

At that time the Air Staff's energies were focused on the next generation of bombers and little thought was given to emerging missile technology. The unfortunate tendency of the bomber mafia to insist on doctrinal loyalty had shown itself again. The Army, on the other hand, regarded all missiles, surface-to-surface as well as antiaircraft, as a natural outgrowth of artillery.

At the close of World War II as part of Operation Paperclip, a program to bring German scientists to America before the Russians captured them, the Army assembled, primarily at Huntsville, Alabama, a team of German rocket experts augmented by U.S. scientists. I remember watching some of their early firings. It was hard to believe, in spite of the German V-2s, that rockets were the coming weapons. They looked then more like expensive toys than the future arbiters of international power. Then, a host of scientific advances—air bearings, high-temperature-resistant metals, more powerful propulsion systems—arrived to move the missile into its present position as the dominant strategic nuclear weapon.

When in 1951 the Army started serious development of mid-range missiles, no range limits were placed on the distance an Army missile could fly. In those halcyon days the Army and the Navy were even sharing missile parts. The Navy was focused on further carrier development and, like the Air Force, felt no threat from missile development. Indeed, with the Korean War in progress, there was not much interest anywhere in the Defense Department in missile development. The Army was allowed to go ahead, but was never able to obtain the $25 million annually that it wanted for missiles. Borrowing from what meager funds it had available during the Korean War, the Army slowly began to build a team of German and American scientists, who developed a 1,500-mile missile to be known as the Jupiter.

The Navy next began serious missile research. It reasoned that rockets carried close to the enemy shores on ships might be the next step in naval power. Ship-launched missiles would be easier and cheaper to build since, having less distance to fly, they could be smaller. Obviously, shipborne rockets would give the Navy a wider role to play in the strategic deterrent. Following the reasonably successful launch of a surplus German V-2 from the carrier *Midway* in 1947, the Navy began to cast about for a rocket system of its own. The rocket selected, the Viking, later modified and called Vanguard, was a newer and more experimental system than the Army's and one that unfortunately was to prove inadequate. But in the eyes of "Engine Charlie" Wilson, Eisenhower's Secretary of Defense, the Vanguard had one overriding plus: It was designed and built by private enterprise. The Army missile, Redstone, from which the Jupiter developed, was built in a government facility.

By 1954, radio intercepts and radar monitoring of Soviet missile tests, plus other intelligence sources, predicted that the Soviets would launch a space vehicle—some sources claimed a space weapon—in mid-1957. Led by Generals Ridgway and Gavin, the Army began a concerted program to beat the Russians by a year and place a satellite in orbit by late summer of 1956. But starting in the spring of 1956 the roof fell in upon the Army missile program. By a JCS vote of two to one, Air Force and Navy against the Army, with Secretary Wilson siding with the majority, the Army's midrange missile program was removed from the Army and given to the Navy. This was part of a complex deal that involved naval backing for an Air Force weapon called Navaho, designated as an unmanned bomber and best left to rust unremembered.

Then the Army was ordered by Secretary Wilson to develop no missile with a range of more than 200 miles, though some continuing research of Redstone was permitted. In May 1956 Wilson sent the Army's research and development chief, General James M. Gavin, a written order: "The Redstone and Jupiter missiles will *not* be used to launch a satellite." Gavin was further ordered to report personally to Wilson, before any Army missile could be fired, that there was no satellite on the missile's nose. "I'm not going to have some missile developed by the government beat out private industry," Wilson averred. In a divorce, one party often denies any accomplishment by the other.

In September 1956 the Army successfully fired a Jupiter-C missile with sufficient power to launch a satellite; but with no satellite on board. Another such firing occurred in August 1957; each time the Army dutifully reported to Secretary Wilson that there was no satellite in the missile's nose. Finally, on 4 October 1957, the Soviets launched a satellite into space.

One might have thought the Army would have been given immediate permission to recoup some American prestige and launch a satellite. But the directive held. The Navy, Air Force, and Wilson would rather have no American satellite than have the Army's government-built missile first into space. The Soviets launched an even larger satellite on 3 November. On 6 December the Navy attempted to launch a satellite with its industry-built Vanguard system. The missile failed. Still the Army was ordered not to launch. In mid-January the Navy twice tried unsuccessfully to launch a satellite with Vanguard. By then political pressure had built on the Eisenhower administration and the Army was finally permitted to ready its Redstone. On 31 January 1958, the Redstone at last launched America's first satellite, one that could have been in orbit two years earlier.

After the Soviet satellites had beaten America's into space there were congressional investigations and many words of analysis to explain the U.S. failure. The culprit usually blamed was American education, the lack of scientific training in schools. The truth lay elsewhere. America had been defeated by a combination of Interservice Rivalry and the first of a series of Defense Secretaries who, as products of the Great Divorce, lacked the hands-on experience necessary to master their job.

Occasionally Interservice Rivalry would help force a service to develop a weapon that later proved highly effective. The helicopter gunship and the submarine-launched ballistic missile were two examples of this infrequent and fortuitous event.

In the middle Eisenhower years the Air Force grew concerned that the Army would put weapons on light aircraft and so get back into the air-warfare mission. In 1956 it and the Navy got the Joint Chiefs and Secretary Wilson to forbid the Army to arm aircraft. At the same time, the Army was forbidden to buy any aircraft heavier than 5,000 pounds (a plane roughly equivalent to the average crop-duster). Initially the Army was also forbidden to buy helicopters weighing more than 10,000 pounds. However, the Air Force and Navy regarded helicopters as a joke. The weight restriction on helicopters was lifted after a few months of Pentagon battle so the Army could buy them "to use as trucks." "Engine Charlie" from GM knew what a truck was and that it didn't fight. It was understood that no helicopters were to be armed, but that tacit agreement was never put in writing.

Forbidden by JCS directive and secretarial order from buying or arming battleworthy fixed-wing aircraft, the Army in desperation began putting rockets on helicopters. After all, it reasoned, some trucks were armed. However, in the early fifties to believe the helicopter was a fighting weapons system seemed a flight of poetic fancy. I remember a demonstration at the Infantry Center at Fort Benning, Georgia, where an early-model helicopter with two bazookas wired to its skids came skimming over the loblolly pines trying hard to impersonate a tank-killer. The blast from the bazooka rockets—they both accidentally fired at the same time—so rocked the helicopter that it oscillated violently in the air and almost crashed. As for the accuracy of the bazookas, the best that can be said is that they killed no observers. The fighting helicopter appeared to be one of these weapons now and then designed that turn out to be far more dangerous to user than to target.

Yet within ten years the helicopter was a vital part of America's Vietnam War effort, and today is a mainstay of NATO's antitank defense. As I have flown in them since, I occasionally remember my incredulous reaction to that early, stricken, bazooka-firing whirlybird, a recollection that tempers my instinctive criticism of weapons that appear too futuristic. Bad weapons arrive and judgments against them must be given; but criticisms based on past performance or the imperfections of early models are not always correct.

Interservice Rivalry was also responsible for the early development of what may be the most effective strategic weapons system today: submarine-launched ballistic missiles. This weapons system would undoubtedly have seen service eventually; but its rapid procurement and enthusiastic support by the Navy came in part because submarine missiles were so effective against the Air Force. Why were these missiles placed on submarines rather than aircraft carriers? Why were they not emplaced on surplus freighters that slowly rusted in mothballs up and down our coasts? The first naval missile program had envisaged missiles fired from surface ships. In the Eisenhower years the whole world of satellite detection and sea search from airborne radars was in the future. The first sea-launched ballistic missiles, the Polaris series, were placed on submarines as much to make certain they remained Navy as for strategic reasons.

I remember an Air Force assistant secretary of the Eisenhower years assuring me: "It makes no difference, Hadley, if the missile is on land or on a boat; it belongs to us. And the Secretary of Defense [Wilson] agrees with us. We have won that one."

"What about the missiles the Navy plans to put on submarines? Will they be Air Force too?"

"They just might belong to the Navy. But they'll never work."

Navy fears of an attempted Air Force takeover were later proven justified. In Eisenhower's second term the then Defense Secretary, Thomas S. Gates, Jr., discovered that over three hundred vital Soviet installations had been cross-targeted for nuclear destruction with different weapons by at least two separate commands, and no one knew this. Some installations, like airfields, considered vital by both services, had even been cross-targeted three or four times. In European Russia and its satellites there were 21 airfields cross-targeted by two U.S. forces and 31 by three. Other targets considered vital by CIA or consulting economists were not even to be struck at all. (It's hard to believe that no one would know for several years that 300 vital parts of Russia's war machine had been targeted by more than one commander; but secrecy and Interservice Rivalry make a deadly mixture.)

The Air Force answer to this problem was a bureaucratic power play to put all strategic nuclear weapons under the Strategic Air Command, then led by General Thomas Powers. The Navy fought off the Air Force move successfully, a vital part of its argument being that the submarine missiles most certainly could not be considered Air Force.

For once a logical and effective compromise resulted. A Single Integrated Operations Plan (SIOP, pronounced "psyop") was ordered created and kept up-to-date by the Joint Strategic Target Planning staff located at SAC headquarters in Omaha, commanded by an Air Force general with an admiral as his deputy. The Chief of Naval Operations, Admiral Arleigh A. Burke, in August 1960 personally protested to President Eisenhower that this remarkable piece of sanity was gravely damaging to national defense and the Navy. Shades of Admiral King and unification. The President stuck with Gates, and the SIOP remains the basic strategic war fighting document of the United States.

"What happens next?" they ask at midpoint in serious secret war games.

"The 'psyop' takes over," someone growls in reply.

End of phase one.

The problem with SIOP targeting today involves Intraservice Rivalry rather than Interservice Rivalry, and arises because neither the Navy nor the Air Force fully believes in missiles. The senior officers in charge of the targeting program tend to assign targets first to aircraft, second to missiles. The submarine-launched ballistic missile program, Trident, is actively fought by much of the Navy today because it takes funds away from surface ships, particularly carriers. Testifying on the Trident program in 1980, Vice Admiral Charles H. Griffiths fought off efforts to specifically fund that program, saying the size of the Trident budget should depend on "what percentage of the defense budget, what percentage of the country's budget will go to the Navy."

I believe that much of the opposition to missiles arises not just because of their newness (new weapons always threaten established systems) but also from the "war is a game" fallacy. Real men don't sit in missile submarines or Minuteman bunkers, watch radars, program computers, push buttons, and turn keys. They jet into the wild blue yonder or march onto the field and have it out man to man. The missileers in both the Air Force and the Navy are not suspect, but they remain not quite in the mainstream either. For example, Admiral Griffith was successful before Congress. He got the specific submarine missile funds shifted to the Navy as a whole. Then the dominant carrier admirals spent part of those funds on surface ships.

The fifties and the massive retaliation strategy passed into history. President John F. Kennedy and the sixties came onto the stage. As the Kennedy administration began, the forces in the field—the soldiers, sailors, airmen, and marines who in any future conflict would find themselves on the dirty end—were, I believe, the strongest of any in the period covered by this book, specifically including World War II. America still had a large lead in nuclear weapons, strategic and tactical. Basic fighting units in all three services were led by veteran noncoms and officers, many of whom had seen combat in two successful wars. The draft functioned: It was large enough to be representative but small enough to be selective about those chosen. The Korean War had increased the degree of service integration in the field.

The permissive tides of the late sixties, so damaging to inner discipline and communal effort, had not yet lapped the pilings beneath national will. The troops in Europe, for example, returned to their barracks by midnight and often moved into attack positions at dawn. The Navy's carrier task forces were still relatively safe from guided munitions and the ever-increasing fleet of Soviet submarines. France remained a part of NATO, so the supply lines across Europe were not the present irrational tangle. General Curtis LeMay, the Strategic Air Commander, had both the bombers and the newly produced missiles of SAC almost 200 percent ready.

Each of the 2,021 priority targets behind the Iron Curtain

contained in the 1960 SIOP was assigned to a specific bomber or land-based or submarine-based missile. If the bomber or missile developed any failure that imperiled its immediate operation, another was assigned the target within the half hour. A commander who took longer was most probably relieved. Fifteen years later this excellence had been dissipated by the war in Vietnam.

By the time of Kennedy's arrival the growth of Soviet nuclear power had made the inadequacy of massive retaliation generally apparent. The new administration replaced that doctrine with two concepts of its own. Massive retaliation itself gave way to deterrence, which eventually became known as Mutually Assured Destruction (MAD). Simply stated, this doctrine holds that peace is best assured when both sides have enough secure nuclear power so that each can destroy the other, even if attacked first. The metaphor most used to describe this strategic situation is that of two scorpions in a bottle. If either starts to sting the other, the second scorpion will sting back and both will die.

To this strategic doctrine of Mutually Assured Destruction was added the tactical doctrine of "flexible response." Flexible response holds that the United States should be able to answer hostile force with many options, from a few Green Berets through a division of marines or paratroopers to a conventional ground army and finally to nuclear weapons. Ideally, America should be able to deal with a variety of nonnuclear challenges, such as the Cuban missile crisis of Kennedy's time or Lebanon in 1984, with exactly the amount of deadly force necessary.

Describing this doctrine, President Kennedy said: "Our defense posture must be both flexible and determined. Any potential aggressor contemplating an attack on any part of the free world with any kind of weapons, conventional or nuclear, must know that our response will be suitable, selective, swift and effective."

After Vietnam this doctrine of flexible response became discredited in its turn. A variety of groups blamed the doctrine itself, rather than its unintelligent application, for America's involvement and defeat in that war. Under the most recent Presidents, Nixon, Ford, Carter, and Reagan, the draft has remained halted and, until Reagan, conventional forces were cut. The country went back to relying almost entirely on strategic nuclear weapons, though Presidents still talked the language of flexible response. In Carter's first years, funding for military forces returned, in constant dollars, to pre-Korean lows. Equipment deteriorated and military professionalism and morale plummeted. The fiasco in the Iran desert and the murder of the marines in Beirut followed directly from such posturing.

During his brief presidency, Kennedy remained ambivalent about the military. On the one hand, he appreciated military power and elevated the weight given to military advice. On the other hand, he diminished the importance of the people in the armed services by topping them with additional layers of civilians. For the first time the tendency to overcontrol appeared as the White House and the top civilians in the Defense Department began sending overly detailed directives to the forces in the field, a process that was to continue disastrously through Vietnam and into today.

For example, during the Berlin crisis of 1961, when the Soviets closed one of the highways to Berlin, President Kennedy himself issued orders to the lieutenant in charge of the truck column probing the blockade, instructing him as to how long he was to stare at the Russians blocking the road, and what he was to say. It did not occur to the President, the assistant defense secretaries present, or their advisors, all gathered in the White House, that the lieutenant and his captain standing on the wet concrete under the soggy German skies might have a better idea of how to handle that particular Russian outpost than they. Each time, after receiving new instructions, the lieutenant went out to talk to the Russians. Then he would come back to the telephone at the border for a new briefing. If that set of instructions didn't open up the road, he was told, he should come back and report again. In any event, he was to report to the White House as soon as he was safe in Berlin.

Finally the lieutenant went forth and like some ancient champion did not return. The President, assistant secretaries, and communications experts in the White House situation room all believed him safely rolling down the autobahn toward Berlin. But the hours passed and no phone call announced his arrival. By now the convoy was gravely overdue, and still there was no phone call. Frantic exchanges with Berlin reported that the trucks were not in sight. A crisis atmosphere developed among the President and his advisors. Finally, over three hours late, the lieutenant reported in. The convoy had reached Berlin safely.

"What took you so long?" asked an assistant secretary of defense.

"The Russian told me I could drive my trucks off the road and around his tank and proceed that way," said the lieutenant. "I figured that was wrong and that if I just stood and stared at him, he would move his tank. After a couple of hours he did." Electronic equipment makes instantaneous communications to all parts of the globe possible. From the President as Commander in Chief on down, the natural inclination of commanders, many of them detail-obsessive, is to do as much as possible themselves.

Napoleon himself believed that an officer had a right to refuse an order unless his superior was standing beside him as the order was issued. Obviously the President and senior commanders cannot be everywhere. Should they then issue so many detailed orders? The British do not. Politicians and senior commanders pressed those fighting in the Falklands when they felt the campaign was going too slowly. But the War Cabinet in London never issued detailed orders of the type that would probably have emanated from the White House and National Security Council. The control mechanisms wisely devised to prevent an accidental nuclear war have too often become a method of aiming the ordinary soldier's simple gun.

As his Defense Secretary, President Kennedy brought in Robert S. McNamara, former chief executive officer of Ford. It would seem that automobile executives do what Yeats believed of certain fine women. They "eat a crazy salad with their meat." McNamara of Ford arrived at the Pentagon in the same style as had Charlie Wilson of General Motors. He arrogantly insulted the professionals with whom he had to work. Officers were relieved who disagreed even privately with him and his appointed subordinates.

McNamara and those around him never realized, or perhaps they did not care, that in place of the outspoken professionals they removed, there rose up instead a bunch of uniformed yes-men; that men who could command in combat had been replaced with managers who could swing the bureaucratic lead. McNamara accomplished much with his reforms of the budget process and supply services. Unfortunately, the problems created by the new layers of civilian bureaucracy he emplaced in the Pentagon and the hatreds engendered by his own hubris and that of his followers far overbalanced his successes.

McNamara approached the armed services like a Victorian divine arriving at some Pacific island to convert the native heathens. The religion about which he had such messianic convictions was systems analysis. Like the Reverend Alfred Davidson in Maugham's *Rain*, he would show the Pentagon natives the meaning of sin, translated as the crime of inefficiency. To help him in his ministry he brought with him into the Pentagon "McNamara's Band" of management experts and systems analysts. They styled themselves the whiz-kids and were so called by those around them. The press and service professionals were informed that the bad old days were gone and things were going to improve drastically. Weapons would cost less; generals and admirals would toe the line; military and foreign policy would perfectly mesh; the Russians would be cajoled and tamed.

Two of America's most distinguished service figures, one an admiral, the other a general, later described the McNamara years to me using the same words: "The last four years of my service career were the most miserable of my service life." Both men remarked that they were treated by McNamara as they had never been treated before, even in their most junior years, not only as men of little worth, but probably as self-serving liars. "I might just as well have been cleaning toilets," said the general.

I remarked that when an officer or a civilian from the Forrestal, Marshall, Lovett years died, everyone, military and civilian, was at the funeral, sharing memories. Now the military went to the military funerals, the civilians to the civilian. "Why would I go to McNamara's funeral but to spit," remarked the general. I quoted this to the admiral. "I wouldn't go even to spit," he said. I am protecting both these men since our conversation was private, but they are no composite, they are individuals of power, expertise, dignity, and worth. One can disagree completely over this or that policy with such men. I have. But the secure can disagree over policy without insulting a man's worth.

Which brings up a strange characteristic of McNamara himself and those he brought into the higher echelons of the Defense Department. Very few had seen combat. Products of the Great Divorce, they were at best ambivalent about those they had to lead. Again, combat is not the sine qua non of good defense decisions. General Omar Bradley, one of America's great World War II combat leaders, had not been under fire in World War I. And certainly exceptional talents, such as language fluency or science aptitude, must be used by the armed services. Still, still,

still, these men were of the World War II and Korean War generation and practically all of them had drawn safe billets. Surely a little more battle experience would have helped them distrust statistics as a measure of what was happening in Vietnam. Nor would McNamara have nodded approvingly while one of his systems analysts in Saigon, who had not been in the field, told him the Vietnamese liked being bombed because it kept the Viet Cong from their villages.

Henry Kissinger, who wielded power comparable to McNamara's under President Nixon, is not without ego and has been many things; he had also been a sergeant in an infantry division. In the World War II defense hierarchy, the top three men, Stimson, Patterson, and Lovett, had been World War I heroes. In the Vietnam defense hierarchy there were few such men. As Dr. Samuel Johnson remarked with his usual pith, "Every man thinks meanly of himself for not having been a soldier." McNamara and his band flipped back and forth from overadmiration of things military to overassertiveness against the military.

The doctrine of the McNamara years was later codified in a book by systems analysts Alain C. Enthoven and K. Wayne Smith, *How Much Is Enough: Shaping the Defense Program, 1961–1969.* The book outlined a procedure called the Planning, Programming, and Budgeting System. None who undertook to lead the Pentagon into more perfect ways through reliance on such measures seemed to have heard of Napoleon's great maxim "The moral is to the physical as seven is to one." Nor read Clausewitz, who felt that economics "[stands] in about the same relationship to combat as the craft of the swordsmith to the art of fencing." Nor had they looked around them in the Department to try to understand the strengths and weaknesses of its structure and of the men and women serving there.

How McNamara and his band felt about those they were to lead can be judged by a quotation from *How Much Is Enough*: "What is commonly called 'military science' is not scientific in the same sense as law or medicine or engineering. . . . The so-called 'principles of war' are really a set of platitudes that can be twisted to suit almost any situation. . . . The point is that military professionalism is largely in the conduct of military operations, not in the analysis and design of broad strategies."

One might remark that law is seldom scientific, or reflect on the psychosomatic nature of much illness, but more to the point, anyone entering the Pentagon with such an attitude is in for trouble. Every veteran reporter knows that the stories you really get wrong are the ones where you know the absolute truth before you start.

In an effort to manage the three armed services more efficiently, McNamara added a new layer of bureaucracy at the top of the Pentagon. The Defense Department had been designed with the civilians exercising overall policy control and the military making decisions within that policy. Now, under McNamara, the civilian bureaucracy gathered more and more power into its grasp and began to make the day-to-day decisions also. Overcontrol and "the Russification of the American armed forces" marched forward. Those at the top were unaware of the seductive trap into which they had fallen. Day-to-day decisions often appear easier to make than policy. In the end, the systems analysts tried to conduct daily military operations in Vietnam while neglecting to examine rigorously the strategic reasons for and costs of that war.

When they had failed, they then departed—sometimes into the antiwar movement—leaving behind the professionals they had insulted. Those service professionals now had to try to rebuild the Atlantic alliance and bring some sort of resolution to the war in Vietnam, a war which the systems analysts had believed could be won by such painless inventions as isolating South Vietnam from the North with an electronic fence.

In fairness to the new defense managers of the Kennedy-Johnson years, the military advice coming up from the Joint Chiefs and the services was at a low ebb. Something began to happen inside the Pentagon in the late fifties—a certain élan left, a feeling of urgency evaporated, careerism began to flourish. No one has given a satisfactory answer why this happened. Perhaps the trend was merely cyclical. In any event, while in the field the forces remained finely honed, all was not well at the center. The whiz kids did not move in a vacuum, but they didn't dash their heads up against any George Marshalls, Forrest Shermans, or "Tommy" Whites either.

McNamara made the initial mistake of dissipating his energy among many programs, his "seventy-six trombones" approach. For example, on taking office McNamara decided he would change the strategic nuclear targeting doctrine of the United States. The changes McNamara made (I am simplifying drastically) basically shifted U.S. policy from one that deterred nuclear war by preparing to reply to a Soviet attack with everything the United States possessed to one that relied on many nuclear options. Basically this plan separated out attacks on Soviet military forces, particularly strategic forces, from attacks on the Soviet industrial base and other war-waging abilities. The Soviet strategic forces would be attacked first. The attacks on cities might or might not follow.

The plan was an immediate disaster for these reasons: First, to thoughtful critics in the United States and Europe it looked like a strategy for first strike, that is, the United States hits first to take out Soviet weapons, and so escapes devastation itself, and then imposes its own peace terms. Second, European governments, particularly the French and British, saw the new doctrine as an attempt to uncouple the defense of the United States from that of Western Europe. Third, the Soviets let it be known they wouldn't play. If there was any nuclear attack on their territory, they would hit the United States with everything they had. Finally, the new theory was impossible to execute, since many of the military targets the plan envisaged attacking were inside or close to major Soviet population centers. After announcing his new strategy with fanfare, McNamara quietly dropped it several months later.

The plan had been around in academic defense circles for a number of years and still has adherents today. From the first it has seemed ridiculous to me. How could one possibly tell in the real world during a nuclear exchange that your enemy was using limited-option plan 36 and ½ and not delivering an all-out attack? "Chicago, Los Angeles, Bismarck, and Washington have gone, Mr. President, but New York, San Francisco, and Atlanta still stand. I think he's just probing. Let's hit only Omsk, Pinsk, Leningrad, and Vladivostok in reply."

I can give you the complex, technical arguments about why communications among our own forces, or between ourselves and our allies and ourselves and our enemies, won't work well enough in the electromagnetically disturbed postattack environment for such a strategy to be effective. But I think here science is both unnecessary and profoundly misleading. McNamara and his followers tended then and tend now to overintellectualize all defense issues, including the war in Vietnam and nuclear weapons. If those mushroom clouds ever start to blossom, the world will not behave as academics wish. In the Carter presidency, Secretary of Defense Harold Brown, a former whiz kid himself, tried to revive the plan and then backed down. Reagan's Secretary of Defense, Caspar W. Weinberger, also tried, but changed his mind.

Buying weapons was the area where McNamara believed he and the systems analysts round him would make their greatest improvements. They would produce better weapons for less money. Comparison of a major McNamara weapons program with an earlier one reveals the difference between myth and reality with respect to the purchase of weapons and illuminates the reasons for excessive Pentagon costs.

McNamara chose to demonstrate the excellence of his concepts by imposing his management methods on the next fighter plane the services were to buy. He decreed that the Navy and Air Force would buy the same new "fighter." The joint plane the services were to develop became known as the TFX (Tactical Fighter Experimental). It also became one of the most expensive weapons buys in Pentagon history, and one of the least successful aircraft. Why was this program, produced by minds of obvious brilliance, so disastrously different from the successes of previous administrations, such as the building of the first intercontinental ballistic missiles?

This book has stressed that the Defense Department is not newborn each morning but has a long history that determines attitudes and decisions. To understand McNamara's failure with the TFX, one should realize where each service stood on fighter development at that time. What were the hidden agendas? In the Pentagon, even simple things like words can lead the uninitiated astray. In the Navy a "fighter" is a plane that does high-altitude, air-to-air combat. The Air Force calls that plane an "interceptor." The Air Force calls a "fighter" a plane that primarily does ground attack and secondarily does air-to-air combat. The Navy calls that plane an "attack aircraft." That sounds simple to understand, but the evidence indicates that those ordering the Navy and Air Force to produce a common "fighter" did not appreciate how vast were the differences between "fighters." Weapons are built to do things, to perform their missions. The TFX designers were being asked to produce one plane to accomplish two very different missions.

The Defense Department moves forward like the rest of mankind by expending human brainpower and energy. In programs that have achieved fame for speed, efficiency, and reasonable cost (General Bernard Schriever's ballistic missile program, Admiral Hyman Rickover's nuclear submarine program), people work seven-day weeks and twelve- to fourteen-hour days. And they often share a feeling of communion and elation as they labor. If that kind of energy is locked in bureaucratic battle rather than solving problems, or if the minds assigned to the project are second-rate, there will be little progress. In the TFX program, about one-tenth of the energy was going to designing the plane. The rest was expended fighting McNamara and the whiz kids or in trying to battle the other service or to compromise on a least-bad design. Besides, development of the TFX, though it was a difficult and experimental idea, never had the necessary overriding priority. Other projects of equal priority went forward at the same time.

Before describing where the Navy and Air Force were coming from as they developed their "fighter" for the 1970s, I feel it necessary to register a caveat. I am not as familiar with the procurement processes of the armed services as I am with other areas. However, it has always appeared to me that, on the average, the Navy does a better job of plane design and purchase than the Air Force, though the Air Force performs superbly on a few priority jobs. The design and procurement programs of the two services are totally different. One is organized by project, the other by major parts. They are in different cities miles apart. They use different criteria to make judgments. The programs fit the strengths and styles of the two services. The Navy, with its greater depth of midrange talent, can take the component-parts approach. The Air Force, with a few outstanding managers but lacking the Navy's wealth of midmanagement or command talent, does better by concentrating on a few high-priority projects.

The Navy, by and large, assigns abler officers to its procurement process than does the Air Force. I think the reason for this is historic. Naval officers have had to design large portions of their own ships, and participate more in the specialized designs of battleship, submarine, or carrier aircraft. Air Force plane design, on the other hand, was pretty much left to the aircraft industry. (The aircraft industry devoted time and skill to working on Air Force planes, particularly the bombers, because development of these weapons helped them build civilian transport planes, a lucrative program. Military aircraft and civilian aircraft specifications are now diverging, and military aircraft are no longer designed so well.) Others believe that the relative superiority of naval procurement arises because the Navy deals with fewer contractors than the Air Force. That may be a factor. But the Army deals with only a few contractors in tank procurement; and historically that program has been a disaster.

However, as usual there are losses with the gains. The Navy seems more inhibited than the Air Force by the NIH factor (Not Invented Here). The Air Force, after some initial resistance, purchased the Navy-developed F-4 in large quantities, used the aircraft extensively in Vietnam, and was lavish in its praise. I doubt the Navy would do the same with an Air Force plane. Even after the Falkland Islands war, where Britain's Harrier jump jets were a spectacular success, the Navy is resisting the Harrier, though the Marines are not.*

To turn to the hidden agendas, the histories behind the two aircraft that McNamara ordered merged: The Navy had just finished designing and buying that tremendously efficient fighter, the F-4. The Navy now wanted to design and build what the Air Force called an interceptor. The admirals wanted a plane to protect their carrier task forces from the growing threat of Soviet plane-launched missiles—next-generation weapons like the Exocets, which were to sink the British ships in the Falklands.

The plane the Navy had developed was the Missileer. The Missileer was the first aircraft designed around a missile, the Eagle. The plane was subsonic, had a large nose to accommodate the five-foot radar dish then required for long-range missile launch, and could stay aloft (loiter) a long time. Again let me acknowledge my prejudice. I am certain we are moving into the world of precision guided weapons and that the planes of the future will be built around their electronics systems. The Missileer was just such a plane. I have grave doubts about how well, if at all, large aircraft carriers can survive, and large airfields too, for that matter. But if you want to remain with large, easy-to-locate, immensely valuable targets, than it makes sense to try to defend them with a plane like the Missileer, an aircraft with advanced electronics

---

* The Harrier, which can take off almost vertically, obviates the need for large carriers and so threatens the dominant Navy faction.

and a long-range supersonic missile. Since it takes longer to design and develop a missile than a plane, the Navy had already spent time and funds on the Eagle.

As with any new idea, there had been bitter battles within the Navy during the refining of the Eagle/Missileer concept. Pilots are pilots and they like to fly fast, hot planes. The idea of flying something slow and fat and letting a bit of electronic gimmickery do the killing is a strictly nonpilot idea. It also conflicts with that damn game metaphor. Then too, pilots, being human, like to stay alive; and there is nothing like an extra turn of speed to help one bug out. (Do not smile in derision if you have not been shot at. Your gallant author has quit the field at top speed in jeep, tank, and on foot.) There was also a much-researched argument that the Missileer was so slow it could be "spoofed"—it would respond to a fake attack from the north and not get back in time to stop the real attack from the south.

That was where the Navy was coming from, with an experimental airplane that had friends and foes of its own inside that service. In the battle over the TFX, that plane got lost. Another missile, the Sparrow, was later hung on a variety of high-performance fighters, such as the F-4s and F-15s, by both the Air Force and Navy. But without the large surveillance radar proposed for the Missileer, the Sparrow failed to perform well over North Vietnam. Today parts of the fighter mafia point to the failure of the Sparrow to perform under that handicap as an example of why you cannot rely on electronic gimmickery. And reporters, divided from service experience by the Great Divorce, get looked in the eye by fighter-jocks exuding the "right stuff" and report to the public that electronics will not work.*

For its "fighter" the Air Force had a totally different hidden agenda. Not surprisingly, the TAC versus SAC battle was the

---

* Several recent weapons—the DIVAD antiaircraft gun and the Maverick antitank missile, for example—have featured electronic systems that have functioned miserably. Some reporters have used these failures to point to electronics as an expensive and unreliable luxury that contributes to excessive weapons costs and failures. The weapons mentioned have certainly been faulty. However, in 1930, to test horses against trucks, the Army moved the 2nd platoon of Troop E of the 1st Cavalry from Fort D. A. Russell, Texas, to Fort Clark, Texas. By horse, the trip always took two days. This first time by truck it took five. Fortunately, the Army did not lose faith in the internal combustion engine.

dominant issue. The Air Force fighter, the TFX, was being designed because of the Tactical Air Command's correct belief that
its fighters were not getting a full share of the nuclear pie and
therefore of the Defense budget. The TFX was to be a plane
capable of carrying nuclear weapons in "on the deck" at supersonic speeds so that it could escape radar detection. It also was to
be able to operate from smaller, less developed airfields, so it
would not be restricted to large, vulnerable bases, as were SAC
bombers. To give the aircraft even more flexibility, the TFX
would be capable of flying great distances at subsonic speeds.
To accomplish the difficult mating of supersonic speeds close to
the ground with the ability to fly far, the plane was to have a
revolutionary movable wing that had just been developed. This
wing would sweep back and so become delta-shaped and smaller
for the supersonic portion of the flight. The plane was also to
contain some exceptionally complex electronics to enable it to
operate close to the ground at high speeds.

The specifications for the TFX added a bit of rubric about
the plane's ability to fly ordinary rockets and bombs for interdiction or in close support of the Army. No one really believed
the plane would ever do that. The bomb bay was not designed
large enough to be able to carry the needed conventional explosives. As part of its price for agreeing to work with the Navy, the
Air Force successfully insisted that the requirement for the plane
to support the Army be dropped.*

The TFX, though not primarily an interceptor, would also
have the ability to engage in high-altitude air-to-air combat. A
plane with a revolutionary wing that could fly supersonic close
to the deck and carry enough gas to be global was bound to be
very heavy. It was: over 70,000 pounds. The Missileer weighed
50,000 pounds. There was not as much opposition to the TFX
inside the Air Force as there was to the Missileer inside the Navy;
the dominant bomber generals reasoned that if the plane worked
at all, they'd just make bombers of them and assign them to SAC.
Which is what happened to a large portion of the TFXs finally
bought, as F-111s, the production name of the TFX.

Two totally different aircraft to perform two separate, largely

---

* "Close support" is attacking enemy troops actually in contact with the
friendly ground forces. "Interdiction" is isolating the battlefield by attacking
supplies, troops, bridges, supply dumps, etc., in the rear area.

different missions had been ordered merged. One plane was light, fat, and slow, with advanced missiles and electronics. The other was long, sleek, heavy, and fast, with a revolutionary wing. To put together these two aircraft would be like mating your washing machine and your dishwasher just because they both clean household items. The resulting hybrid would be expensive and most likely would not clean anything particularly well.

The inception of the TFX program exposes a major, perhaps the major, factor behind excessive weapons costs: the presence of impossible requirements. If the requirements are imperfect, then expensive, poorly performing weapons follow. The selection of General Dynamics over Boeing to make the aircraft finally agreed upon drew the headlines on the TFX because that was "sexy" news: McNamara all alone reversing the admirals, generals, and career civilian experts and taking on the Pentagon. But that wasn't the question that should have been asked. The key question was "Should anyone have ordered such a plane?"

If McNamara had wished to save money, there were things that he might have done. He could have said that the TFX was designed to do too many missions and requested a test model to see if the movable wing would work. He could have moved directly against the idea of supercarriers and risked a Navy in revolt, which he got anyway. He could have questioned the Missileer concept and asked the Navy to examine a more conventional, supersonic interceptor. That would have generated support in large parts of the Navy. But McNamara had his secret agenda. He intended to use the TFX to demonstrate he could design and build a cost-efficient airplane, and to show the generals and admirals who controlled the armed services. The TFX was the battleground on which he elected to fight his Pentagon battle.

The Missileer was canceled and the Navy, realizing that it was the TFX or nothing, began to negotiate seriously with the Air Force over specifications. When ordering that there be but one aircraft, McNamara had stipulated that the Air Force should take into account the Navy's concerns. I have talked to negotiators on both sides, and most of those on both sides are dubious that the other was negotiating in good faith. I cannot pass judgment. Building such a plane seems to me to have been impossible; and when you set an impossible task, people duck and weave, particularly when their promotions are involved.

Further, the Missileer threatened the Air Force in a number of ways. It was a single-mission aircraft, and the Air Force had long argued against single-mission aircraft, partly from belief that one fighter should be able to perform a variety of missions, partly to avoid designing a separate aircraft for Army close air support. The Air Force wished to handle air defense with small supersonic fighters, both for reasons of tactics and also because of doctrinal fights with the Army over the antiaircraft mission. The Missileer challenged this outlook. Then the Air Force had been much slower than the Navy to develop air-to-air missiles. The most effective air-to-air missile, one still in use by both Air Force and Navy, was the Navy's infrared heat-seeker, the Sidewinder. Ironically, the Air Force later forbid the FB-111s that were built from engaging in air-to-air combat because the violent maneuvers threw off the complex electronics necessary for low-level bombing.

On the other hand, the Navy didn't like the idea of a fighter that could cross oceans and come in on the deck and deliver nuclear weapons. That called into question the need for carrier aircraft in strategic warfare. Not only were the two planes that McNamara had ordered merged significantly different; each was psychologically threatening to the opposing service.

As the negotiations dragged on, it became clear that not one TFX was being talked about but five. The situation resembled the three Johns in Oliver Wendell Holmes's *The Autocrat of the Breakfast Table*: At breakfast sat John as John saw himself, John as others saw him, and the real John, known only to God. Upon the Pentagon negotiating table was the ideal Air Force TFX and the ideal Navy TFX. Then there was the ideal Air Force TFX as seen by the Navy; and the ideal Navy TFX as seen by the Air Force, and the Defense TFX as seen by McNamara. Everyone had different figures to describe the weights, speeds, fuel capacity, loiter time, climb rate, and so forth, of the five different airplanes.

While all this was in progress, the contractors, sensing a big buy, were going wild, submitting bids and trying to find the locus of power, where the true decision would be made. They soon discovered that no matter what the services decided, the decision would be made by McNamara. So they tailored the information they put into the process for the efficiency experts, not the fighters. A three-star general involved in the process said to me, "Here it is, the biggest weapons-buy in five years, and my phone is not

ringing. Any time there's a big buy and the contractors are not
putting pressure on you, you know you are out of the loop."

By that time the decisions had taken so long and the criteria
had been changed so often, making the plane such a hybrid, that
both services were trying to bypass the TFX and design the next
aircraft. The Navy already had specifications for the F-14 in the
works and was trying to figure ways to move that through the
Defense hierarchy. The Air Force was planning for the F-16.
Since both services were already looking beyond the TFX to
planes they believed in, many of the ablest design people were
no longer working on the TFX.

McNamara had decided that procurement of the TFX/FB-111
would be by competitive bids. Boeing actually put in the low
bid, but McNamara gave the contract to General Dynamics. His
explanation later was that he believed Boeing's bid was artificially
low, an effort to buy in and then raise the cost afterward. This had
been the way things operated in the past, and McNamara correctly
insisted that should cease. However, no one believed him. Lockheed did not believe him a year later when bidding on the C-5A,
the gigantic transport. As a result, that company headed toward
bankruptcy when the cost estimates were enforced.

Both Navy and Air Force officers had favored Boeing as the
builder of the TFX. Boeing's design was more experimental,
"state of the art," and used a variety of new metals. I believe the
military felt that since the plane as designed would never amount
to much anyway, they might just as well learn what they could
from the few models built. When somebody tells you around the
Pentagon, "The primary purpose for which we funded this
weapons system was to advance the state of the art," he means,
"We've spent millions on this dog and we can't even get the
doors to close."

The final buy decision was made in great secrecy by McNamara
acting alone. He did not even thoroughly study the recommendations of the various military boards, all of which had recommended the contract go to Boeing rather than General Dynamics.
The military officers and service professionals who had been
studying the Boeing and General Dynamics designs had often
been excluded from the room where the progress reports were
made to the Service Secretaries by the whiz kids. In fairness to
McNamara, he had been getting his own backdoor reports on

the plane all along from his own people in the decision processes, just as Kennedy was getting backdoor reports on McNamara from his own people in the Navy. The number-two man in the Defense Department, Deputy Secretary Roswell L. Gilpatric, reports that from the look on President Kennedy's face, it appeared he was totally surprised when he heard the contract was going to General Dynamics and Texas.

There were the usual immediate cries of political foul, particularly from those who did not get the contract. Many thought the contract had gone to General Dynamics as part of a deal by Vice President Lyndon Johnson to help his Texas friends. Another theory was that General Dynamics executives had supplied the street money with which President Kennedy had carried Chicago. Others claimed this or that Pentagon official or service officer had secret interests in the company. You can find people who will tell you exactly how the deal was swung and claim to have seen cash-filled attaché cases. But when you check their stories—and I spent (wasted) a great deal of time doing this—the leads all vanish. The Justice Department, under Attorney General Robert Kennedy, held no investigation, which doesn't prove much one way or the other. A congressional committee looked into the TFX award at long and vituperative length. Indeed, they were so nasty they accomplished the close to impossible, getting the Navy and Air Force to support McNamara to a limited extent.

I have my own informed guess as to why, against the advice of the service boards studying the TFX, McNamara decided to buy the less advanced, more expensive aircraft. I think the secret lies in his personality. McNamara was not a bad man; his reforms of the Pentagon supply services were mostly excellent and overdue; but he possessed an ego that blinded him. One of McNamara's friends and assistants, Henry S. ("Harry") Rowen, defended him in the early days of the Vietnam War, saying, "The war is difficult for him. Vietnam is a combination of people and ideas and these are the two areas in which he is weak."

McNamara would be laughable, a weapon-wielding Candide, had not the results of his arrogance been so tragic for the armed services, in Vietnam and elsewhere. He believed that in systems analysis he had the answer to all problems, and that since he most perfectly understood this new faith, he was entitled to rule. He picked the General Dynamics design because unconsciously he thought by so doing he would humble the military and demon-strate his superiority by acting exactly contrary to their judgment. If he thought he could humble these professionals, he was wrong. If he thought he could damage their morale and that able men would hasten their exit from the service, he was right. In the twenty-twenty hindsight of history, two things are certain. One: He incurred such hostility that the Defense Department function-ing was damaged. Two: He picked a dog.

While those that fly in the FB-111 are loyal to it publicly, after the manner of combat pilots everywhere, privately there is little enthusiasm for the plane. The FB-111 exists primarily as a nuclear bomber of small payload; it sits around on the ground while committees try to dream up missions to fit its limited capabilities.

The ridiculousness of relying on systems analysis and computer printouts to determine weapons buys was vividly brought home to me because I was once part of the military industrial complex. In those TFX days, credit card companies were stickier about issuing credit cards to individuals, particularly such oddball types as writers, directors, actresses, than they are now. To help myself and some others obtain credit cards, I formed a fictitious tank company, known as Hadley Tank. (Or notional tank com-pany, if you prefer the jargon of intelligence.) Of the fortunes of Hadley Tank I have written elsewhere: how the company was eventually listed in various business directories and its officers were asked to lecture at defense symposiums; the difficulties we had avoiding secret clearances; the troubles we had refusing your money.

What is important to record here is that McNamara's office invited me down to Washington to receive the Defense Depart-ment's E for Excellence for my company because we had "never had a shortfall." What more is there to say about relying solely on efficiency experts and their computers? We not only had no shortfall, we had no long fall, we didn't even have a windfall. We had never built a damn thing. Yet in McNamara's world, Hadley Tank was one of the most efficiently run companies in the United States. To think that with a little bad luck, had I been Hadley Plane instead of Hadley Tank, we might have been stuck building the TFX.

The Air Force ICBM program under General Bernard A. Schriever, which led to the design and production during Eisenhower's presidency of the Minuteman missile, serves as a contrast to the TFX. Rather than statistics and Pentagon committee work, command responsibility and human skills were stressed.

The directive setting up the program stated: "The present successive levels of review place an onerous burden upon personnel actually administering the ICBM programs. . . . therefore, to assure program acceleration commensurate with technological progress *maximum authority for program approval and implementation should be delegated to the lowest possible echelon* [italics mine]."

The critical importance of making the proper decisions at the correct level burst on me in such compelling fashion during World War II that it is worth a brief detour to record the moment. At one time, one of my loudspeaking tanks had gotten a bit chewed up. Not only could it no longer loudspeak, it couldn't even croak. I clanked back to division headquarters and got a priority order to have the tank repaired, and then clanked off to the repair battalion. I arrived at the tent of the lieutenant colonel commanding the maintenance battalion at the same time as did a jeep that belonged to one of the assistant division commanders, a brigadier general. The jeep needed a new roll bar welded to it.

The lieutenant colonel in charge of the maintenance battalion called in his heavy maintenance and repair officer, a captain, and said to him, "Here is the loudspeaking tank that has to get back to combat right away and here is the general's jeep that needs a roll bar. Get them fixed up."

"Yes, sir," said the captain. "Which one has priority?"

"Give them equal priority," said the lieutenant colonel.

The general's jeep and the talking tank followed the captain into an apple orchard, where beneath the trees we met the repair officer, a first lieutenant, my own rank.

"Lieutenant," said the captain, "here is the talking tank for a new loudspeaker and the general's jeep for a roll bar. Work on them first."

"Yes, sir," said the lieutenant. "Which one has priority?"

"They have equal priority."

Now following the lieutenant, jeep and tank arrived at the welding section, where stood one corporal with one blowtorch with one jet of flame coming out the end of that one blowtorch.

"Corporal," said the lieutenant, "here is the loudspeaking tank for a new loudspeaker and the general's jeep for a roll bar. Stop what you are doing and work on them first."

"Yes, sir," said the corporal. "Which one has priority?"

"They have equal priority."

The corporal looked at his single blowtorch with its single jet of flame and shook his head.

To return to the big picture and the ICBM program, the civilian leadership of the Pentagon, having helped General Schriever and the other professionals in the service set up the operation, and having secured for it from the President and National Security Council an overriding priority for materials and able people, left further management to the military. Air Force Secretary Donald A. Quarles and his Secretary for Research, Trevor Gardner, both scientists, reviewed the program quarterly. The only other Pentagon involvement was two small special committees set up to make sure the rest of the Pentagon did not get involved.

Even the Secretary of Defense, recognizing the importance of technical knowledge, delegated his legal authority to manage the program to the Secretary of the Air Force. As a result, the thirty-seven committees, individuals, or organizations that those developing the missile would have had to report to in an ordinary major weapons program were reduced to seven. Compare this with the TFX program, where not only was the number of committees increased but the aircraft specifications were passed through the committees four times.

To further remove the missile design and production from obstacles in the Pentagon corridors, the management of the program itself was removed from Washington to California, where the Western Development Command was created. Here the effort was not run out of a set of glorious offices. An old two-story Catholic school and chapel across an asphalt street from a gas station in Inglewood served as headquarters. An outstanding team of scientists, including two of great fame, John von Neumann and George Kistiakowsky, advised the program.

A separate company composed of scientists and engineers was created to design, test, and build the first missiles. As for the officers and civilians assigned to his Western Development Command, General Schriever got the authority to write their efficiency reports himself so that they could not be penalized for supporting the program by some superior who wanted his ideas to rule. He had the money coming to him directly and he had the promotions of his people in his hands. Also, he was tough enough to resist the blandishments of and pressure from various industrialists who wanted to get the missile contracts away from his specially created company. As for Interservice Rivalry, Schriever was meeting privately in motels with his Navy counterparts to pass on and receive information.

Congress, more disciplined and better qualified than today, but nonetheless containing some rather difficult and crusty powers, was brought on board by briefings in terms of five-year periods rather than the customary one-year budget requests. This gave the Congress a feeling of participation, as each year it could check the progress of the ICBM program against what it had been told to expect. As Schriever describes the days of effort: "It was just like the war, everyone was driving as hard as they could. . . . We were working 7 days a week, 12 hours a day. Really we were never off; all our waking time we were working. The only time we were not working was the time we took off for sleep. Nobody complained but the wives."

In 1955 and 1956 those in the Western Development Command did paper studies and designed, built, and tested difficult hardware items. By 1957 they were designing the prototype Minuteman missile. On 28 February 1957, Secretary of Defense Neil H. McElroy was briefed on the program's progress. Two weeks later he authorized the $50 million necessary to complete development of the solid-fuel missile. Three years later came the first firing, in February 1961. A year later, in December 1962, on cost and on time the first squadron of twenty missiles became operational outside of Cheyenne, Wyoming.

Having examined the ICBM and TFX program, one can appreciate the mix of reasons behind excessive weapons costs. There are sometimes villains and crooks in defense procurement, but by far the most likely reasons for ineffective, expensive weapons are impossible requirements written by uninformed committees. Requirements drive the weapons process. However, few people understand requirements or know who makes them— where they "get generated," to use the jargon. Here the services must shoulder much of the blame. Pride and priority in the armed services go to the combat forces, combat command, and the service staffs. Able people all too rarely enter the field of weapons design, and their promotions are apt to be slow. The Navy tried to fire Rickover as a captain because he lacked combat experience. An ongoing horror story is the ordnance design of supertanks for the Army. No matter what the tankers themselves request, out roll behemoths that are too big and too expensive, burn too much fuel, and may be too complicated for today's tanker.

Confronted with close-to-impossible requirements, defense contractors bid low, believing that the specifications will be modified later and large, extra charges for the modifications will be allowed. This is the infamous "buy in," where the contractor, having won the contract with a low bid, makes his money on construction of modifications and sale of spare parts. This is where those $500 hammers and $75 washers enter the picture. Another trick of the trade is known as "bow waving." Here you make something at less than cost for, say, four years and then recoup with enormous costs in the fifth year, after your company, the Defense Department, and the Congress are all locked into the program. Competitive bidding is not the total answer either. That just leads to companies without experience, such as Hadley Tank, buying in with low bids. In most large weapons buys, parts of the system are subcontracted out to plants in which powerful senators and congressmen have a political interest, even though these parts could be made at less cost elsewhere.

Supposing you, as a Defense Department official, come to me and say, "Hadley, please design us an elephant that will climb trees. We need to reach those choice leaves at the top."

And I say to you, "I don't really think you can produce a tree-climbing elephant. How about a very little elephant with a very long trunk; and a mobile ramp."

And you bark, "No. I want a tree-climbing elephant."

"I don't think you can—"

"We are going to get a tree-climbing elephant, Mr. Hadley. It's just a question of big suckers on the feet. And besides, Lockheed, McDonnell Douglas, Ford, and General Motors are already bidding on the wonder tusker."

"OK, times are tough, count Hadley Tank in."

Then I win the competition with a low bid and try unsuccessfully for four years to design a climbing elephant. Finally you realize that the best that can be done is a very small elephant with a long trunk and a movable ramp. You should see what the wheels on the ramp are going to cost you, the ones with their cotter pins manufactured in Senator Budget-Cutter's hometown. And the screws that hold the planks together will be made of gold. That's what you get for asking for a tree-climbing elephant.

The famous whistle-blowers, whom Congress and the press love to interview, expose some of these excessive charges from time to time. They perform a service and one that should be neither minimized nor exaggerated. But the whistle-blowers habitually expose symptoms, like the $500 hammers, rather than major causes. And some in power are glad to have attention focused on such small items while the real culprits, impossible requirements, underbidding, and the ability of powerful senators and congressmen to get contracts for their areas, go publicly unobserved.

Sadly, many on Capitol Hill regard national defense as just another part of the pork barrel. Many of the impossible requirements are the result of legislative fiat. Take the intertwining of defense costs and the construction of the Tennessee-Tombigbee Waterway, a nine-foot ditch and presumptive barge canal that duplicates the Mississippi River and that may just be the most expensive flim-flam ever put over on the taxpayers. Lobbying hard for Ten-Tom over the past several years has been Senator John C. Stennis of Mississippi, through whose state the ditch slices. Stennis carries a little book listing who votes how on this project, and the defense contracts and bases they have in their districts or want to have. Stennis is chairman of the Senate Armed Services Committee and one of the first to denounce expensive weapons and bases.

Congressman Duncan L. Hunter of San Diego, California, came up with a plan that would have required the naval ships stationed in Japan to return to California for periodic overhaul, increasing maintenance costs on these ships ten times. He compromised—only one destroyer had to return, at an added cost of $14 million. Coal state politicians force the troops in Germany to burn U.S. coal, rather than convert to oil or burn German coal; this adds $45 a ton in shipping costs alone. Senator Ted Stevens of Alaska held up the entire Air Force budget until the

Air Force agreed to purchase more expensive Alaskan milk. Senator Alan Cranston of California, who campaigns as an enthusiastic supporter of the nuclear freeze, also votes additional funds for the B-1 bomber, built to carry the weapons he would outlaw. While he was a senator, Roger W. Jepsen of Iowa had a Marine colonel on his staff, paid for by the Navy, whose job was to help Iowans get more defense contracts.

More than pork-barrel politics is involved. In 1984, in the name of efficiency, Congress required more than 20,000 pages of documents from the Pentagon justifying the dollars spent. These ranged from reports on "Military Jacket Linings" and "Hawaiian Milk" to studies of business contracts signed on Indian reservations. While these requirements have been increasing, the Great Divorce has caused a decline in the expertise of Congress. In 1975, 71 percent of the House Appropriations Committee members had seen military service. Ten years later the percentage was 55 percent. The same decline in experience has occurred among congressional staffers, who, as sixties products, have ambivalent feelings about the military and can get just as parochial about a favorite strategy or weapon as their bosses. The press, which often sets the congressional agenda, also lacks a depth of military knowledge. Besides, stories explaining the complex reasons for excessive weapons costs are difficult to write with clarity and verve. Assistant Secretary of Defense Lawrence J. Korb estimates that congressional plums plus the additional paperwork cost the Defense Department roughly $10 billion a year.

The NIH (Not Invented Here) factor also drives up weapons costs. Even though they could save millions by not having to develop their own, each service finds it close to impossible to accept a weapon designed by another service—or even something as simple as a broom. Representatives and senators would almost rather kill than see a weapons buy of any size "go off shore."

The Infantry Fighting Vehicle reveals the NIH problem. The West Germans have a superb vehicle, known as the Marder, which has been in the service for five years and costs $400,000. Almost without exception, infantrymen and tankers who have been around the Marder want the United States not only to buy it now but to have bought it long ago. But the NIH factor has forced on the Army a rather dubious $500,000 vehicle called the Bradley. The Bradley was meant to be in operation by 1975 but arrived in 1984. It is meant to be able to cross rivers on its own. When in 1980 the test model was rolled out at Fort Knox for a bunch of generals and reporters, the Bradley proudly drove into the Ohio River and sank. Its silhouette is higher than the tanks it follows.

The Defense budget has always gone through periods of feast followed by periods of famine. In times of feast, those writing weapons requirements acutely remember the famines. They see the weapon they are designing as having to last through the next lean cycle. (The Minuteman missiles and B-52 bombers are examples of this process.) The weapons designer, aware that this weapon must last a long time, longer than he would like, pushes the frontiers of science and technology as hard and far as he can with the money he has now. When you try to reach far into the future, unless you are both lucky and wise, expensive mistakes result.

Our unwillingness to draft the best and the brightest of our young men also drives up weapons costs. The designer knows that his new weapon, whose construction is already stretching the possible, will be maintained not by a cross section of society but by those who volunteer to become privates, airmen, sailors. In times of depression, such as 1979 to 1983, the volunteers will be better than those who enter in times of prosperity, but they will still not be as able as those who would enter if America would support a just draft. So the designer orders weapons that not only are complex but that can, he hopes, be operated and maintained by high school dropouts.

Weapons are built with technical solutions to replace human initiative and intelligence. For example, our tanks are given a laser range finder with a computer attached to a wind sensor, because figuring corrections for wind will be beyond the capacity of the gunner. But each increase in complexity usually lowers reliability and forces up costs. The Giant loses rather than gains strength because expensive technological advances are used to design weapons that will prevent the less able from failing rather than aid the more able in winning.

A final reason for escalating weapons costs is the excessive use of committees. All those bad jokes about committees are true. A camel is a horse designed by a committee. My favorite committee description was coined by General Frederick E. Morgan, Eisenhower's British deputy for D day: Committees are "assemblies of open—and on occasion vacant—minds brought together for nebulous negative purposes." The Hummer, the Army's 1985 replacement for the World War II jeep, had to travel through the committees of sixty-three agencies and commands, including the Air Force Air Weather Service. Not surprisingly it is bigger, heavier, faster, and more expensive than the old jeep.

I am not sure why committees spring up so frequently in the Defense Department. Indeed the committee seems to me a present curse of America, with even books being produced by "brainstorming committees." In the military, I believe the proliferation of committees results from Flawed Organization, the fact that there is no true location of power and therefore, to do anything of great importance, one has to touch a great number of bases. And the easiest way to do this is by putting a committee on each base. The reforms of the Defense Department advocated in the last chapter—reforms, I should say now, that are generated from within the armed services—should go a good ways toward replacing the many committees by fewer commanders.

As the Eisenhower/Kennedy era drew to a close there occurred a change inside the Other America of Defense, one largely invisible from outside. The ablest, most highly motivated, most original officers began to leave the armed services in increasing numbers. This was the group who had entered the armed forces in the depression years, or during World War II, or even in the surge of patriotism in the early days of the Korean War. They were tired physically from a series of tough assignments and prolonged separation from their families; and they were tired mentally and morally from having been paid inadequately and hazed by Congress and insulted by Defense Department civilians, who then hid behind them when the going got tough. The departures of the famous attracted press attention—for example, that of airborne hero and military iconoclast General James M. Gavin. Gavin left for a variety of reasons, not the least of which was that the then senator Lyndon Johnson lied to him and released testimony he had said would be kept secret. But for the most part, the vast exodus, the vital hemorrhage, was remarked on only by those who remained.

How could able men and women in the services help noticing

that when a congressman retired and immediately came back as a lobbyist, that was fine, or when a high-ranking defense civilian went into a law firm and represented contractors, that was fine, but when an officer retired, took the pension for which he had worked and suffered low pay and perhaps been wounded, and then went into government, he was called a double-dipper and was investigated by Congress? And if he went to work for a defense contractor, a whole host of legal restrictions were placed on what he could do—restrictions that were not placed on civilians who had worked for the Defense Department at his level.

Sometimes, when I get really discouraged, I think that Congress actually wants to see nothing but dumb, subservient officers in the services because legislators fear challenges to their power. They want to be able to bend America's defenses to their own purposes more easily. After all, prior to the 1914 World War, the French parliament preferred an inefficient, horsey officer corps to an efficient one that might have Napoleonic ambitions. I know that most senators and congressmen don't really want the armed services to be commanded by a bunch of Reverend William Collinses. But I can understand why those in the services sometimes feel that they and their staffs do.

Each time an able man left, at whatever level, the atmosphere became a little less pleasant for those with initiative and intelligence who soldiered on. General Matthew B. Ridgway, a forceful and intelligent airborne hero in World War II, and successful United Nations Commander during the Korean War, was once asked what he thought his most important role had been as Army Chief of Staff in the mid-1950s. Those asking expected some such answer as "to work for interservice harmony," or "to avoid a land war in Asia," or "to develop a lighter infantry division." Instead he said, "To protect the mavericks."

Ridgway went on to explain that, like wars in the past, any future war was apt to be completely different from what the planners had forecast. Yet when such a crisis came, there would have to be plans and methods ready to meet the unforeseen challenge. All he could hope to do was to have some mavericks around who were looking at the future from points of view different from the orthodox beliefs and school solutions. Since the Army, Navy, and Air Force were powerful and rigid institutions, such maverick officers were not always popular and their careers were usually at risk. He felt his chief contribution had been in protecting such men. Starting in the late fifties, there were few around who protected the mavericks in any of the three services.

So we came to Vietnam.

I sat in the headquarters of the Americal Division in Phu Bai in 1970 with some officers I had known since we were all juniors in World War II, or from lectures at West Point. We began to run down the names of the able men we knew who had retired. It was a long and discouraging list. It was as if a whole group of possible future Nobel Prize winners in physics and chemistry had suddenly decided to quit practicing in the world of science when they were young. For me it was even more poignant because I knew that two of the best men around the table were also planning to retire at the end of this, their second, Vietnam tour. One of them had been arguing eloquently against our involvement in Vietnam since before the French defeat at Dien Bien Phu in 1954.

In an atmosphere of discouragement and conformity inside the Other America of Defense, and of indifference and even derision from outside, the wonder is not that so many able men left the services, but that many stayed on. I have nothing but respect for those superior few who served first through Charlie Wilson's haranguing, through McNamara and the whiz kid's arrogant foolishness, the horrors of an unpopular war in Vietnam, followed by peacetime service with funds cut and all things military reviled, and then, in the end were whipsawed by the further capricious budget cuts and mind-numbing sanctimonies of James Earl Carter. We went into Vietnam with the supply of able men and women in the services stretched perilously thin. We came out with many of them dead or retired and few replacements in sight. Then some within the services and many outside did their best to make life miserable for the able few who remained.

SIX

Vietnam –
The Giant Stumbles

In popular belief wars spring up suddenly, following explosive events such as the Japanese attack at Pearl Harbor, the 12 April 1861 firing on Fort Sumter, or the assassination of the Archduke Ferdinand at Sarajevo in 1914. Though historians have demonstrated that these wars had long-term causes, they tend to be remembered as commencing with a thunderclap. The Vietnam War is different. We remember its arrival accurately, as a slow misunderstood growth into a national disaster.

From the early fifties on, when Indochina, as Vietnam was then called, first came to their attention, those in the Other America of Defense were ambivalent about what course to follow there. Having been challenged by the Russians in Europe and by the Chinese and North Koreans in Korea, they felt a natural, reflexive reaction to come to the aid of the French, who were resisting Communist infiltration. However, surveying the strategic realities, many inside the services grew concerned that the costs of "victory" in Vietnam might be more than America was willing to bear and might not be justified by any forecastable gain. Once again, attitudes toward involvement in a war tended to differ by service. The Joint Chiefs constantly divided over the forces necessary and the prospects of success in Vietnam, with the Air Force and the Navy usually the more sanguine, as the Korean pattern was repeated.

Eisenhower's diaries of 17 March 1951, before he became President, when he was still NATO's first commander, reveal his early interest in the Indochina problem. He wrote of the French war effort there: "I'd favor heavy reinforcement to get the thing over at once; but I'm convinced that no military victory is possible in that kind of theater. Even if Indochina were completely cleared of Communists, right across the border is China with inexhaustible manpower."

A year later, with the Korean War still in progress, I reported from the Pentagon to *Newsweek* of an Army staff study that saw Indochina as the key to Southeast Asia. However, the study reasoned further that to hold that country effectively would require a "heavy commitment" of ground troops, and it was doubtful the American public would approve such action. The study waffled on whether it was in the strategic interests of the United States to make the commitment anyway.

The first serious effort to use U.S. armed forces in Vietnam occurred in 1954. At that time the Joint Chiefs disagreed over whether to launch a carrier air strike to aid the French troops trapped inside the fort of Dien Bien Phu. Both the Air Force and Navy members favored employing air power to avoid a French defeat, as did the JCS Chairman, Arthur W. Radford, a carrier admiral. The Army member, General Matthew B. Ridgway, strongly disagreed, convinced that American air power by itself could not provide the French with a victory. Ridgway carried his "split" from the other Chiefs to President Eisenhower, who sided with the Army's position. The Army's Deputy for Plans, at that time General James M. Gavin, has written: "I well remember my feeling of relief when President Eisenhower's decision went against the strike. A feeling that was regrettably brief."

Then in 1956, after the French defeat in Indochina, the same split on the Joint Chiefs occurred, with the Navy and Air Force members voting to mine the ports in the Haiphong/Hanoi area, and even land American forces there to protect the fleet from shore attack. Once more the embattled Ridgway carried his case to President Eisenhower, arguing that it would take at least eight American divisions to handle the North Vietnamese alone—more if the Chinese Communists were to intervene. Again Ridgway carried the day.*

However, from this argument within the Chiefs there emerged a compromise, fully supported by the Army, stipulating that military aid would be given to the South Vietnamese government. A U.S. Military Assistance Advisory Group was created, averaging around 650 officers and men during the rest of Eisenhower's presidency.

When President Kennedy and Secretary McNamara arrived on stage, the early idealism that permeated the new presidency unfortunately fused with important faults inside the Department of Defense. The new President and high officials in his administration were intrigued by, and believed in, guerrilla warfare and Special Forces. To please him, these Army forces were expanded from about 3,000 officers and men in 1960 to 12,000 in 1964. Many of the officer specialists in irregular warfare in these forces who went out to aid the Army of the Republican of Vietnam (ARVN) in the early sixties were thoughtful, complicated, liberal men—among the best the armed services had to offer. Typical of these were Lieutenant Colonel John Paul Vann of the Army and the legendary Air Force general James Lansdale . The latter had helped the Philippine Army defeat the Huk Communist insurgents using novel and imaginative counterinsurgency tactics.†

Inside the military, however, KAFCA, Keeping the Able From Contributing to the Action, was still a fact of life, and service with foreign troops generally remained a stigma. The regulars never believed in the Special Forces or those who served in them. Army general Paul Harkins's more conventional ideas of what to do in Vietnam won over those of Lansdale in 1962, when the Military Assistance Advisory Group was replaced by the Military Assistance Command Vietnam (MACV). Though officers piously intoned that Vietnam was "a war for the hearts and minds of the Vietnamese people," one saw on their desks the sign "Grab them by their balls

---

* In 1968, at peak U.S. strength, there would be somewhat over nine American divisions in Vietnam.

† By 1974 the Special Forces had been cut back to 5,000. Indeed, such irregular formations labored for a time under the additional handicap of having been supported by those very liberals who later turned against the Vietnam War.

and their hearts and minds will follow." At the same time most officers did their best to avoid serving with Vietnamese troops.

With the strength, particularly the psychological strength, of the enemy greater than perceived and the Special Forces never fully supported or their limitations understood, the United States began to drift into general war.* On whirlwind fact-finding tours of Vietnam, McNamara and his entourage were fed the type of data that they wished to hear, for the Great Divorce was intensifying and the Defense Secretary had already begun to surround himself with officers who agreed with him and used his jargon of statistics and game theory. Important service caveats over the use of military power in Vietnam were becoming muted.

Secretary of State Henry Kissinger later described the type of officer now being promoted: "A new breed of military officer emerged: men who had learned the new jargon, who could present the systems analysis arguments so much in vogue, more articulate than the older generation and more skillful in bureaucratic maneuvering. On some levels it eased civilian-military relationships; on a deeper level it deprived the policy process of the simpler, cruder, but perhaps more relevant assessments which in the final analysis are needed when issues are reduced to a test of arms."

After returning from a flying visit to Vietnam in 1963, McNamara had the White House issue the following statement: "The military program in Vietnam has made progress and is sound in principle, though improvements are being energetically sought. . . . [By] the end of this year [1963] the U.S. program for training Vietnamese should have progressed to the point that one thousand U.S. military personnel assigned to South Vietnam can be withdrawn."

The ability of the top civilian and military officials in Washington to jet back and forth to Vietnam, as well as to be in constant electronic contact, greatly increased problems of Overcontrol. Indeed in 1962–1963, so many generals were making the trip and then holding conferences and writing reports that President

* *Parthian Shot*, by Loyd Little (Viking Press, 1973), a humorous, disturbing, and unfortunately rather overlooked novel, captures the spirit of the early Special Forces time in Vietnam. *Free in the Forest* (Yale University Press, 1982), the second volume of Gerald C. Hickey's definitive ethnohistory of the Central Highlands, includes heartbreaking material on the same period.

Kennedy finally issued an executive order which in effect made presidential approval necessary before a general or admiral could visit Vietnam.

Unfortunately, the full danger of such flying visits and masses of electronically transmitted statistics was not realized. Strategic questions were neglected while the White House and Pentagon became mired in questions of technique and tactics that should have been decided by those in the field. In perhaps the most unfortunate example, President Kennedy and his advisors became so involved in the details of a coup against President Ngo Dinh Diem in late 1963 that the vital question of whether the United States should support such an action escaped thorough examination. Unlike Truman and his advisors, who during the Korean War had avoided the details on the military cabal but faced the moral and political implications squarely, the Kennedy administration became deeply implicated in the illegal overthrow of Diem's government and his subsequent murder. This action forced upon America a greatly increased responsibility for Vietnam's future.

On 22 November 1963, President Kennedy was assassinated and Lyndon B. Johnson became President. David Halberstam has pointed out that while Kennedy may possibly have been experiencing private doubts about Vietnam, publicly he was taking a hard anti-Communist line. Johnson, who tended to be an activist anyway and certainly did not wish to seem less manly than his predecessor, soon began to increase the size of the U.S. commitment. In August 1964 two U.S. destroyers were attacked by North Vietnamese PT boats, and in the wave of patriotism following this attack the President ordered American air power into active combat in Vietnam. Then in March 1965 the marines landed in Danang to be followed by more ground forces within six months. Colonel Harry G. Summers, Jr., in his incisive book *On Strategy: A Critical Analysis of the Vietnam War*, argues that it was at this moment strategic policy broke down: "It was here that the basic error was made in the conduct of the war. Instead of leaving ARVN to pursue the counterinsurgency mission, assisted at least initially by U.S. combat forces, and concentrating U.S. efforts on repelling North Vietnamese aggression, the U.S. instead committed the United States forces in support of counterinsurgency." Summers goes on to point out that the American military forces in Vietnam had no concrete objectives but were rather pursuing political platitudes. A Clausewitzian principle had been over-looked: Do not "take the first step without considering the last."

In a reverse twist of history, some of the more intelligent staff officers in all three services swallowed their doubts over Vietnam policy because of the knowledge that they had been wrong to ignore European politics as they fought World War II. They had fought that war as a ball game, and in the overriding effort to win they had trusted the Russians, against the advice of the British and a few prescient State Department officials, such as Charles Bohlen. General Marshall himself had almost court-martialed General Lauris Norstad for agreeing with the British on the need to keep the Russians out of the Balkans. Perhaps, these officers now felt, the politicians were right this time. The military should fight in Vietnam for political objectives, however difficult these might be to obtain by military force.

Neglecting the thorough consideration of basic war aims and issues, White House and Pentagon continued to be bogged down in details that should have been left to the field commanders. The discussions on how to begin the bombing campaign against North Vietnam make an apt example. The strategic question of what such bombing would accomplish, based on analysis of World War II and the Korean War, was submerged in a series of technical questions on how to carry out the bombing. Chief among these was whether the bombing should begin at a relatively low level and then slowly escalate, the course favored by the whiz kids, led by McNamara's assistant secretary of defense John T. Mc-Naughton, or whether maximum force should be applied hard and fast from the beginning.

This latter course was favored by the Joint Chiefs of Staff, who argued that to affect North Vietnamese will America had to show a willingness to go all out. Also applying maximum force from the beginning would get the job done with far fewer American casualties. McNaughton argued that his "slow squeeze" policy would be understood by Ho Chi Minh, and the Communist leader would behave rationally and stop the war before his homeland received maximum destruction. (This approach was similar to the nuclear-target-options strategy favored by the same group of war-gamers.)

The Joint Chiefs were not alone in arguing for the initial maximum use of force. The intelligence organizations involved in the policy planning—the CIA, the Defense Intelligence Agency, and the State Department's Bureau of Intelligence—all agreed with the military's position. President Johnson overrode both the intelligence estimate and the military recommendation to side with McNamara and a policy of "graduated response."

The policy dispute may never have reached Johnson's ears. To quote Colonel Summers again: "Indeed, it is not at all clear whether Secretary McNamara ever even bothered to convey their [the Joint Chiefs'] arguments to him."

Even today it is hard to know what professional military advice was reaching the President during this period. Johnson had inherited the somewhat messy and informal organizational structure that President Kennedy, like Roosevelt before him, had enjoyed. Between June 1965 and June 1966 the Chief of Staff of the Army saw the President privately only twice. The Air Chief of Staff had four private meetings with the President. In those months the buildup of combat troops in Vietnam had surged upward with the arrival of four infantry divisions and several independent brigades, and the total number of U.S. troops in Vietnam had climbed to 252,000. In the same period the air war also intensified, with the first B-52 bomber raids in the South, the downing of the first U.S. aircraft by a missile over the North, and the creation of an Air Force headquarters, the Seventh, inside Vietnam.

Later in 1965, as high Pentagon civilians continued to be obsessed with tactical details, the three Joint Chiefs actually considered resigning. McNamara had forbidden them to bomb the antiaircraft missile sites in North Vietnam as they were being constructed. Then policy changed and orders were issued to bomb the completed antiaircraft missile installations. In these raids the Air Force suffered heavy casualties. The three Chiefs considered that the orders prohibiting them from bombing the missile sites while they were under construction bordered on a criminal offense. The civilians never seemed to address the increased aircrew casualties that resulted from their policy of slow escalation. Because of the Great Divorce, in the lost aircrews were neither their family members nor friends.

Finally, the neglect of strategic questions and the Overcontrol of tactical details were epitomized by President Lyndon Johnson's lying on the floor of the Oval Office, picking out bombing targets for fighters from the aerial photos spread on his rug. He once said, "I don't want those Air Force generals to bomb the smallest

shit-house north of the 17th parallel without checking with me."
So he did the job of some lieutenant colonel, while the reasons for
the war went unexplored and the consensus for continuing the
dying broke down. Recall that on the final day of the U.S. involvement in Vietnam, when defeat was absolute and the American
embassy in Saigon was being evacuated, the White House requested the tail numbers of the helicopters being used to lift the
Americans off the embassy roof.

In Vietnam itself Overcontrol from the apex of the armed
services stretched down to those walking on patrol. I would stand
alongside a captain or a lieutenant in the jungle or crouch behind
a paddy dike while he attempted to fight his company. Orbiting
above at 700 feet was his battalion commander, issuing orders
from a helicopter. Above his battalion commander, hovering at
1,000 feet, was his brigade commander, issuing another set of
orders. And if the firefight got really intense, the assistant division
commander might arrive on the scene at 1,200 feet, as per the
textbook, and issue a new set of orders. The poor junior on the
ground, with the solid stuff cracking around him, was spending
more time saying "Roger all that, sir" on his radio than commanding his men. And battle conditions as seen from the air, even from
as close as 700 or 1,000 feet, often looked completely different from
what they actually were on the ground.

While senior commanders in Vietnam were keeping such tight
rein on battlefield details, they too were neglecting the more difficult question of broad policy. One wet night following a monsoon
I was asleep in a ruined hooch ringed by the pup tents of part of
an infantry company. Though we were out on patrol, the situation
seemed so safe I had taken off my boots. Suddenly my sleep was
shattered by an explosion, the sound of rifle fire, and cries of
"Incoming. Incoming."

I was off my bed and cowering in the mud with my hands over
my head and my arms shaking as two more explosions sent steel
splattering through the hooch like heavy drops of rain. The radio
operator had hit the dirt on top of me. Machine guns, rifles, and
the grenade-launcher began firing. There were cries of "Medic,
medic."

The captain in command of the patrol called for artillery and
the forward observer traveling with us replied that he was already
cranking it up. I got my boots back on. Men took up firing positions; flashlights were turned on so that wounds could be dressed.

"Where's the goddamn artillery?" the captain kept asking.

"We can't get clearance to fire."

"What?"

"The Vietnamese say there are friendlies there."

But we had just been hit from there.

"Give me that radio." The captain took the radio mike from the artillery lieutenant, who had been pleading into it for twenty minutes.

"This is Socket Six. This is a combat emergency. I want those fires now. My initials are L.G."

Here at the end of the line, a cold, wet, and tired twenty-two-year-old captain, his men dying around him, had been forced to accept the moral responsibility of which his superiors—from the President and Congress to his battalion commander—had, like Pontius Pilate, washed their hands. President Truman had a sign on his desk: "The buck stops here." Because broad policy issues had been avoided all down the line while tactical details had been pored over, the decision of which came first, his men or the rules of engagement in Vietnam, had been passed to this junior officer.

Decisions made in Washington reached the field in Vietnam only after a tortuous passage. From the debating circles of the Joint Chiefs the orders were passed not to the Military Assistance Command Vietnam, MACV, which supposedly ran the war, but to CINCPAC, Commander In Chief Pacific, an admiral stationed in Honolulu. From there, after further delay for more Joint Staff debate, the orders were sent to Saigon. Imagine Eisenhower fighting his World War II battles in Europe with an extra headquarters stationed over him in Iceland.

There was no reason for such nonsense except that the Navy did not wish to be left out of the war and the Flawed Organization of the Defense Department could not align itself to fight efficiently. When a JCS decision finally reached Vietnam, it then passed through MACV to the United States Army Vietnam, perhaps pausing briefly on the way at the Army Republic of Vietnam Joint General Staff, or the "Free World Military Forces." If air power was involved there were four Air Forces that had to be coordinated. As General William C. Westmoreland, the longtime commander in Vietnam, noted afterward: "MACV functioned not directly under the Joint Chiefs of Staff in Washington but through CINCPAC. . . . not I, but Admiral Sharp [Admiral U.S. Grant Sharp, Commander in Chief Pacific Command] was the theater commander in the sense that General Eisenhower, for example, was the theater commander in World War II."

The draft's unfairness and the maldistribution of abilities and risks inside the armed services found in both World War II and the Korean War grew worse in Vietnam. The same old sieve was sifting out those who went into the infantry. By avoiding the draft, cultivating a noncombat specialty, merely dragging his feet, or doing something almost, if not actually, criminal, a man could assure himself of, at worst, a safe rear-area assignment. I watched a lieutenant reluctantly assign to such a job a man who, when on patrol, constantly threw away his equipment. As a result, infantry companies were once again peopled by a group of men unrepresentative of the nation as a whole.

Notably absent were Ivy Leaguers and graduates of other prestigious non-Catholic universities. In my three-plus months in Vietnam, I found only four junior officers from any of the prestigious universities along both coasts. Yale University lost only thirty-four sons in Vietnam, including the grandson of General John J. Pershing, commander of the American forces in France during World War I. Harvard has not felt it necessary to tally its Vietnam losses. By 1972, Army statistics showed no draftees serving in Vietnam from category I, which corresponded to the roughly 8 percent of America's population with the highest intelligence. And at a time when 75 percent of Americans had received high school degrees, compared with 38 percent before World War II, 30 percent of those in Vietnam had not graduated from high school.

Unlike the situation in the early eighties, when blacks made up roughly 50 percent of the combat units, for most of the war there was not an excessive percentage of black faces present in battle. The reports that in Vietnam blacks died in disproportionate numbers were false. Judging from the number of black faces in the rear, they were probably drafted out of proportion to their numbers, but in the dying units or the hospital wards, the ratio of blacks to whites seemed to reflect the civilian population. About 10 percent of the units I walked on patrol with, give or take a few points either way, were black. When, under pressure in 1984, the Defense Department finally released the statistics on black casualties, they showed that blacks had made up 13 percent of the casualties, almost their exact proportion of the draft age population over those years.*

The psychological and physical health of those raised in poverty or badly fractured families often is insufficient to withstand the strains of battle. As a result, the very poor are usually absent from the front. In Vietnam, black faces in the combat units were, like white faces, mostly middle-class. The Vietnam War, which many wealthy radicals so violently protested, actually united them and the poor in safety, while the "hard chargers" of the middle class got blown away.

The unfair sharing of the Vietnam combat burden raises questions that persist today. Would the war have ended sooner if the children of the elites had been present in the paddies, to give those in power back home personal touchstones about conditions "in country"? Would such nonsense as the belief that infiltration from the north could be stopped by the construction of an expensive electronic fence linked to computers have been laughed out of court if sons of Pentagon civilians had returned to report that the DMZ was not a solid line on a map but a rolling, hummocking mass of hills, water, fields, and jungle? Would scientists who had served in Vietnam or had relatives fighting there have built a People Sniffer that, when hung beneath a helicopter, could supposedly hunt down guerrillas from the ammonia and methane given off by their urine? Inside Vietnam such meaningless, tremendously expensive nonsense was known as "blip krieg."

Finally, how is defense legislation affected, when out of the 103 congressmen in the 96th Congress of the right age to have been drafted during Vietnam, 94 held at least a bachelor's degree, but only 4 served in Vietnam? Of the Vietnam generation in that Congress, 36 percent had seen some form of military service, compared with 41 percent of their age group in other occupations. Contrast this with the fact that of the senators in the World War II and Korean cohorts, 70 percent saw active duty.

As the Vietnam War wound down, the alienation of those inside

---

* The problem of black casualties is complicated, because during the initial Vietnam buildup of 1965–1966, airborne units were among the first to arrive. Blacks made up a high proportion of these peacetime units, and for a period black casualties amounted to almost one-quarter of the total U.S. enlisted losses.

the Other America of Defense from the rest of the country's elites became more complete.

"You see what's happening, don't you?" said a young general late one night in his hooch, the highland rains pelting down outside. "You don't need me to tell you. We are economizing on everything else to spend our psychic energy and blood.

"And who are the young men we are asking to go into action against such solid odds? You've met them. You know. They are the best we have. But they are not McNamara's sons, or [National Security Advisor McGeorge] Bundy's; I doubt they're yours. And they know they're at the end of the pipeline. That no one cares. They know."

In late 1970, after saying "these are what guide my life," a colonel handed me a three-by-five card. On the card was typed the number of rifle bullets, Claymore Mines, 81-mm mortar rounds, artillery shells, and so forth, that his battalion could fire each month. In World War II and the Korean War, such restrictions were imposed from time to time; but the restrictions on this card were much tougher. When it came to 81-mm mortar ammunition, I noted, a unit in World War II would often have fired his monthly quota in less than a week.

On another card the colonel kept track of the number of hours each day he could fly the various helicopters assigned to him. This limitation, called the blade-hour limitation and in force throughout Vietnam, was the most rigid cost-control tool used to wind down the war. For example, in 1970 helicopters flew roughly one-sixth the hours they had flown in 1969. Such controls wound down the war all right; they also killed people.

It seemed that from the very beginning in Vietnam all the armies fighting there were invisible—the Viet Cong and the Viet Minh in the jungle and the American middle class in their green fatigues. Those being wounded and dying for America were products of the Great Divorce; they lacked personal and emotional ties to the press, the Pentagon civilians, or the leaders of the antiwar movement. They were not totally real to any Americans other than their own families and themselves. I never saw the blade-hour limitation and its effects reported by anyone but myself, or questioned in Congress.

The military came to resent and close themselves off from questions about their actions. One night a patrol I was walking with came under attack and we called for 105-mm artillery illumination rounds over ourselves to make bright the night. I knew the rounds were being fired correctly because I could hear them pop overhead. Supposedly, that pop pushes out a canister that burns with a brilliant light as it floats slowly to earth beneath its parachute. But that night about half of the rounds did not light up after the pop. Three days later I got to the base from which the illumination shells had been shot and was able to get the serial numbers off the boxes of ammunition so that the faulty rounds could be traced.

On my return to America I asked the Army to track down these rounds for me so I could try to figure out what had happened and why. I was told that the investigation had proved there was nothing wrong with any of that lot of ammunition. Further, I got a desperate letter from the commander of the base in Vietnam saying that he had been ordered to court-martial the sergeant who had let me copy the serial numbers.

In the Air Force, bitter over the extra casualties caused by the target limitations occasionally imposed, there was equal alienation. At least twice the cameras that record operations were removed from a number of airplanes and illegal bombing missions were run.

Finally, from time to time I ran across hints that a few American officers had started their own secret society, the Sin Loy society. (Sin Loy is a universal Vietnamese expression roughly translated as "Sorry about that but such is life.") Vietnam is a culture permeated by secret societies, some of them perhaps dating back to the first Chinese occupation around 111 B.C. During the war they were a powerful and usually overlooked part of that nation's life. Communist and Nationalist commanders, who fought each other by day, might meet by night in these societies to plan at least limited aspects of a joint future. Undoubtedly remnants of these societies function today under the Communists.

The Sin Loy's purpose, as I pieced it together from bits and snatches of information, was to meet with the enemy and pass information about American operations and in return receive information about Communist operations. In this way both sides could avoid each other and reduce their casualties, as a war already decided dragged to its end. The Sin Loy was definitely no radical effort to help the detested Communists win the war. If it was ever more than an idea—and I am not certain that it ever went beyond debate and discussion—the society's purpose was a mutual effort to limit casualties on both sides. The information exchanged secretly —for instance, I won't go there if you don't go there—could be likened to the temporary truces sometimes agreed to in other wars so that the dead could be buried and the wounded evacuated.

To turn from strategic questions such as Overcontrol and Flawed Organization to Interservice/Intraservice Rivalry, battlefield cooperation between services was certainly better in Vietnam than in Korea. In some instances it even surpassed that of World War II. On MACV's Joint Staff in Saigon, officers of all three services worked alongside each other in greater harmony than in previous wars. The doctrinal disputes that had restricted the use of air power in Korea had largely faded, and World War II practices had been resumed. The Air Force, after a few initial joustings at the JCS level, did not place limitations on the use of firepower by Army helicopters. Army long-range patrols in the enemy rear were skillfully emplaced and supplied by the Air Force. The fly in the ointment was that by and large the good work was stitched together by desperate and needy pilots and soldiers in Vietnam, not rationally constructed by senior Air Force, Navy, and Army officers working harmoniously in Washington. Indeed on one occasion, General Curtis LeMay, the Air Force Chief of Staff, became so enraged at the way the Army was using helicopters to support ground troops that he challenged the Army Chief of Staff to an aerial duel.

Inside the Air Force the Intraservice Rivalry between TAC and SAC markedly lessened. Pilots served in Vietnam for a year and then rotated elsewhere. To fill the shortage created by this constant turnover, many SAC pilots flew with TAC for the first time, while TAC pilots flew with SAC. Both sides began to appreciate the problems of the other and also to sympathize increasingly with the plight of those on the ground. At war's end, the practical monopoly of senior Air Force positions by SAC also ended. As already mentioned, in 1981 "Chuck" Gabriel became the first Air Force Chief of Staff who was a pure fighter pilot, and in 1982 for the first time the majority of high Air Staff billets were filled by non-SAC officers. (There is a real question of how long the benefits of the job rotations in Vietnam will last because there has been no comparable peacetime exchange of SAC/TAC assignments and training. Also, with the lavish budgets of the Reagan years, close working relationships have begun to erode as each commander thinks he can get the whole pie without having to compromise with other parts of his service or with other services.)

If the lessening of the TAC/SAC rivalry was one of the brighter results of Vietnam, other parts of the air war were less praiseworthy. Command over the B-52 bombers was divided between Air Force headquarters in Vietnam and Strategic Air Command headquarters in Omaha, with SAC controls predominating. SAC dictated the altitude at which the bombers would fly, the direction from which they would attack, and the length of their final bomb runs to the target. The rigidly dictated times, distances, maneuvers, and altitudes had been developed for nuclear warfare and did not fit the conditions of Vietnam. As soon as the B-52s, during such operations as Linebacker, began their customary left turn toward the target, the North Vietnamese knew where and when to fire their missiles.

The armed services are quite properly worried about the ability of some junior officer to launch a nuclear weapon on his (and increasingly on her) own. Complex electronic communications nets make constant detailed monitoring of nuclear weapons possible. But preoccupation with this justified concern has robbed other junior officers of the ability to use their battlefield experiences, the capabilities of their nonnuclear weapons, and their own initiative.

Interservice Rivalry resulted in four more or less coordinated air wars. There was the Air Force air war; the Republic of Vietnam Air Force war; the Marine air war in support of the Marine ground troops; and the Navy air war in the North. After 1968 Air Force/Navy cooperation became better than in previous wars. However, as General Bruce Palmer, Jr., commander of the American Army in Vietnam was later to write: ". . . undivided responsibility and unified direction of the [air] war was conspicuously absent."

The most damaging air war conflict in terms of time spent and lives unnecessarily lost was that between the Marines and other parts of the armed services. Until late 1967 the Marine Corps had refused to share its aircraft with any other service. Then, when the marines were in danger of being overrun at Khe San, in return for increased Army and the Air Force help, the Corps finally agreed to put its planes in the Air Force/Navy common pool. The Marines tried to go back on that agreement within the month. This was the only issue over which General Westmoreland threatened to resign while in Vietnam, and because of his action the Marine aircraft stayed somewhat available to aid beleaguered Americans and Vietnamese other than marines.*

General James Hollingsworth, when commander of the 1st Division, used to tell his new lieutenants and sergeants to remember that if they got into trouble, all the artillery of the division and all the power of the U.S. Air Force would be behind them. This was largely true, but to get around the effects of Interservice Rivalry and bring air power into action, a great deal of human energy was expended in unnecessary games.

For example, in the Saigon area the Air Force maintained a headquarters of some 400 men who "generated" (discovered and planned) targets for the next few days. But since by the very nature of the Vietnam War the enemy was often invisible and usually fleeting, many of the targets assigned by headquarters one day were not there the next. When the planes arrived to attack the nonexistent targets, real enemy who were actually present were substituted and attached instead. This worked, but for reasons of service doctrine, both Air Force and Army were going through the elaborate fiction of "developing targets" to get aircraft over the battlefield so that they could then perform real missions. This personnel-wasting charade had not been necessary in World War II.

Even combat itself was often complicated by service priorities. If an Army captain on the ground had no Air Force Forward Air Controller with him—as usually happened—and wished to bring air power to bear on those firing at him and his men, he gave out the number and location of the enemy over his radio. What usually happened next was that a slow propeller-driven aircraft arrived over his head. This plane carried the airborne Forward Air Controller, known as the Airborne FAC, who was an Air Force officer. The problem of whether an Army officer or an Air Force officer should call in air power, which had plagued American

---

* The relief of the marines at Khe San by the Army's 1st Cavalry Division is brilliantly described in Michael Herr's *Dispatches* (New York: Knopf, 1977).

forces since before World War II, had been solved by adding a new bureaucratic layer in combat. The Army captain had now called in an Air Force officer, who was aloft in a slow plane. That officer then called in the jets with the weapons on board to do the actual job of destruction.

Further, the marines put rockets in their slow spotter planes so their FACs could work over a target themselves while waiting for the jets to arrive. The Air Force never put such rockets in its planes. Rockets fired from a slow, light propeller-driven plane might have led to the Army's getting back part of the battlefield air mission. Though official objections had been stilled, many Air Force officers felt the Army was already regaining too much of this with its rocket-firing, gun-ship helicopters.

Other armed services besides our own increase their chances of defeat through Interservice Rivalry. The British RAF, like the American Air Force, is constantly fearful of losing some of its independence to the Army or Marine commander on the ground. The RAF therefore also insists that the FAC, who travels with the forward troops and guides aircraft to the target, must be a pilot.

No first-rate pilot wants to sit in a hole with his feet wet waiting for the occasional chance to radio targets to his friends aloft. Not surprisingly therefore FACs tend to be not-very-good pilots or overage pilots. In the critical Falkland Islands attack on Goose Green, the Forward Air Controller expected to "yomp" in freezing weather for two days with the paratroopers was a fifty-four-year-old RAF squadron leader. He dropped out totally exhausted after the first four hours. The paratroopers proceeded with less effective air support. One cannot blame the RAF officer, who was an honorable man and tried hard. His superiors, however, once again had placed service doctrinal loyalty ahead of victory.

Looking back at Vietnam, those inside the Other America of Defense are more apt to dwell on the shattering psychological effect of that war on themselves and their service than on the dying. And their residue of bitterness, frustration, and anger comes not just from the strain of having had part of their troops in deadly revolt, or the constant, debilitating fear of being fragged, but from their frustration at having seen the military institution they believed in torn apart by the lies juniors were forced to tell. These distortions and omissions were used to produce the bogus indications of progress desired by their superiors. And often the better the man, the more intense his revulsion over the system.

Knowing that the body-count statistics were false, but also knowing that their careers depended on the manipulation of these and other equally meaningless statistics, many officers lost their morale. They realized the war had grown unpopular back home. Many of them, particularly in the Army, had been against ground involvement in Vietnam since the days of Ridgway and Gavin. They knew that the restrictions on ammunition, maintenance funds, rules of engagement, construction, and flight hours were killing their men. They knew that the draft-age members of the elites were avoiding service. What were they to do?

Not only the officers suffered. The backbone of the armed services, the senior noncommissioned officers—sergeant majors, first sergeants, and platoon sergeants—were battered in the same fashion. They too, at the summit of a long career, had found not rewards but frustration and threats. Their love affair with the Army had turned sour and their remarks about the military were often more violently antagonistic than those of any peace radical. I recall one first sergeant, a scholarly man and an early refugee from Hitler's persecutions, who had been a platoon sergeant with the 1st Infantry Division in Aachen. "I'm on my third tour in my third war," he said. "I'd been wounded twice before some of these sons of bitches calling me pig and motherfucker were born."

Other sergeants had gathered around us and agreed. "The officers lie to the public. They stand before a graph with all the arrows pointing up. They should deal with the scum we get."

"We're the professionals."

"The forgotten men."

Like their officers, the sergeants wanted to show that they were doing a good job. And again the better the man, the more pressure he was apt to put on himself to produce. But his performance was measured by those obviously false statistics. So NCOs, like the officers, often either gave up or produced the desired numbers, both courses of action that were damaging to themselves, the armed services, and the war. As they say in service argot: "Mission motivates estimates."

Working with Vietnam veterans after the war, psychologist Jeffrey Jay pinpointed where this demand for numbers led. "The need to accumulate body counts pressured officers to produce dead

Vietcong. This led to the working rule that a dead Vietnamese was a Vietcong. The paradox for the soldiers was clear: civilians were to be protected; soldiers were to be court-martialed for harming civilians; once dead, civilians could be counted as Vietcong—and dead Vietcong were the only spoil rewarded by superiors."

Under a multitude of such pressures, those inside the Other America of Defense began to move further away from the rest of society, and the military services themselves started to break apart. As early as June 1970 an Army War College survey of that service's officers found ". . . there is a disharmony between traditional, accepted ideals and the prevailing institutional pressures. These pressures seem to stem from a combination of self-oriented, success-motivated actions and a lack of professional skills on the part of the middle and senior grade officers."

From the beginning of 1970 onward, many of the best in the military had begun to lose confidence in themselves. They either left the service or modified their behavior to become more like the pusillanimous bureaucratic managers they saw being promoted around them, and being undeservedly decorated. One of the Army's senior generals today walks around wearing a silver star he did nothing to earn and many officers and senior NCOs know it.

Two years after the war's official end another Army War College study found that unit readiness reporting, the system by which the fighting ability of military formations is measured, had become corrupt. Seventy percent of those answering that 1976 survey agreed that official readiness reports did not reflect the true condition of their unit. There was a consensus that the whole system was "held in disrepute by the Army personnel most familiar with it." As one officer stated, "Readiness reporting has continued to be a lie since I've been in the Army."

As late as 1985 the Army surveyed 23,000 officers, from lieutenants to colonels, on their attitudes about their profession. Over two-thirds believed that "the officer corps is focused on personal gain rather than selflessness." And just under half believed "the bold, original, creative officer cannot survive in today's Army." As one wanders through the corridors of the Pentagon or visits the field, one hears the same complaints about the decline of standards in their services voiced by naval and Air Force officers.

A final psychological burden carried by a large number of those who served in Vietnam (and this includes veterans as well as those who remain inside the military) is guilt feelings over what they see as the abandonment and betrayal of the South Vietnamese. Many of the finest officers and NCOs came to appreciate and respect the people they were there to aid. This was particularly true of the more junior officers and senior NCOs, who worked in conditions of intimacy and danger with their ARVN counterparts. Even for a reporter whose involvement never came that close, the memories sear.

Once the Bru had been a strong and numerous tribe among the Montagnards (the Vietnamese mountain peoples), some 14,000 of them living not far from the border between North Vietnam and South Vietnam. By 1970, hunted and killed by the Communists, recruited by CIA, occasionally bombed by the South Vietnamese and U.S. air forces, and forcibly relocated by the South Vietnamese government, the Bru were down to a few thousand. They had been forced to abandon their traditional long houses on stilts. Their new village, in a forest clearing near the Lao Bao pass not far from the border between North and South Vietnam, consisted of a group of low, almost square, sandbagged huts with squat wooden sides and woven roofs. The bullet scars on the boards above the sandbags were a dull, milky white, which made them about four days old.

An interpreter, the American advisor, who was a lieutenant, and I sat with the Bru chieftain in his hut. Before the clan leader on a crate stood the symbol of his authority, an ancient typewriter, the kind with a carriage that dropped rather than a platten that rose. The chief wore blue cotton trousers and a white, short-sleeved shirt. We drank a clear liquor, slightly green in color, that the tribe made locally. We did not really need the interpreter; the lieutenant and I spoke adequate French, and the chieftain's was better than adequate.

The chief was describing to me, the visiting reporter, village life under intermittent attack for ten years. From time to time, he interrupted his narrative to ask me, who supposedly knew about the outside world and America, what was going to happen to his people. I knew what was going to happen. The lieutenant knew. The United States was going to pull out and abandon him and all the Bru. Then the Viet Minh were going to hunt him and his people down and slaughter or send to prison the leaders who had, like him, been on the democratic side. His tribe would be forcibly relocated to some other part of Vietnam, to be integrated into the victor's totalitarian society.

That is what happened. I kept ducking and gave no answer.

As the lieutenant and I walked back to his jeep at the end of the afternoon, he turned to me, his features stiff with the conscious effort to hold them together, and asked, "What do I say when they ask me that question? What do I say?" To remember his face in the damp, forest-flecked sunlight is to understand the depth of conviction with which service people speak when they say they never again wish to see military force used without an American commitment to stay the course.

General William T. ("War Is Hell") Sherman, the brilliant Civil War leader, had a military-intellectual protégé, General Emory Upton. Trying to reorganize the War Department in the years of peace between the Civil War and the Spanish-American War of 1898, Upton lamented that military reform was made close to impossible because "Ultimate success in all our wars has steeped the people in the delusion that our military policy is correct and that any departure from it would be no less difficult than dangerous."

In Vietnam, our flawed military organization and policy led to defeat, and that disaster has been followed by the Iranian and Beirut fiascoes. The defects in both defense planning and structure blossom forth to be seen by all but the most parochial. Not blinded by the successes of Upton's day or World War II, a number of thoughtful critics both inside and outside the Other America of Defense have used the mistakes of Vietnam as a platform from which to intelligently examine America's defense posture. If the Vietnam War should lead to armed service reform, the Giant can then say, as Abraham Lincoln did after his defeat in the race for the Senate, "It's a slip; not a fall."

SEVEN

The
Accuracy Revolution

(How the Future Affects the Present)

I n May 1972 two Air Force F-4 fighters using infrared-guided bombs knocked out the Than Hoa and Paul Doaumier bridges in North Vietnam. No aircraft were lost. For the preceding six years, ton after ton of conventional bombs had been dropped on these bridges and they still stood, though eighteen of our aircraft had been lost in these attacks. A year later in the Sinai, during the Yom Kippur war, the Israeli 190th Armored Brigade lost over 130 tanks in two flaming hours to Russian-made, wire-guided anti-tank missiles. At the same time Russian-made surface-to-air heat-seeking missiles (SAM 6s) temporarily drove the Israeli aircraft from the skies; ninety aircraft were downed in two days. Off the Falkland Islands the Argentine cruiser *General Belgrano* was sunk by the first two British homing torpedoes fired at her; 368 men were lost, a stinging Argentine defeat. These events are the vanguard of what is certainly a new evolution in warfare. Some, myself among them, would even call it a revolution: the accuracy revolution. The changes being driven by this revolution affect the forces we have today, those we design for the future, and all our arms control policies and negotiations.

When man first picked up a stone or stick to hurl at his enemy, his expectation was that he would probably miss. Until recently—in spite of the claims made on the rifle range or in weapons brochures—weapons missed far more often than they hit. During World War II it took 300,000 fired bullets to hit an infantryman. The Than Hoa and Paul Doaumier bridges still stood after six years of bombing. That is changing. Smart weapons, known as PGMs, for Precision Guided Munitions, are arriving that can hit their target 50 percent of the time. Within a few years, if you can see a target, you can kill it; if it moves, you can kill it; if it has iron in it, you can kill it; and if it emits, you can kill it. To "emit" means to produce nonvisual signals, called emitter signatures, which include infrared exhausts from jet engines, radio waves, radar beams, or even the body heat of people massed together.

There are ways to protect against smart weapons: hide behind smoke, build dummy emitters, shift radio frequencies, wait for clouds, rain, or night. But in the main, the battlefield—and the world—has become a more complex and deadly place. And, unfortunately, more expensive. In one week of the 1973 war the Israelis used up $2.5 billion of military equipment. And that was a small war, against an underequipped power, using what would now be considered antiquated weapons.

Because, historically, weapons were so inaccurate, people, in their efforts to kill one another, turned to exploiting ever more powerful forms of released energy. Man first used sinew or levers like the club or catapult, then gunpowder and cordite; and finally, nuclear explosives, which gave a new order of magnitude to destructive power. Now, with smart weapons, the pattern shifts, because with a limited amount of explosive energy one can do things that formerly required a great deal. This has a profound effect on both nuclear and conventional (high-explosive) warfare. Our strategic nuclear weapons are becoming more vulnerable because they can be attacked with ever-increasing accuracy. On the other hand, accurate conventional high-explosive weapons can now destroy targets that earlier could have been killed with certainty only by nuclear weapons.

On the old-fashioned battlefield, one expended great numbers of relatively cheap munitions, like bullets or bombs, and hoped that they hit something. Since the weapons were only generally accurate, one needed to know only roughly where the target was. And because, until the first atomic bombs, explosives were relatively cheap, a lot of them were used. Volume substituted for accuracy. You knew the enemy was behind that hill, or beneath those clouds, or on that bearing, and you threw tonnage at him in hopes that some of the weight of steel would hit.

Since the Bien Hoa bridges and the Yom Kippur war, this is changing. Now you locate the target accurately and launch a few expensive weapons at that specific target and kill it. You don't fire thousands of rounds behind that hill; you look behind it in some way and fire ten smart rounds. You don't miss so often anymore. Unfortunately, this also means you don't get missed so often.

There is a vital corollary to all this, one that makes Interservice Rivalry even more dangerous. In the old days, if you misidentified some of your friends as enemy and attacked them, you usually missed them, too. I admit to having fired once at British tanks. I missed. I have been bombed twice and rocketed once by friendly aircraft during World War II; and shelled once by friendly fire in Vietnam. I was missed. And that was normal for those times. It's not anymore. Now, if you have located the target accurately, you will probably kill it, even if it is a friend. So accurate location must include the close to absolute certainty that the target is an enemy. Historically, the process of sorting out friend from foe has broken down when it had to be done across service boundaries.

All three armed services are experiencing great trouble adapting to the arrival of the PGM age. The three services feel that smart weapons threaten weapons systems basic to their identity. Therefore, they believe their budgets, their doctrine, perhaps their very existence as a separate service, are under attack by these new weapons. Further, smart weapons cause the services problems because their successful use requires the crossing of present service boundaries and so increases Interservice Rivalry.

The Navy, particularly since the Falklands war, has the greatest fears over the changes PGMs will bring. A large surface ship moves relatively slowly, emits, is made in part of iron, and is easily visible on the surface of the water to all sorts of sensors. This makes ships, other than submarines, particularly vulnerable, as they turned out to be in the Falklands. But the Navy's problem goes deeper than the fear of losing ships. Since missiles of all kinds can go vast distances and sink ships and so control vital areas of the seas, like the Strait of Malacca or the Persian Gulf, why have so many large, expensive ships? The question of which service should develop and control a cruise missile launched from land to strike at a ship found by a satellite raises conflicting problems of interservice interests that paralyze today's Joint Chiefs.

Since the larger a target is, the easier it is to locate and destroy, isn't the whole system of convoys obsolete? Instead of convoys, perhaps what is needed is freighters with helicopters on them, dispatched at random across the oceans. (There is a project, called Arapahoe, to research this approach, but the idea so conflicts with naval doctrine that it has received only token funds.) The submariners are benefiting from smart weapons because targets beneath the water are probably harder to find than all other targets. But the surface Navy, particularly that of the dominant carrier admirals, feels threatened.

The bitter World War II interservice debate that occurred over whether the then Army Air Corps could aid the Navy in combating enemy submarines continues unabated today. The current B-52 on a sea-control mission can fly 2,000 miles from its base carrying antisubmarine missiles and loiter up to two hours in place without refueling. Under pressure, the Navy has permitted the Air Force to modify an AWACS to receive data from the Navy Outlaw Shark over-the-horizon submarine and surface targeting system. Plans called for two squadrons of sea-control B-52s to be operating with the modified AWACS by the end of 1984. This goal was not met.

The Air Force believes that smart weapons gravely threaten the bomber. The air, like the surface of the sea, is an easy medium in which to pick out targets electronically. The bomber does not appear as immediately vulnerable as the surface ship because it is smaller and can hide its "signatures" better, vary its flight and attack pattern, and operate at very high speeds to get away faster. Still, PGMs call into question the future existence of any bomber that is not made "invisible," to the extent that is scientifically possible. And if a few smart bombs can do the work of many conventional bombs, why not deliver the bombs by fighter aircraft, which are smaller and more easily hidden? The smaller aircraft do not need the large airfields, which PGMs can already easily locate and destroy. Further, if smart missiles can do many of the fighter and bomber missions at less cost, the need for both planes and pilots is decreased. Inside the Air Force, the dominant faction, the bomber generals of SAC, feels the greatest threat from the coming increases in accuracy.

These Air Force fears have already led to military inefficiency.

The forefathers of the smart bombs that hit the Bien Hoa bridge had been on the Air Force "shelf" since their use in the Mediterranean theater in World War II. Since 1964, "radicals" in the Air Force, chiefly at Eglin Air Force Base, led by General John D. Lavelle (who never thought of himself as a radical), had been trying to get the Air Force to use such weapons in Vietnam. But the Seventh Air Force in Vietnam and headquarters in Washington refused. The overt argument used against them was that it made no sense to drop a $3,000 smart bomb on a $1,000 truck. This overlooked the fact that they had been dropping ten $1,000 bombs on the truck and missing. Not until General Lavelle himself became head of the Air Force in Vietnam were the smart bombs used.

The Army, too, fears to examine closely what smart weapons do to its choice weapons and battle plans. Its heavy and expensive tanks are vulnerable to smart antitank weapons. Even more vulnerable are the huge supply dumps in the Army's tail and the large, static headquarters dedicated to electronic chatter. The dumps are easily spotted by satellite or secret agents and can therefore be killed, while the headquarters can not only be seen but also emit great quantities of radio messages, which direction finders can readily locate and on which beam-riding missiles can home. This raises questions about the worth of the whole elaborately controlled and choreographed scenario by which the Army intends to fight. There are 176 nuclear supply points in Europe. Someone has thought a great deal about the vulnerability of those weapons. There is only one large conventional weapons supply point in Europe. That part of the future has not been faced.

One of the most accurate methods of locating a ground target on the battlefield is to point a laser beam at it and have a weapon home on the reflected invisible light. (This is known as lasing the target, the method employed to destroy the Vietnam bridges. The target is lased from a laser source known as a designator.) One would think this an ideal function for long-range patrols in the enemy's rear. Such patrols, composed of Army Rangers, were effective in both Korea and Vietnam, even before PGMs. But until very recently such patrols could not use lasers to designate targets. This came about because target designation is a G-2, intelligence, function. Long-range patrols are composed of infantrymen. The assistant G-3 (operations) officer of the Army was an old infantryman. He didn't want infantrymen demeaned by performing an intelligence function.

The chief doctrinal reason why smart weapons pose such an external threat to all three services and increase Interservice Rivalry is easy to explain but hard to eradicate. The problem comes with target-finding. *If* you can accurately locate the target, you can kill it, and so finding the target becomes at least as important as delivering (firing) the smart weapon. And unfortunately—and this is the key—the target is often found by a sensor (eyeball, infrared, satellite, sonabuoy, etc.) belonging to one service, while the weapon fired at that target belongs to another service. The services have great difficulty exchanging this target information and firing data.

Why did the battleship *New Jersey* fire almost at random into the Lebanese hills in 1983 and not use the Army radars, which can locate an enemy artillery piece within several feet, seconds after the hostile shell has been fired? And when the Army radars did finally start operation, why couldn't their information be processed on board the battleship? In modern, smart-weapon warfare, targets turn up everywhere; but the services are at present unable to pass information about them or attack them across their doctrinal boundaries.

For example, the land battle is the responsibility of the Army, the air battle of the Air Force. Who will pay for the Air Force satellite that spots by infrared sensors the Russian infantry headquarters behind the front, a target that will then be attacked by smart Army artillery shells? Or another problem: The Air Force wants to penetrate to the rear of the enemy to destroy hostile air bases. Who pays for the ground-based antiradar missiles that attack the enemy antiaircraft radars along the front so the Air Force can get through? Who will see that such complex missiles are manned by soldiers at least as able as those that fire the antitank rockets?

Pentagon-CIA rivalry transforms such problems from a can of worms to a nest of vipers. Secret agents now can locate major targets with laser designators; they were quite effective using only radios in Korea. By presidential order, giving target designators to agents is a CIA responsibility. But the CIA doesn't want to run this type of low-level agent, who would function only in time of war. It is after the big payoff, the agent who penetrates the Czech or Soviet defense ministry. At the same time, the CIA doesn't want the Army or the Air Force organizing stay-behind agents and competing with it for a few brave bodies. Nor does the ambassador want the armed services recruiting secret agents to whom they will hand designators. The ambassador has enough trouble with the CIA and knows all too well the sort of officers the armed services traditionally shuffle off into intelligence.

In NATO, the West Germans don't want the secret agent designator responsibility; they have been so penetrated by Russian intelligence that they won't even give their own agents encoded radios, for fear the codes will be compromised. Besides, by a still-secret arrangement we struck with the British when the Germans entered NATO, we have to inform the British of any intelligence deal we make with the Germans. We don't always do this; but designators are so important that the British will find out even if we don't tell them, and trust, on which NATO eventually rests, will be damaged. But given the recent security leaks inside British intelligence, should the British be told? Who can blame an overworked general on the Joint Staff if he decides to leave the problem of giving designators to agents until next year?

There are other perplexing Pentagon-CIA questions, such as who will steal some of the enemy's black boxes—for example, the Identification Friend or Foe (IFF) equipment at his antiaircraft missile batteries—so that we learn what those emissions he is bouncing off us will do in wartime? Who tries to buy or steal these electronic devices—CIA agents, Air Force agents, or Army agents?

Our Defense Department does have in experimental form an electronic system for the transmission of data and IFF that is supposed to work across service boundaries. It is called JTIDS (Joint Tactical Information Distribution System, pronounced "Jay-tids"). This system is eight years late. The Air Force and the Navy have been unable to agree on one of the complex electronics parts within the system. The next time some senior Pentagon official, in or out of uniform, tells you the present organization works as is, or needs only "fine tuning," ask about JTIDS.

To some extent, smart weapons are resisted because such weapons have often been oversold by their advocates. Here, the Great Divorce rather than Interservice Rivalry strikes. Smart weapons are advocated by some partisans as part of new, painless strategies, relying more on mobility and science, which will allow the United States to reduce its forces. Those who hold this view are often sincere, and some of their observations are acute and their suggestions excellent. A nation with high technology and few people should incline toward mobility for its forces, more mobility than we have now. But as former Speaker of the House Sam Rayburn remarked of those brilliant bureaucrats entering the Kennedy administration, "I'd feel a whole lot better about them if just one of them had run for sheriff once." Those inside the armed services would be happier if more of the smart weapons tub-thumpers had been shot at.

General Sherman's question "Who ever saw a dead cavalryman?" appears deadly valid. Mobility is fine, but you also have to stay and fight, have firepower. The 1st Cavalry Division, although one of the most mobile and most successful in Vietnam, took 30,536 casualties. There are times when mobility runs out and heavy firepower is necessary. The battles of Stalingrad, Iron Bottom Sound, and Shiloh, and the RAF's defeat of the Luftwaffe all come to mind. Too much of the change-ringing by some advocates for smart weapons and small mobile forces appears to be code for small, cheap, and unsophisticated enough so that the present low-IQ volunteers can operate them. And we don't need the draft.

The unfortunate result of overselling these weapons is that service attitudes against change harden. Those who might be persuaded to make an important beginning resist, fearing they will be pushed too far. For example, I believe that the future for large aircraft carriers is short and that most of them should be replaced by smaller ones. But how many large carriers and how many smaller ones are needed? I do not blame admirals for fearing that if they conclude that smaller carriers are better for most missions, they will be trapped by the mobility extremists in Congress into having small carriers only. I think they should examine the problem and face down the opposition. But that sort of moral courage is rare everywhere in America today.

The charge is also leveled against smart weapons that planning for their use will divide our alliances, particularly NATO. Professor Michael Howard of Oxford, whose brilliant analyses of the military past so often enlighten our defense present, has exposed this bogus fear. Alliances are split by selfish national interests and knit by leadership. Those who wish to weaken the West will try to use the advent of smart weapons, like the cruise missile, to lever the democracies apart. Others will find in the same weapons methods of deterring the Soviets and lessening the dangers of nuclear war. The weapons themselves remain neutral.

Smart weapons introduce uncertainty into both the modern battlefield and the military future. We Americans tend to like the "sure shot," the "blue chip," the "100 percent guarantee." Europeans, unsheltered by our oceans and lacking our wealth, size, and strength, have historically been more sanguine about uncertainty. I believe that the European attitude is correct, and that properly employed smart weapons can increase American security and strengthen the NATO alliance. Doubt is an effective peacekeeper. If you are not certain you are going to win, you just may not start something. Uncertainty of outcome is a further increment of deterrence, to use the jargon.

Precision guided munitions offer a way out of our present Russian roulette choice of being defeated in conventional warfare in Europe or going to nuclear holocaust. Recall that there are two methods of killing targets: to use a great deal of explosives, or to be accurate. Until smart weapons came along and brought phenomenal increases in accuracy, there were a great many vital Soviet targets we could be certain of destroying only if we attacked them with nuclear weapons: bridges, railyards, headquarters, mountain passes, fuel dumps, radar units, airfields. So to make up for our weakness in conventional forces we planned to use nuclear weapons against such targets.

PGMs, if we are willing to buy them in sufficient numbers—and assuming that the Great Divorce has healed sufficiently so that we have troops that can use these complex and deadly weapons—remove this nuclear necessity. Take the vital bridges across the Vistula and Bug rivers. At present, these are targeted by tactical nuclear weapons. In the immediate future these bridges, located by satellite, can be taken out using precision weapons and conventional high explosive. The weapons system used would most probably be ground-launched cruise missiles or the invisible airplane. Headquarters destruction is another mission ideally suited to smart weapons. Even if the staff was relatively safe in some deep underground bunker, conventional explosive weapons that home on radio emissions would make the headquarters incapable of command. The possibility of using PGMs in this fashion also gives the Western alliance the opportunity for hard and meaningful negotiations with the Russians for the removal of nuclear weapons from Western and Eastern Europe, or at least their numerical restriction.

Smart weapons are so deadly that in order to survive on the battlefield of the future, everyone and everything will have to be spread out and dispersed over a wide area. This is precisely the military posture that limits the damage done by nuclear attack. In coping with smart weapons, tactics are used that make nuclear attack less promising and, therefore, less likely. Smart weapons not only increase our ability to defend Western Europe without resorting to nuclear weapons; they also widen the nuclear firebreak by removing tempting nuclear targets.

So far the effects of increased accuracy on tactical, or battlefield, weapons have been considered. The accuracy revolution also affects strategic weapons such as the land-based and submarine-launched ballistic missiles, the long-range bombers, and more futuristic systems such as the Strategic Defense Initiatives, or "Star Wars."

The explosive revolution, the quantum jump in destructive power that occurred with the invention of nuclear weapons, has run its course. There are far too many nuclear weapons in the world; but neither their growing numbers nor any increase in their destructive power is the cause of the present strategic turmoil. If the Russians had 30 percent more nuclear weapons than they now possess, but if those weapons had merely the same accuracy they had in the early sixties, we would be a great deal more secure. They must feel the same way about our arsenal. The crisis in today's strategic world has come about not because of an increase in weapons numbers, horrendous as these numbers are, but because of the accuracy revolution.

Smart strategic weapons are shifting the concern of both sides from weapons that kill populations to the so-called counterforce weapons, strategic weapons accurate enough to kill other strategic weapons. Both sides fear that a successful first strike—one side hitting the other hard enough to destroy most of the other side's weapons—could again become a possibility. This is a challenge both to arms control negotiations and to the design of our strategic weapons. Though there is an unnecessary amount of nuclear explosive in the world, we and the Russians have at least negotiated some limits on weapons numbers. But to negotiate about both numbers and accuracy at the same time is a harder task.*

When we talk about the accuracy revolution and increasingly complex weapons, the Readiness question again comes to the fore. For example, the Soviet strategic missile forces are not as ready to go as our own, and are kept at a much lower level of alert. Russian launch procedures are more complex than ours, with the KGB sharing control of missile firings with the armed services. Students of Soviet behavior conclude from this that the Soviets know enough about our open society to believe we are unlikely to strike first, and that they feel their agents have so penetrated our defenses that they should have ample warning of first-strike preparations.†

Russia has roughly sixty submarines equipped to launch nuclear long-range missiles. At any one time roughly 20 percent, or about thirteen, of these sixty submarines are in firing positions at sea. In marked contrast, the United States keeps 50 percent of its fleet of roughly thirty-five active ballistic-missile submarines at sea. Both sides end up with the numbers somewhat in balance. The probable reason for the few Soviet submarines on patrol is that Soviet society is not producing the efficient reactors and skilled crews necessary for prolonged submarine operations.

To make up for the low number of submarines regularly at sea, about every four years the Soviets hold practice surges, in which 90 percent of their submarine force leaves port. To get into firing positions from their home bases, the Soviet submarines must sail out through two ocean gaps, the Bear Island gap off Greenland and the Aleutian gap northeast of Japan. These gaps are almost as extensively wired for sound as a Hollywood studio. In addition, our own nuclear attack submarines patrol the areas regularly.

* The throw weight/accuracy relationship is thoroughly understood by the Soviets. Marshal Sergei F. Akhromeyev stated in an 18 October 1985 interview: "One should not assess the power of missiles solely by . . . their throw weight. . . . A more important criterion is the accuracy of the warhead. A twofold increase in accuracy leads to an eightfold growth in warhead yield."

† Just how accurate Soviet ICBMs are now is a complex question involving science, intelligence, and secrecy. Experts disagree among themselves by factors of two to four. It is probable that Soviet ICBMs can now land within an eighth to a quarter of a mile of their targets—and that in five years they will be able to land within a tenth of a mile of their targets.

When the United States learns of a Soviet surge, the United States' strategic forces often go to a higher state of alert. Were the Soviets to improve their submarine forces so that they kept 50 percent of the ballistic-missile submarines at sea, this increase in Readiness would pose a far greater threat than, say, a 10 percent increase in their land-based missiles.

Soviet nuclear doctrine is different from that of America and NATO, stressing war fighting and first strike more, and deterrence less. However, my own fears of a nuclear sneak attack are tempered by the amount of time I have spent in the field. I have seen too many weapons that were listed as ready-to-go not work in practice. The day of the accuracy revolution has certainly dawned. But the day of the foolproof weapon lies far ahead.

The arsenals of both the East and West undoubtedly contain a certain number of what I term Wonk missiles. These are the missiles fired by Joe and Josephus ("Wapper") Wonk, who, even when not hung over, can be relied on to set the wrong number in the computer. In the real world of defense, the happy grin of good old Joe Wonk is ever present. I am not being facetious when I state that his existence on both sides of the curtain is a great buttress of world peace. Neither side can calculate how effective their attack, surprise or not, will be because of those missiles fired, submarines navigated, or bombers recently repaired by old Joe Wonk. May God bless and preserve his fouled-up head forever.

The accuracy revolution not only calls into question the survivability of many of our strategic weapons, it makes their replacements tremendously expensive. Cost of a B-1 bomber wing are still under debate, but $2 billion plus seems a fair estimate, while a Navy nuclear supercarrier comes in at $6.8 billion. When President Carter first proposed the MX system in 1979 he put the program's cost at $33.2 billion. Six months later the estimated costs had escalated to $60 billion and by late 1980 the Pentagon was admitting to an MX cost of $108 billion.

While I am certain that present versions of the MX will never be built, its huge price tag, and that of other strategic weapons, dictate the stern necessity to think cost. Not only will public opinion quite rightly refuse to stand for the large expenses entailed in buying excessive numbers of these weapons, but the possibility of national bankruptcy is very real. And there is every indication that Interservice Rivalry once again is trapping us into buying weapons we do not need, with each service insisting that its weapons systems, and its alone, can secure the safety of the United States.

The MX, which continues to be modified, is a 12-story-high, 192,000-pound missile. The MX's 92-inch diameter is the maximum girth possible under the terms of SALT II, and naturally we built to the maximum. The MX was designed to move from hardened shelter to hardened shelter on its own gigantic 200-foot-long, 1-million-pound truck, built like the gantries that move the satellite launch rockets at Cape Canaveral, only bigger. The 226 MXs in the original plan, which keeps being modified, were to shuttle between some 4,500 hardened shelters dug in an area covering roughly 6,000 square miles. The Soviets could never be certain which hole was empty, which lethal, and would be unable to target all of them. The MX counters the effects of increased accuracy by both hiding and hardening.

The term "hiding" is self-explanatory: it means having the missile in a hole or beneath the sea, where the enemy cannot be certain enough of its location to fire at it accurately. Hardening weapons, putting them in shelters that make them as impervious as possible to nuclear blast, is a method of protection that, while still valuable, is under direct attack from the effects of the accuracy revolution. Hardening is measured in psi, pounds per square inch of overpressure. Overpressure is any weight above the weight of the one atmosphere that we constantly bear. Five thousand psi is the upper limit of hardening believed to be attainable. To damage a missile hardened to this degree, the warheads of present Soviet weapons would have to burst within 1,000 feet of the target. (Or so the conventional wisdom holds. I am extremely skeptical that any weapon could survive that close to the nuclear fireball. This would be particularly true if the weapon was designed to penetrate deeply into the ground before exploding.) The United States hopes to obtain such missile accuracies within five to ten years.*

* Weapon accuracy also involves weapon numbers and so encompasses both science and arms control. If one weapon has a 50 percent chance of destroying a target, two weapons have a much greater chance. If more than one warhead aimed at the same target is placed on a missile, the law of averages improves the accuracy of that missile. Present arms control agreements, in addition to putting a ceiling on missiles, limit to ten the number of nuclear weapons

To me, discussion of the MX, no matter how serious, always seemed to deal more with wish than with reality. For one thing, to construct and operate one Air Force version of the MX system for twenty years would require 190 billion gallons of water. Construction alone by Air Force estimates would require 42 billion gallons. It would also require more concrete than there is at present in the entire federal highway structure. It is highly doubtful that there is the water available west of the Rockies to construct such a system.

Recently, a series of compromises on the MX has been developed by Congress and a Defense task force. There are tentative plans to replace Minuteman with a smaller and more mobile missile, somewhat jokingly called Midget Man. This missile, a scaled-down MX, would be trucked about the country to be hidden and sheltered on various Army and Air Force bases. For the present, some Minuteman silos are being further hardened, and the first MX missiles are now scheduled to be placed in them. Operationally, both these solutions make more sense than the gigantic and expensive original system. But there is a disturbing air of service logrolling and adhockery about the new answers. Time is truly running out on the Minutemen. However, all the replacements in sight appear to offer us very little additional defense for a great deal of money.

---

each side may put on any given missile. (Whether the Soviets have violated arms control agreements and tested a missile with more than ten nuclear weapons on board is a heated question that divides the scientific-intelligence community.)

Each individual nuclear weapon carried aloft by a missile is called an IRV (Independently Targeted Reentry Vehicle). The final stage of the missile's warhead that goes aloft is called the bus. As it flies through space, the bus fires out IRVs at different targets, or several IRVs at the same target. Since the bus has more than one IRV on board, the missile is said to be MIRVed, or to be a MIRV (Multiple Independently Targeted Reentry Vehicle). If the IRV can maneuver after it enters the atmosphere to better hit its target, the IRV is then known as a MARV (Maneuvering Reentry Vehicle). The MIRVs are then said to have been MARVed. MARVed MIRVs (people really talk in these terms) are the next step in accuracy. Since smart strategic weapons, rather than numbers of nuclear missiles, are the root cause of present strategic dangers and problems, believers in arms control, like myself, see restricting MARVs before they have been deployed as far more important than, say, negotiating a verifiable and mutually beneficial nuclear freeze.

The cost of a weapons system is tied to its length of life. The longer a weapon will last, the longer the period over which its costs can be prorated. This does not mean that everything about the weapons system must stay the same—merely that a number of vital and expensive parts must continue to be usable. Our B-52 bombers, designed at the close of World War II, continue to play an important defense role. This makes the B-52 an excellent example of an expensive weapons system whose long life has made it inexpensive in the end. Paradoxically, both Congress and the military shy away from building weapons that can last a long time through modifications. When the ability to be modified is built into a weapon, the initial cost is raised, and this makes Congress unhappy. At the same time the military fears it may not get the monies necessary for modernization at a later date. The obsolescent computers aboard most of our aircraft are a case in point. These are "hard wired"; what capacity they have is built into them. Congress has not been willing to authorize the purchase of more sophisticated computers that could take successive generations of software. Nor has the military pressed hard for such systems, though they are vital both to counter enemy missiles and to assist weapon accuracy.

While the life of the B-52 bomber has been long, the life of its successor, the B-1 bomber, appears likely to be short. The B-1 is designed as a penetration bomber. Its ability to penetrate hostile Soviet airspace deeply drives up the plane's cost, because the plane must be capable of extreme speeds and must carry complex electronic equipment to render it relatively immune to enemy missiles as it comes in close to the target. But why penetrate? Why spend such huge sums merely to get closer to or even overfly the target? Standoff missiles, either cruise or short-range attack, fired from the aircraft will deliver the nuclear blow. And the stealth bomber, which is far harder to spot, will be able to deliver these more efficiently in a few years.*

When pressed, the Air Force replies that the B-1 must be capable of deep penetration to determine with certainty that the target has been destroyed. But whether or not the target is de-

---

* I am aware of the complex arguments on all sides of this issue. I can only hope that those who would like a fuller discussion of it will reread the last paragraph of the preface to this book.

troyed can be determined by satellite or high-flying reconnaissance aircraft. The B-1 turns out to be an expensive weapons system with a short life designed to do much that other weapons systems do better. One is entitled to the suspicion that, as is the case with large aircraft carriers, an anointed weapon system is being defended after its peak usefulness has passed.

Recently the possibility has appeared that strategic weapons and, enthusiasts claim, all of the United States can be defended with lasers and charged-particle beams primarily launched from satellites in space. President Reagan's Strategic Defense Initiative, nicknamed Star Wars, proposes this option. The idea burst on press and public as something new; however, charged-particle weapons had been under secret development by the Air Force since the end of the Ford administration. And the Army had been publicly spending about $3 million a year on a program called Sippau, an American Indian word for "sacred fire," that would fire from the ground a charged-particle beam of antimatter hydrogen to kill incoming missiles. Reagan has in part gone public with decades-old secret tests, plans, and proposals.

Informed debate is difficult about future strategic weapons of a radically different kind. With such weapons, complex scientific questions predominate. Unfortunately, scientists disagree violently among themselves on the answers. A great many reputable scientists, including Vannevar Bush, head of President Roosevelt's own Office of Scientific Research and Development, believed the atom bomb would never go off. Things have not changed. The debate over the Strategic Defense Initiative follows this pattern. Difficult scientific questions have been answered by extravagant claims, charges, and countercharges from both supporters and opponents.

Proponents speak of beam weapons orbiting in space that could destroy all Soviet rocket weapons as they lift off and so make the United States and our allies close to 100 percent safe. Opponents say that since beam weapons could never be 100 percent successful, exploring this expensive option is purposeless. There are no 100 percent sure and safe answers in defense. The best that beam weapons might be able to do, and that is a great deal, is to destroy enough attacking missiles so that we would be less fearful of a successful first strike.

A secure deterrent without the ability to be decisive in a first strike has helped to keep the nuclear peace since the end of World War II. There appears a distinct possibility that within ten years we can protect a limited number of missile sites with a system of charged beams at heavy but not prohibitive expense. Some of the beam weapons would be space-based, others placed on the ground around our offensive missile systems. Were they to adopt the same system, the Russians would reap the same benefits of increased security for themselves.

U.S. attitudes toward the possibility of beam weapons seem to suffer from the Manichean nature of so much military debate since Vietnam, with questions framed in terms of right and wrong. Technology is neutral. Several leading scientists, persuasively led by Freeman J. Dyson, argue that the key to a more secure future is a system of such beam weapons to protect a small number of strategic offensive nuclear missiles. The remaining missiles would be rigidly limited by effective arms control agreements. A combination of research on beam weapons and diplomacy has already restarted the arms control negotiations between ourselves and the Soviets.

If beam weapons do work, that portion of the accuracy revolution will give the United States a military advantage, because beam weapons appear to be most effective against long-range, fixed-based land missiles; and that is the weapons basket in which the Soviets have placed most of their nuclear eggs. However, another facet of the accuracy revolution is the increased ability to closely track submarines beneath the seas through a network of underwater microphones linked to computers. The United States already follows much of the Soviet submarine fleet through such a system.

When a Soviet submarine sank in the Pacific, the United States was able to locate the hull and recover parts of the sub, using the spy ship *Glomar Explorer*. In ten to fifteen years the Soviets will probably be able to follow our own submarine fleet accurately enough to threaten that part of our deterrent missile system. That is to the Soviet's advantage, because we have put a large portion of our nuclear capability into submarine-launched missiles. Full exploration of the possibilities of beam weapons, coupled with constant negotiations over arms control, would seem to be a wise national course.

The accuracy revolution makes negotiations with the Soviet

Union over arms control even more difficult. Imposing verifiable limits on the numbers of strategic nuclear weapons that both sides may possess has been an almost impossible task. Now, in addition to limits on numbers, secure agreements must be reached on the type of guidance system permitted on the missile's nose or inside the ground radar station. Reliable verification is an item the Soviets find most threatening to their control over their police society. They have not wanted us even to know if their leaders are married or how many children they have, much less allow inspection of the guidance systems of their missiles.

The increases in accuracy make the goals of the nuclear freeze movement difficult to achieve. President Lyndon Johnson was among the first to call for a nuclear freeze, suggesting in 1964, a "verified freeze of the number and characteristics of strategic nuclear offensive and defensive vehicles." The problem with Johnson's freeze and with the majority of freeze proposals since then lies in that word "characteristics." In these times of rapidly improving weapon accuracy, how do we verify "characteristics" in ways which both we and the Soviets can tolerate? In desperation over finding acceptable methods of verification, some freeze supporters have even advocated a return to the "launch on warning" posture of the fifties. This means that one fires one's missiles not after having been attacked, but when one judges an attack imminent. This negates all the small steps of progress we have made since President Kennedy first proposed serious negotiations on arms control.

Other versions of the nuclear freeze do away with all attempts to control improvements in accuracy and merely advocate holding constant the present numbers and types of weapons. Far from making the world more secure, such proposals threaten both ourselves and the Soviets. A great many older, land-based Soviet missiles are vulnerable to the increasing accuracy of our weapons. The Soviets should be allowed to substitute for these weapons others that make them feel less vulnerable to sneak attack. On the other side, if and when a major breakthrough in underwater detection makes submarines far more vulnerable, the United States will be forced into making major changes in its strategic weapons systems.

On the positive side, ever since the early 1960s, a nuclear freeze that would bring to a halt the production of nuclear explosive material has seemed a difficult but promising goal. Nuclear explosive plants require vast amounts of power and are hard to hide from satellite inspection. There are not many of them; they do not need a great number of inspectors to ensure compliance; and they are usually located in remote areas, so that international inspectors at such plants would not disrupt the rest of society. A freeze of the production of nuclear explosive material could be a promising start toward a halt in the nuclear arms race.

This chapter on the accuracy revolution and our defense future must close with a warning and an ancient truth. First the warning: When considering new weapons, including some touched on in this book, beware what I term the rain dance. The rain dance is what officials in the Defense Department are performing when they tell you that they have this new weapon that solves all your problems. The question to ask immediately about this extraordinary weapon is, just where do they have it? All too often the weapon exists only on paper, or at best the development contract has been let out.

> "—Methinks I see a wonder weapon."
> "O, where, my lord?"
> "In my mind's eye, Horatio."

They can really boogie with the rain dance along the prestigious E ring of the Pentagon puzzle palace. Unfortunately, many weapons talked about have a tendency not to perform up to the expectations of their advocates. Or to arrive late rather than soon. This is particularly true of strategic weapons at the frontiers of science. An old notebook informs me that on 12 June 1978 Dr. William J. Perry, an energetic and dedicated Under Secretary of Defense for Research and Engineering, predicted that the first squadron of B-52 bombers armed with cruise missiles would be operational by September 1981. In late 1984, one squadron was finally formed.

The ancient truth is that—though this chapter has focused on change and the future—one aspect of warfare, like brave Horatius, remains constant. Wars kill and hurt people. They are meant to. Even when kept small, wars are expensive, violent, bloody, and painful. Wounds, even invisible ones, hurt those who get them. Death hurts those who grieve. Fear is an integral part of battle. Causing fear, both to prevent and to win wars, is the purpose of our Defense Department. Weapons, organization, thoughtful strategy, and effective tactics will help us; but the courage of the American citizen makes the rest possible. I know these words smack of tinsel and high school graduations. I know they turn people off; they do me at times. But I do keep meeting fine and intelligent people who believe modern weapons have abrogated the need for courage.

I was the first or second tank in the column that liberated a major concentration camp, Magdeburg. When I came round the corner of that pine forest lane and saw the human skeletons hanging from the barbed wire enclosing the camp, I thought, how barbarous of men to string up corpses. Then some of the skeletons moved slightly and I realized I was looking at the starved living. There was a horror beyond the horror of all the dying I had seen. I learned a lesson that day. There are worse events than battle. When they come to take you off to the camp, fight. And people who tell you that you will be better off in the camps than resisting are not your friends.

We Americans have not had a war fought on our soil since Lincoln's time. We want, quite naturally, to see the fighting and the dying, if there must be any, happen to other people, elsewhere. In World War II Americans did not join with Europe in feeling "we are all in this together" until we ourselves were attacked at Pearl Harbor. We are so afraid of nuclear weapons that we sporadically try to restrict our involvements beyond our shores. It's a natural reaction, though one that frightens our allies and is exploited by our enemies. We repeat our diplomatic and strategic history. In our fear of nuclear war we have taken, since the close of World War II, action after action that make such a war more likely against not just our allies but ourselves. Abolishing the draft, we field less efficient conventional forces, which increases our reliance on nuclear weapons. The perfect example of how to avoid looking at the lion: We stick our head in his mouth.

After the inhabitants of Samos, rather than continuing the battle, had surrendered to the Athenians, Pericles sent them the following letter: "Of the Gods we believe and of men we know that whatever they can do they will. Therefore, we are about to do to you what you would do to us, had you the power." The Athenians then descended on the Samians, killed all the males over eight, cut the right hands off the boys under that age, and sold the women and girls into slavery. Perilous choices are not unique to the nuclear age. It is only that they are forced on us and not on the Athenians or the Samians. Strength, courage, wisdom, justice—a nation and her citizens need all four. The need for such qualities remains, despite the continuing revolution in weapons.

EIGHT

Today's Strategic Forces –
Expensively Unready

T he airplane is older than the copilot. It is five in the morning in June 1979, for military operations, real and practice, always seem to start in the dark, and I am standing before an eight-engine B-52 at Barksdale Air Force Base, Shreveport, Louisiana. Beside me, in addition to the copilot, is Tom, a captain, who is the pilot; and Bruce, a major and a B-52 instructor pilot. Bruce is there both as my chaperone and to see how the copilot shapes up. A calm and competent former tobacco farmer from Arkansas, Bruce lived through the Vietnam War flying small airplanes low over the jungle to lift people we claimed were never there in and out of places we denied existed. We are going to take this BUF (Big Ugly Fucker, as the pilots lovingly call their B-52s) at 400 miles an hour 200 feet above the badlands of Oklahoma and Kansas, simulating an attack somewhere behind the Iron Curtain. Part of the time the pilots will not be looking out the window. They will be flying instead by a combination of radar, Forward Looking Infra-Red (FLIR), and television, all of which appear on a screen like a TV screen in front of the pilot.

Washington calls the low-level attack by B-52 bombers "part of our first line of defense." Armed with bombs, nuclear cruise missiles, and short-range attack missiles, the B-52s are meant to be effective weapons systems well into the 1990s. Bombers still carry 50 percent of the megatonnage we plan to deliver if our policy of deterrence fails and America has to strike back after being attacked.

For deterrence to be effective at keeping the peace, as it has been since the close of World War II, both our friends and our enemies must believe we can strike back after being attacked. This is called delivering a second strike, or a sure second-strike weapons system. One key to our secure second strike is the reliability of the B-52 bombers. Can enough of them survive and penetrate enemy airspace so that they, along with the land-based and submarine-launched missiles, can inflict unacceptable damage on the enemy?*

I am standing before this particular plane, call sign *Biggs 99*, because surprise is an important ingredient in obtaining accurate answers about readiness. I have seldom been deliberately lied to by the professional military. But in all large organizations, even the press, truth tends to get diluted as it rises toward the top. Members of the armed services are human and, like the rest of us, can confuse what they would like to see happen with what is actually happening. Strategic Air Command (SAC) headquarters had arranged for me to take a B-52 flight out of Carswell Air Force Base in Texas. At the last moment I had been able to switch from that long-prearranged flight to one here at Barksdale, chosen suddenly and I hope more at random.

Carrying our lunches of sandwiches, junk food, apples, and a great deal of fruit juice and milk—we will be airborne for nine hours—we stand before *Biggs 99*, with its drooping wings and eight engines. The B-52s were originally designed back in the 1940s to be aircraft powered by turboprops and not jet engines. By the time B-52s got into production, more powerful jet engines had arrived. These were hung on the plane to make it a high-altitude bomber. Today improvements in radar and homing antiaircraft missiles make the high altitudes no longer safe. So

---

* Such terms as "unacceptable damage" accentuate the psychological factor in warfare. Military power is directed against both an adversary's physical power and his will. What is "unacceptable damage" to one nation may be "a necessary sacrifice for victory" to another nation.

now war plans call for the B-52s to carry in their bombs and missiles at a low level, 200 feet, to get beneath the radar screen. In this way, either unseen or spotted only briefly by radar, they can reach their targets inside Russia.

I watch the pilots' faces as they examine the logs of the airplane and I realize I certainly have picked a bird at random. Neither Bruce nor Tom likes what he sees. The plane is twenty years old. It flew in Vietnam. It has 9,994.04 hours on it. (Some BUFs, the first of which were delivered to the Air Force in 1952, have over 13,000 hours.) The number-two engine is turning over too slowly. There are serious problems with the instrument lighting system. The pitch and roll instruments on both the pilot's and the copilot's side, necessary for blind flying, are behaving erratically. The forward-looking TV, vital for low-level flying in bad weather, is inoperative in some positions and erratic in others. Further, the plane is a fly-through. This means it has recently landed after flying all night. The mechanics have had no chance either to fix the noted defects or to check out the rest of the plane. Tom, serious and left-handed, signs off on *Biggs 99*. It's all his to fly now. No commercial airliner would take off with one-quarter of *Biggs 99*'s problems.

Bruce and I walk around the outside of the B-52 for the preflight check. The tires are very, very worn. Not only do they have no tread but the cord is also showing through in places. "They grip better that way," says Bruce with a smile. The B-52s have a "wet wing." This means that if a bullet goes through it, the wing leaks and probably catches fire. Later aircraft have wings that seal closed when hit. "I guess they don't expect these planes to be used more than once." Bruce smiles again.

One of the ways the military test you is to keep bouncing their little inside jokes off you. If the jokes stop, you know you are in trouble. Military humor, like doctors' humor, tends to be wry, laconic, and black. My favorite from Vietnam remains: "A sucking chest wound is nature's own way of telling you war is hell."

At 7:10, eight of us, three pilots, myself, and the rest of the crew, in green flameproof clothes (even the name tag is flameproof) climb up through a small hole in the belly of the aircraft. Each man begins to make some part of the huge aircraft his own particular niche, as men do everywhere when they plan to be in some place a long time. My place is right in back of the two pilots and alongside Bruce. Behind us the gunner sergeant is wearing a pistol, in case I, the stranger, get out of hand. As we begin to check out the plane, the gas gives out on the ground starting-generator. The electric current fails in the plane. The ground crew blames a faulty gas gauge on the starting generator. Tom's guess is that it's part of the mechanic shortage. With the draft stopped and the military budgets low, able mechanics are no longer joining the Air Force to escape the draft, or for pay benefits.

We have trouble starting the engines. Bruce's magic finally works on number four on the left side; but number-five engine on the right is intransigent. Under Bruce's guidance, the crew tries a series of tricks that would make Lindbergh proud. The old plane rocks and shakes as if a herd of moose were stampeding through the cockpit. Old five will not grab hold. "We have a no-start on number five," Tom reports sadly to his headquarters. Twenty minutes later the master mechanics arrive in their truck and take the cover off number-five engine. They stick the leads from the starting generator into the innards to jump-start it, just as you do with your car when the battery is dead.

"Let me know when she hits forty percent so as I can pull out my wires," the master mechanic on the ground yells up to us.

"Whack her up to forty, Tom," says Bruce.

Old *Biggs 99* racks and shakes like an agued wino. "Now. Now. NOW! Forty percent," hollers Tom. The mechanic reaches in a gloved hand and pulls the wires out of the spinning engine's gut. The second time we try this trick number five finally starts. *Biggs 99*, part of America's first line of defense, is finally ready to fly. Would you take off on your next civilian flight in a plane one of whose engines had to be jump-started? In part because of the Great Divorce, inside the Other America of Defense standards are tolerated that would not be allowed in our civilian life.

Taxiing out to the runway, everybody is dead serious; the attention to detail meticulous.

Fighter pilots and bomber pilots are quite different types of people. Drop me in an Air Force bar anywhere with my ears plugged and no insignia on anyone, and I think within a minute I could tell you what sort of pilots are at the bar. A bomber pilot's feeling for his plane is not as sexual as a fighter pilot's and is gentler. Where fighter pilots idealize and adore their planes, bomber pilots love and respect theirs, imperfections and all. Flying his plane, a fighter pilot thinks, "We're one, kid; we're one; and I am going to have you do some fantastic tricks." A bomber pilot thinks, "We're in this together, old girl; and if we just look after each other we are going to be OK."

After flying, fighter pilots stand at the bar in their uniforms, get a bit smashed, flap their hands, and talk about tactics. BUF pilots go home, take their wives out to dinner for a treat, and talk about insurance and the kids' school. Fighter pilots are always "exploring the edges of the envelope," pushing to see what their planes can do. Bomber pilots know that when you are 200 feet off the ground and the wing span of the B-52 is 400 feet, there is no time for fast maneuvers. Should you attempt to recover from a mistake too quickly, the BUF is, as they say in the trade, "apt to exceed its critical limits."

By the time *Biggs 99* has reached its cruising altitude, 23,000 feet, and leveled off, the crew has learned enough about the aircraft to feel secure and relax. Beside me on the floor Bruce has gone to sleep in the lotus position. The gunner sergeant, head cradled in arms, is nodding off. Tom leaves the pilot's seat and pushes by me with difficulty for a glass of water. An hour later the tanker that is to refuel us in the air shows up as a white dot on our infrared screen. Tom turns *Biggs 99* to a northeast heading. Inside the aircraft everyone becomes wide awake, and the routine returns to tense professionalism.

The dot on the infrared screen gets bigger and bigger. Finally there is the tanker aircraft in our windshield, straight ahead and 1,000 feet above us. The navigator keeps calling out the tanker's position. "Coming up on a mile and a half. Coming up on a mile . . ." We have all seen hundreds of pictures of aerial refueling in magazines, TV, and movies. It remains a consummate piece of flying. Nor is there any way to escape the mating image. The great swollen, red-tipped pizzle of the tanker trailing down and behind. The two silver beasts bobbing and weaving like two ancient dinosaurs, only moving at 225 miles an hour. The tense white face of the boom guider peering out the rear window of the tanker. The dull, hard *thunk* as the fuel boom penetrates the hole right above us in the cockpit.

The first time we hear the dull *thunk* we are a bit too much in a right-hand swing and the boom nozzle pulls out of the bomber's hole. His hands massaging all eight throttles gently, Tom lets the B-52 drift back, then edges her slowly forward again. *Clunk.* This time the fuel boom stays in and we fly along connected in the sky. Tom has his own method of keeping the two planes together. He lines up a known spot on his windshield with the radio antenna in the belly of the tanker and flies to keep this alignment perfect. About us the plane creaks and groans as the full weight of fuel enters her wings and the wrinkles in her skin stretch out to smooth.

We finish refueling and now, for practice, the copilot tries the mating dance. Twice under Tom's careful coaching he brings the huge plane forward. Each time he fails to make secure contact. As yet he lacks the piloting skills to bring off this complex maneuver.

This symbiotic relationship of bomber and tanker is a concise illustration of the need to think about defense not in terms of weapons but at the very least in terms of weapons systems, to realize why Tooth and Tail are one fighting unit, as in any effective dragon. The bomber is useless without the tanker. It cannot make it to the target. It does no good to spend millions on bombers and not have sufficient tankers, as the British found in the Falklands. *Biggs 99* is also useless without pilots skillful enough to refuel in the air. So the cost of pilot training, a Readiness problem, is part of the cost of the bomber weapons system, as is the cost of guarding and maintaining the bases from which bombers, tankers, and guardian fighters fly.

Finally, our refueling period over, *Biggs 99* breaks off its rendezvous with the tanker and we head for the Kansas-Oklahoma low-level range. Several hours later, at 200 feet, *Biggs 99* weaves across the deserted countryside where northeast New Mexico, southeast Colorado, the Oklahoma panhandle, and southwest Kansas all fuse. We are practicing the maneuvers that would let us press home an attack safely beneath an enemy radar screen. The ground is less than half a wing-length away: barren low hills, rolling fields, brown earth, and an occasional farm silo. As we fly across a road I can read one of the road signs. "Welcome to Kansas," it says. That's another little-understood part of the Tooth-to-Tail problem. As weapons get noisier, bigger, and deadlier, the Army and Air Force are running out of places where they can practice driving, flying, and shooting without an ever-growing population complaining. Already, German tank units fly to Canada to practice with live ammunition. The Air Force used to practice over the Iranian desert.

Now, at 200 feet, weaving through the little valleys to avoid our own radar trying to track us for practice, Tom and the copilot pull their seats down and begin flying by the Forward Looking Infra-Red and the radar terrain probe. Even trees stand out on the screen as we sweep across the landscape. On the screen, the terrain probe marking the high spots darts and leaps around, making a nervous graph that looks like the pulse chart of a fevered patient. In the deck below, the navigator with his radar plots directs the pilots toward their targets. Bruce keeps careful watch out the windshield at the real world.

Suddenly the vital gyro instruments that show how a plane is flying, whether it is upright or turning, all begin to spin and tumble on both the pilot's and the copilot's side. Fortunately we are not in the clouds. Up pop the heads back into the real world as we continue to weave above the hills and farmland at 200 feet. Bruce opens a can of apple juice and drinks it down calmly. "This happens all the time," he says.

Obviously it does, for Bruce has no hesitation about the cure. He squeezes the can together with his hands and then jumps on it a bit, making of the juice can a truncated V with a bubble at one end. He takes out his pocketknife and opens up part of the instrument panel, revealing the pumps for the worthless gyros. He wedges his sculpted juice can beneath the forward edge of the vacuum pumps. Then he ties the juice can securely in place with a bandage from the first aid kit. The gyros spin back to life. Bruce fits the instrument panel back together with his pocketknife. We go back to flying the mission.

In the target area, those on the ground report that we on *Biggs 99* have dropped our simulated thermonuclear weapons within 800 feet of the target. That is pretty good, better than average, but the crew is disappointed, having hoped for better than that. Still at 200 feet, we head for another part of the low-level range in New Mexico, where we will simulate the launch of our nuclear Short-Range Attack Missiles (SRAMs).

The little papers they put out for the press at SAC headquarters in Omaha and in the Pentagon—called, not always accurately, fact sheets—describe the SRAM as follows: "The SRAM's range, speed, accuracy, and small radar cross-section greatly improve the penetration ability of SAC's bombers against sophisticated enemy defense." There is only one problem with this today, as far as old *Biggs 99* is concerned. When we get to the range, none of our SRAM missiles work. Even when the radar operator slugs the computer in a special place he says always fires at least one of the missiles, nothing happens.

Two months later I am standing on a SAC field in 32-degrees-below-zero weather outside of Minot. There is a bit of a flap on. A B-52 that took off that morning on a practice run has dropped a whole engine off its wing somewhere over South Dakota. "Got to find it before the governor gets upset." The colonel shakes his head forcefully inside his parka's hood. Others on the field explain to me, none too happily, that the problem is not so tough. Parts drop off the B-52s so often that they have special teams standing by to find fallen engines and other such things. This engine was found within five hours, while I was still there. The air police rushed off by bus and helicopter to guard it from souvenir hunters. The governor never got upset because he never found out. But does the President know the true state of his "first line of defense"?

America's strategic air forces, along with our troops in Europe and to some extent the active fleet, still suffer from a classic case of robbing Peter to pay Paul. During the Vietnam War those parts of the armed services not actively engaged in Vietnam were starved of funds to disguise the true costs of the war. Those who financed that conflict this way believed that when Vietnam was won, the strategic forces and other parts of the armed services would receive extra funds and could then catch up. But that did not happen. Congress and the rest of the United States underwent an antimilitary spasm, as they had at the end of World Wars I and II. Military funds were cut drastically and our armed forces, unable to replace what had deteriorated during the Vietnam years, became dangerously ineffective.

In roughly the same period of time, 1964 to 1977, the Soviets had expanded their number of nuclear weapons by five times, from 649 warheads to 3,228, and had also increased the accuracy of their missiles. They increased the number of their divisions from 140 to 170, with probably 120 of these available to confront NATO. Further, after the Vietnam defeat the draft stopped, and the post–World War II pattern was repeated as able people left the armed services in droves. The American public never realized the actual plight of our defenses (though some of our allies did) because the press, part of that antimilitary reaction, was under-reporting the armed forces. Robbed of facts, and with the Great Divorce working on the elites, the public responded as would be expected. In 1973 only thirteen percent of those polled felt that the United States was spending too little on its armed forces. The vast majority felt then that we were spending too much or about the right amount. Meanwhile those in the Air Force were looking at the ancient planes and smilingly referring to them as "rusty but trusty."

In such a lean period the Pentagon's leaders were using their available dollars to buy weapons for the future rather than spending on Readiness. The purchase and maintenance of complex weapons systems such as the B-52 bomber pose awesome questions of Readiness/Tooth-to-Tail. Suppose you, as an Air Force general, have been given $10 billion by a wise but vigilant Congress to spend on buying and maintaining the "Zapper" jet fighter. This fighter, the "Zapper," will be our first line of defense for the next ten years; after that it will be superseded by some other plane or missile. Each "Zapper" costs $10 million to build. Each of these $10 million "Zappers" can be maintained at a high state of readiness for $2 million a year. Or each can be maintained at a low state of readiness for $1 million a year. Now how is that $10 billion to be divided? Should 500 "Zapper" fighters be bought and then kept at a low state of readiness? Or 333 "Zappers," with these kept at a high state of readiness? That's the mathematics of the choice, though, of course, compromises could be made that would buy parts of both worlds.

Which choice or compromise or mix of programs is going to produce the more "ready" force of fighters? Which choice is going to do the most to deter war now? To promote peace and safety at the end of that ten years? If the tail is slighted, maintenance lowered, and more planes bought, the increased number of planes can be brought up to standard if we have adequate warning before hostilities start. However, in the meantime, some less-well-maintained planes will certainly be lost in crashes. That will affect public opinion and congressional attitudes toward defense. How many crashes can be accepted as a trade-off for more planes? And, remembering Pearl Harbor and Korea, can sufficient warning be counted on to bring the "Zapper" force to a high state of readiness? On the other hand, with superb maintenance and fewer fighters, will we be so outnumbered that our excellent but small force is defeated? What course makes the country most "ready," thus decreasing the risk of war and raising the odds on victory?

In the real world, as an Air Force general you would be under a great deal of pressure to make certain choices in the "Zapper" program. First, Congress talks a lot about Readiness, but except for a very few legislators, like Senator Sam Nunn of Georgia, Senator Robert J. Dole of Kansas, or Representative Les Aspin of Wisconsin, most don't understand it. And Readiness always gets cut first. Always. There are a variety of reasons for this. Big weapons—submarines, bombers, destroyers, or even helicopters —are sexy. They mean major contracts going into someone's political backyard and thousands of jobs. Congressmen love to ride in them and have their pictures taken. Even defense-budget-cutting liberals like Senator Edward M. Kennedy and Senator William Proxmire support big weapons if they are built in their states. Once a big-weapons program is started, you don't save much money by cutting it back. Indeed the cost of the weapon may actually be increased if it is built over a longer time. Probably only about 8 percent of the funds for a single "Zapper" will be spent in any one year.

Whereas to cut Readiness brings quick savings: Just don't buy the spare parts or train the pilots and mechanics; also save on fuel costs by not flying so much. So even if the choice is for fewer planes and more Readiness, when the next economy wave hits, maintenance probably will be cut; we will have fewer planes; *and* they won't be ready. The builders of the "Zapper" will put the heat on Congress for the 500-plane program, as will the unions. On the other hand, if the decision is for a smaller number of planes and more Readiness, they and their supporters in Congress will kick us to death. The next time someone says to you that generals don't earn their pay in peacetime, consider the Readiness problem of the "Zapper" fighter.

What of the other land-based leg of our strategic forces, the missiles in their holes in the ground? The Minutemen missiles that make up the backbone of the land-based missile forces are not as old as the B-52s. They were conceived and designed (with the help of our outstanding team of civilian scientists) in 1952–1953, when, with the Korean War successfully ended by a personally popular President Eisenhower, the effects of the Great Divorce were not as virulent as today. The first operational flight of missiles went into position in 1962 and the last was lowered into its silo in 1970.

The Strategic Air Command and the Pentagon, in another one of those "fact sheets," refer to the Minuteman missile force as "98 percent ready." Missile Readiness is harder to estimate than bomber Readiness, but even with that caveat, there are some disturbing questions about the Minutemen. I am referring not to the arguments about whether they are vulnerable to Soviet missiles, or to the even more complex questions about whether they can be commanded to fire in actual wartime. The basic question is, if they were fired without being attacked, how many of them would actually go off and land anywhere near their target?

The Minutemen were designed to last five years. Those emplaced last, in 1970, have lasted sixteen years; those emplaced first, over twenty years. Parts of the system are much older than that. For example, the Minutemen silos, the six-story-deep holes in the ground inside which the five-story-high missiles live, are meant to be held at temperatures between 68 and 70 degrees. The diesel generators that supply the power to do this and also to keep the missiles' computers functioning were built in the late forties to power the radars of the DEW (Distant Early Warning) line, which was then being built in arctic Canada. When the DEW line was dismantled in the late sixties, the generators were shifted to the Minuteman silos.

Or take a less obvious problem. Inside the guidance system, where the temperature must be highly controlled, there is a little fan slightly bigger than your thumb constantly going round and round. Back in the late fifties, when the system was being built, a contractor offered to design the perfect little fan for $5 million. The Air Force said, "That's too much; pick a less expensive fan and go with it." The contractor did; but three months later he was forced to admit that the fan he'd picked was not reliable enough. The missile defenses of the United States were being held up over a fan. The solution, since the Air Force was pressed for time and money, was to take the little fan that cools your average refrigerator and use that. Those fans usually run for at least ten years without needing to be changed. There was some hostility to putting a commercial refrigerator fan into a defense missile; but no one had a better fan. The Air Force engineers wrapped some more electronic shielding around the fan and bought it.

But this little fan that cools your cola and your strategic deterrent goes round and round only one way. As a result, after fifteen years of going round only one way, the fan has created its own magnetic field. No one knows how much that magnetic field affects the guidance system of the missile. The problem has been computer-gamed, and scientists believe the Minuteman will land on target. But in the restricted test flights made by the Minuteman, the missile has always traveled from east to west, from Vandenberg Air Force Base to Kwajalein Island. If it should ever have to be used, it must fly from west to east. This disturbs a significant number of people.

The effect of such Readiness problems on the Minuteman forces is harder to judge than the effects of Readiness problems on a B-52, a naval ship, or an army unit because there has never been a successful operational test of a Minuteman missile—that is, a test in which, after the nuclear warhead has been removed from a randomly selected missile, the missile is fired out of its silo in Wyoming, Kansas, or North Dakota. Reportedly, there have been three attempts at such tests, and each time the missile failed to make it out of its silo. After that, such tests were canceled. One can understand why. If a missile should make it out of its silo only to blow up over, say, Minneapolis, the Defense Department would have, at best, a public-relations problem. Minutemen are now tested in the following fashion:

The missile to be tested is selected at random by tail number at SAC headquarters outside of Omaha. The wing commander of the missile to be tested then seals off the missile so that it cannot be tampered with. Next, a special crew comes to remove the nuclear warhead and transport the rest of the missile on a special train to Vandenberg Air Force Base in California. Moving missiles is a tricky business, for which the missiles' regular crews do not have sufficient training. Note, however, that only the missile moves. The computers that will tell the missile where and when to fly remain behind in the silo. At Vandenberg the Minuteman is slipped into a special silo and hooked up to special computers to program it to fly to the Kwajalein test range. Note that this silo and its computers are maintained largely by skilled and highly paid engineers. The computers back at the operational silo are maintained by Air Force sergeants.

As the missile is readied at Vandenberg, the test environment becomes even more unreal. The missiles' own guidance system is removed and replaced by a "section 33," programmed especially for the Pacific missile range, and also to report on the missile's inflight performance. When this lengthy, four-month process is finally complete and the engineer experts fire the missile, the results are close to 100 percent successful. But what is being tested, other than structural integrity and the propellants? How much resemblance does this Minuteman being fired bear to the operational missile with its own computers that was sitting in its silo before the test process began?

The Air Force colonels who brief you at SAC headquarters insist the tests are "absolutely valid." Another colonel actually involved in the test program was a bit more cautious. "You have to be concerned," he says, "that there are too many tests in other than the operational environment." A retired general, a friend of some years, who had monitored the test program from the Pentagon, says bluntly, "About the only thing that's the same [on the tested Minuteman and the missile that was in the silo] is the tail number. And that's been polished."

I look at the problems we have experienced with the space shuttle—most dramatically the explosion of *Challenger*. I remember the failures in the Apollo and Mercury programs, in which everything was done at peak effort by scientists. I recall the reliability of other military programs. I look at the several public failures, as well as the successes, in the Navy's missile program, which can run operational tests because they are done over water. If the dark hour ever came and a launch of the Minuteman was ordered, a failure rate of 30 percent would not surprise me. And their readiness could easily fall below that level if they were attacked first.

Each Minuteman in its individual weapons silo is part of a 10-missile flight controlled from a single underground command silo. In turn, each flight of 10 missiles, with its command silo, is interconnected with 4 other flights to make up a squadron of 50 missiles. Three squadrons form together into a strategic missile wing of 150 Minutemen.

What most strikes you about the 91st Strategic Missile Wing as you chopper out to its Oscar One launch control silo is that there is nothing there. At a bomber base or an Army encampment or on an aircraft carrier there is lots and lots to see. When you fly above the awesome destructive power of a Minuteman wing, there is nothing for the eye to grasp—just a few barbed-wire fences surrounding small snow-blown patches of the North Dakota plain. The enclosed spaces aren't large enough for a horse, though they would do for a child's pony. In the center of each of these pony pens humps a small snow-covered mound. Yet beneath that bump is the 7,000-pound multiwarhead Minuteman in its 6-story-high climate-controlled tube; its megaton nose cone feeling slightly waxy to the touch.

The entrance to Oscar One's underground chamber is behind the paper-shredder in a small wooden building about the size of a summer bungalow. It is a massive steel door like that on a bank vault, though Oscar One's door is a bit rusty, not as shiny as the average bank vault. The stage sets constructed for TV or motion pictures to represent missile firing silos are too gadget-filled and modern to resemble the real thing. Because of military's lack of funds, the fictional copy is more awesome than the reality.

The two officers standing beside me coordinate their security numbers with the two on duty below. Then the door opens and we slowly descend sixty feet into the earth in a creaking freight elevator with open sides. When the elevator reaches the bottom, the scene does get otherworldly. Behind two gigantic blastproof doors supported on shock absorbers, each the size of a limousine and designed to take the earthquakelike jolts of a nuclear explosion, is a computer-jammed room forty-one feet long and twenty-six feet wide. The general feeling is that of two equipment-filled minivans jammed hastily together.

Inside this room two officers control the launch of the ten missiles in their Oscar One flight. In an emergency they can pick up control of twenty more "birds" in the flights nearest theirs. There are never less than two officers here on duty. This is a "no lone zone." Wherever there is a possibility that a ready-to-go nuclear weapon can be fired, there are "no lone zones" so nothing can be done unless two people act in coordination. These zones are an important part of arms control, making our own weapons safer and less liable to nuclear accident. Every time I enter one I'm conscious of a few short breaths and an instant prickly feeling on the back of my hands. It is like following the painted yellow footsteps that mark a safe path through a radiation-contaminated area; one stops to think an instant before the first step. The average age of the lieutenants and captains standing watch inside these Minuteman control silos is twenty-five.

At the end of Oscar One's underground room is the firing console with its locked code boxes. Into these two boxes must be fed both the codes of the missile firers on duty and the master codes that in an emergency will be transmitted from the White House. The control console contains the twelve firing-sequence buttons, beginning with "Strategic Alert," progressing through "Warhead Armed," to "Launch in Progress," and finally, "Missile Away." On a status panel along the right wall as you face the launch-control console are a series of small red lights that flash if something is wrong with any one of Oscar One's ten missiles. Other red lights indicate trouble with the additional twenty Minutemen that Oscar One might have to control, were another command silo knocked out in wartime.

I notice that there are quite a few red lights glowing on the board. I count twenty-two. If we are 98 percent ready, I ask, why all these little red lights? One of the pleasant things about getting out in the field, away from Washington, is that the military are usually quite open about their problems as well as their successes. Indeed, I have found them more open than most businessmen or labor leaders. The four officers in Oscar One explain to me that while these red lights do show problems, all of the indicated failures are such that we have merely a "degrade of performance," not birds that will not fly. Obviously there is a great deal of difference between a red light reporting that the barbed-wire fence around the silo has a severed strand and a red light that indicates a Minuteman's gyros are tumbling. The officers assure me that reporting here in the 91st is honest. But they also have stories about being ordered, on other bases, to carry as merely degraded missiles they were certain were "dead birds." Missile readiness appears as much a matter of judgment as statistics.

There is also a feeling throughout the Air Force, as there is in other services, that, since Vietnam, standards of reporting and readiness have slipped. There was a time in the late fifties and early sixties, under the legendary SAC commander General Curtis LeMay and his immediate successors, when each plane and missile had its designated targets inside the Soviet Union. Should there be any indication that a plane or missile was unready to fly, another plane or missile took its place immediately, with the responsibility to destroy those targets. And if the plane or missile was not fully ready to go again within two days, some general or colonel was in trouble. But that was in another intellectual climate; and it was also a time when SAC got a most generous portion of the military budget.

Before leaving Oscar One, I ask the two officers there and their colonel, the squadron commander, if they would run a test for me on the security of the Minuteman missile: have the officers in another launch facility try to fire one of our ten missiles, something that would be possible in an emergency. After some discussion the squadron commander gets on the scrambler phone and, with some lengthy authentication signals, orders another launch facility to try to fire one of our birds. Suddenly little white lights start to glow alongside the panel for number-eight missile in Oscar One's flight. The sequence gets down to just before "Warhead Armed" and the air vibrates with the shriek of alarm bells.

"That's something I never expected to hear in this room," says the captain in command of Oscar One. He pushes a button and takes his missile back under control. Inside our confined space, computers and loudspeakers begin to chatter and question, demanding an explanation. I have to turn and face the door while some rather complicated encoding procedures are followed. That's all rather reassuring. Parts of the strategic weapons system certainly work well. It's those other, untested parts that cause concern.

Here, outside of Minot, North Dakota, another aspect of the Readiness problem is revealed, one that no one wishes to talk about publicly, though both our strategic and our tactical weapons are affected. In the twenty-eight-degrees-below-zero cold a group of new Air Force mechanics is learning how to change the guidance system on a Minuteman. They have hauled the warhead and guidance system off the top of a missile and are loading it onto a special transporter truck to bring it to the base for testing. On its thermonuclear nose, about the height of a tall man, some wag has stuck a little red flag that says, "Remove before flight." The new mechanics have a bit of a problem. The delicate thermonuclear nose and guidance system won't sit on the floor of the truck properly. With a great deal of difficulty the nose gets winched back up off the truck floor.

"Somebody get me a broom," bawls the sergeant, getting back to basics.

His extremely pregnant corporal assistant hands him a broom. After the sergeant sweeps hard, a small washer from no one knows quite where turns up on the floor. Maybe it's from this missile, maybe from the one they put back together yesterday. Ninety-eight percent ready?

The female corporal helping change the nuclear warhead is no aberration but a constant occurrence inside the Other America of Defense. In the early seventies, with the failure of able men to enter the AVF (All-Volunteer Force), all three services began to rely more and more on female volunteers. In 1971 only 1 percent of the armed forces were women. In 1984, of those serving in the active-duty forces, 9.5 percent were women, with the total still rising. These women decisively outscore men on intelligence tests. For example, of the women entering the Army in 1983, 44 percent scored in the top two categories in the entrance test, compared with 35 percent of the men. And 18 percent of the women had some college, compared with 8 percent of the men. In the Marine Corps, women enlisted applicants need a high school diploma or a year of college, while males need merely a tenth-grade education. As a result of their educational superiority, the important technical jobs on which modern warfare rests— nuclear weapons control, aircraft maintenance, electronics, and so forth—are increasingly filled by women.

In 1984, women inside the armed forces were distributed as follows: The greatest number of women, 11.38 percent, were serving in the Air Force, and the fewest, 4.88 percent, in the Marines. The Organization of the Joint Chiefs of Staff had its first woman general, Mary A. Marsh. The number of women with the Joint Chiefs organization had risen from one or two in the early seventies to eighty-eight (twenty-three officers and sixty-five enlisted personnel). The Marine Corps, after a lapse of four years without a female general officer, again had one, the second in its history.

The Air Force, the service with the greatest number of non-combat jobs, has been directed by Congress to raise its level of enlisted women to 22 percent by 1987. There is great pressure on the Air Force to take more women because it is believed that if the Air Force will fill more of its technical jobs with highly qualified women, more highly qualified men will be available to enter the Army. Even in late 1984, when, thanks to unemployment and restrictions on student loans, the enlistment of able young men had risen rapidly, the Army was still short of qualified men to fill combat roles. Historically, the Air Force, where military life is relatively pleasant, has had less trouble in maintaining a quality all-volunteer force than the other services have had.

Today's increased readiness of our armed forces rests decisively on the capable shoulders of our female soldiers, sailors, and Air Force members. But such reliance has also created problems that would be humorous if they did not so affect readiness. Recently the Air Force excluded women officers from serving in Minuteman silos, where two officers are necessary to launch the missile. Previously women had served in Titan silos, where four people were necessary. Then, six months later, the Air Force opened up the two-person Minuteman crews to females. But both officers in the silo had to be female. That restriction will obviously break down in an emergency. The Navy has classified as a combat operation the supply ships and tankers that sail with the fleet. Women cannot command such ships and can serve in them only on temporary duty. But women do serve and can command the Merchant Marine ships that sail with the fleet in the same convoys doing the same jobs.*

Even more controversial than female job opportunities are questions about employment of pregnant women. For example, until 1975 single women in the armed services who got pregnant were discharged. Now, servicewomen, married or not, get ninety days of maternity leave and then are back on duty. In 1977, the

* In 1984 both the Chief of Army Personnel, General Robert M. Elton, and the Chief of Naval Personnel, Admiral William P. Lawrence, had daughters who were officers in their respective services. Admiral Lawrence's daughter is a helicopter pilot. In 1984 female helicopter pilots were finally allowed to serve temporarily on Navy ships. As more male officers have wives or daughters in the armed services, attitudes change.

year in which a statistical study was made, 15 percent of the women soldiers in the Army got pregnant; and the statistics are believed to be comparable in the other services. Morale problems arise because other people have to do the women's jobs during the last months of their pregnancies; and there are no funds or personnel slots for these extra people. The pregnant Air Force corporal in this truck here at Minot cannot assist in changing the missile warhead. In such noncombat environments as military hospitals, females in the last months of pregnancy can't carry stretcher patients from place to place. Military efficiency is lowered and resentment is created among those, male and female, doing the extra work.

Male and female soldiers agree that pregnant women should not be doing heavy work, nor should they go into the field. There are those who will tell you there is no issue here, that the noise is all created by male chauvinists. But in the field, when you look and listen, you see a real-world difficulty. Many of those concerned over the problem presented by the pregnant soldier are enthusiastic about increasing the numbers of women in the armed forces. They would just like to know how to solve their Readiness problem.

The debate is complicated by history. When the numbers of servicewomen began to increase in the mid-seventies, the services were in such horrible shape that any able and dedicated body, male or female, was warmly welcomed. Helicopters were being burned, officers were assaulted, drugs were rampant, over 40 percent of the Army's intake were reading at merely fifth-grade level.*

---

* The categories by which the Army rates the intellectual skills of its personnel have been restructured several times in the last twenty years, most recently in 1981, and the relationship between the categories and reading levels has varied. At present those in category I are comparable to the top 7 percent of the population as a whole; they would score between 600 and 750 on the verbal SATs used for college entrance and between 650 and 800 on the mathematical SATs. Those in category V, the lowest category, are comparable to the bottom 15 percent of the population as a whole in intellectual attainment. The Army does not currently accept any category Vs, but it has done so at certain times, notably just before the Korean War. Today, as a rule of thumb, those in category IV read at the fifth-to-eighth-grade level; those in category III, comparable to roughly the middle third of American youth, read at the eighth-to-twelfth-grade level; and those in category II have skills at the level of twelfth grade through some college. In the mid-seventies the achievement levels of those in categories III and IV would not have been so high.

Back then, statistically, women lost less productive time through pregnancy than men lost through drug abuse and time in jail. Now, in the mid-eighties, when the caliber of the enlisted male personnel has vastly improved, that is probably no longer true. The pregnant servicewoman is a problem no one is willing to face. The average Pentagon official or member of Congress would rather see a bearded PLO terrorist walk through the door with a live grenade in his hand than an action officer with a folder requiring a decision on the pregnancy issue.

The problem of the survivability of all our strategic forces, Minutemen, submarine-launched missiles and bombers, is further complicated by the Tooth-to-Tail fallacy. Most scenarios of how the Soviets would attack our strategic forces assume that their nuclear missiles will go after our teeth: our missile silos and submarines. But what if they go after the tail, the centers that have the firing codes that will enable these missiles to be launched? Suppose they concentrate their nuclear fires on such command centers as Oscar One or the NEACP (National Emergency Airborne Command Post) aircraft that contains all the firing codes.

This aircraft was moved only last year from Andrews Air Force base in Maryland, where it could be reached in seven minutes by a Soviet missile fired from a Yankee-class submarine off our coast, to Grissom Air Force base in Indiana. This happened after a test run by the National Security Council under President Carter uncovered the fact that while a great many U.S. land-based and submarine-based missiles had survived a theoretical Soviet attack, they could not be fired because they had been, in the defense argot, "decapitated." The command and control centers that would transmit their firing codes and targeting orders had either been destroyed or had their ability to transmit messages knocked out by the electromagnetic impulses of high-altitude nuclear explosions.

Again, we had so focused on what was happening to the teeth that the vulnerability of the equally important tail had been overlooked. When I first observed this phenomenon back in 1959, I rhetorically asked: "Does America really plan to use its nuclear arms. . . ? There are definite physical signs that indicate America won't." That situation hasn't changed greatly. Paradoxically, since reassuring the Soviets that we do not plan a first strike is important, this illogical posture has advantages.

We concentrate our war plans on attacking vital parts of the Soviet tail, such as headquarters, rail centers, and vital bridges. Should we not assume that they are wise enough to do the same? The evidence indicates that they do. In 1978 the Soviets staged a satellite "kill" when they successfully crashed one of their space satellites into another. This embarrassed the Defense Department, as top officials there, led by Defense Secretary Harold Brown, had been saying that no killer satellites would be deployed for a number of years. Further, the much-touted Air Force radars of NORAD (North American Aerospace Defense Command) had missed the satellite intercept. The event had been discovered by a group of amateurs in Kettering, England.

Shortly after the successful Soviet intercept I visited Cheyenne Mountain. This is the famous Air Force Headquarters Under the Mountain, mythic home of NORAD, whose computers and radars are meant to keep track of everything that happens in the air and in space that threatens America. One enters this latter-day Niffeleheim through a tunnel cut into the mountainside that is rather less finished than an average automobile tunnel—the lights are few, the center line is worn, the rock walls are lumpy and bare.

Once again you think, as you did when you descended into the Minuteman command post, Hollywood does this better. A movie set of NORAD would look less dingy and neglected. Inside the protected headquarters one can occasionally see the great springs on which the rooms rest to take the shock of a close nuclear hit. The rooms are smaller than expected and are crammed with computers and computer screens. Naturally, when a reporter is there the screens don't show much. The command screen was displaying the weather over the Soviet missile bases. Still, everyone seems to breathe a little harder than normal under the mountain.

I had expected to find NORAD concerned over its failure to detect the satellite intercept and frantically scrambling to find answers to the problem. Instead I found vast indifference. The thirty-nine computer systems and seven operations centers of NORAD's under-the-mountain world have three missions: attack warning, sovereign air space control, and space surveillance. I got the feeling, from the length of time the briefers spent explaining each one, from the size of the room where each mission was monitored, and from the relative rank of the people in the rooms, that space surveillance came last. That attack warning was still thought about in terms of spotting approaching bombers. The junior officers, who were radar and missile experts and almost to a man nonfliers, talking off the record, were both concerned about and eloquent on the shortcomings of U.S. missile and satellite defense. But the senior officers, colonels and generals, all of whom were fliers, never mentioned the problem. Their concern during my visit was to enlist my support for the interceptor aircraft that would replace the F-16, a rather dubious project in the missile age.

Once again I was in the presence of KAFCA. These new space- and strategic-weapons systems, where the action will be, threaten established weapons systems like the aircraft carrier, the bomber fleet, or fighter-interceptors, so able officers fight shy of assignments to the new programs; their development is often left to juniors. The war-as-a-game syndrome reinforces this. Real men should fight in traditional, predictable ways. Several times as I worked on this book naval aviators told me in effect: "The submariners are getting too much money and too many promotions. We pilots have fought two wars since World War II; and no submariner has been under attack."

The Air Force's answer to the increased age and vulnerability of the Minuteman system is the 12-story-high MX missile. Several of the faulty strands that run through our defenses have unfortunately affected the design of the MX. The Minuteman program was assisted by an internationally famous team of scientists. The MX was largely designed by a team of Air Force colonels. I have spent quite a bit of time in both Washington and Santa Barbara, California, with these dedicated officers. Their commanding general for a long period was John W. Hepfer, who has won prizes for his contributions to the theory and design of inertial navigation systems. However, I am certain all these men would have welcomed more assistance. But in the post-Vietnam world in which the MX was conceived, the Great Divorce made scientific help from academia all but impossible to obtain.

Interservice/Intraservice Rivalry also played a part in the development of the MX, and in the alternatives currently being considered by defense task forces and Congress. Both the Navy and the Air Force are concerned that the replacement for the

Minuteman does not threaten their service. The Air Force wishes to be certain the new missile remains definitely an Air Force weapon. The Navy does not want the new missile to infringe on the autonomy of its strategic role.

For example, serious consideration was never given to hiding the MXs in a number of old freighters cruising the oceans. If this had been done, our enemies would never have been sure which freighters held the real missiles, which the dummies. The freighters are already constructed and sitting anchored as a moth-ball fleet. Rehabilitating such ships would have been a lot cheaper and more feasible than pouring all that concrete, and the vessels would have been ready earlier. But the Air Force cannot allow this alternative to be considered, because it would then at least have to share control of these new missiles with the Navy and might lose command over them altogether. Nor can the Navy consider such a system, because the funds for it might come out of money for its cherished aircraft carriers. Further, a missile carried by surface ships might involve some Air Force control over such weapons and so leash traditional naval autonomy.

Back in the summer of 1959 a number of scientists were gathered together outside Boston at the National Academy of Arts and Sciences Summer Study on Arms Control. The method favored by the majority to make missiles secure in the eighties was to have a certain number of ICBMs airborne at all times in slow-flying, propeller-driven planes. The theory behind this was that the airborne mobility of the missiles would make them difficult to target and so difficult to destroy. To be sure, there are drawbacks to this system. The aircraft burn a great deal of fuel; there is a danger of crashes; it is difficult to make ICBMs accurate when they are so extremely mobile. But both Interservice and Intraservice Rivalry make this a weapons system today's Pentagon cannot evaluate. The Air Force missileers, many of whom are not pilots, are not particularly keen to devise another reason for pilots to get the choice jobs in the missile command. And since the planes that would carry such weapons aloft are slow, fuel-efficient, propeller-driven aircraft, pilots, who would rather fly jets, are not too enthusiastic either.

The Air Force insists that all such airborne missiles be air-launched, that is, pulled out of the flying plane by a gigantic parachute and then fired at their distant targets as they drift earthward. This requirement makes the missiles far more expensive and difficult to design. Why is it there? There are deserts, highways, and airfields all over the United States on which the planes could land after nuclear attack and fire their missiles from the ground. Some of these places are going to be highly radioactive and genuinely unpleasant; but so is most of the post-attack world. Is Air Force insistence that the missile must be launched while the plane is aloft an effort to make certain the strategic-missile mission stays all–Air Force? To ensure that the Army never again has a chance to get a handle on such weapons?

In arguing for the land-based MX rather than for mobile flying missiles, the Air Force always assumes the missile-carrying planes will fly only over land. That increases the problems they have with possible plane crashes. The reason for the artificial restriction to overland flight is obvious: Venture out over any body of water larger than a mud puddle and the alert eye of an admiral will see a Navy mission. You don't get to be a general in the Air Force without foreseeing that threat.

I am not certain that putting mobile missiles on freighters or flying them through the air is a valid solution at present. They may not be, though I happen to favor the airborne system. The important point is that the strategic weapons most vital to our defenses for the rest of this century cannot be evaluated on their merits inside today's Department of Defense.

In the warm ocean off Mayport, Florida, between the gray inshore shallows and the clear blues of the Gulf Stream, the carrier USS *Saratoga* is launching and recovering planes. This is Washington's Birthday, 1983. The *Saratoga* has just been refitted in the Philadelphia naval yard and is on her shakedown cruise. At the same time the ship is training and qualifying some new and some out-of-practice pilots for carrier operations. The carrier was built in the early fifties. As each weapons system becomes more and more expensive, the number of modifications that it can receive becomes vitally important. At this time of rapid technological change, weapons tend to become obsolete fast—just as do other products at the forefront of technology, like home computers. The more a weapon is designed for a specific mission or job, the better it will probably perform that mission. And if it is built to do only one thing, it will probably be less expensive. At the same time, such a weapon is more likely to pass rapidly into obsolescence. The more general the weapon design, the greater the likelihood that the weapon will not do anything particularly well and will be expensive, but it will probably be more adaptable to change and therefore have a longer practical life. This produces an always-tantalizing balance between the immediate cost and effectiveness of weapons and their effectiveness and cost in the longer term.

During the day the launching and recovery of aircraft have gone smoothly. Both the new pilots and the older ones, who are re-qualifying for carrier operations after time spent ashore, success-fully arrive and depart in the "controlled crashes" that are the hallmark of carrier landings. Like martins chasing a huge hawk, the 42,000-pound A-7 Corsairs turn onto the final approach path and line themselves up with the carrier deck, relatively stable today in the calm spring seas. Little squirts of black smoke spout out their tail pipes, like jets of cuttlefish ink, as pilots add bursts of power to control their descent. The plane slams onto the deck and comes to a quivering halt straining against the arresting wire, engines shrieking at full power. Immediately after hitting the deck the jet goes to full power just in case the plane's tail hook has not grabbed the arresting wire. Unless the engines are at full power and the plane is handled perfectly, it will crash into the sea as the pilot goes round again to attempt another landing. In daylight most of the plane's hooks grabbed the wire on the first pass. Not so tonight.

On board a carrier at the rear (stern) of the flight deck are three arresting wires. On the bottom of a carrier plane is a hook that grabs one of these wires as the plane lands. Ideally, when a pilot lands perfectly, his hook grabs the rearmost of the arresting wires, the one closest to the stern of the ship. Even in the day-light that wire is easy to miss. There is an almost overpowering urge to land just a tad long, be certain one is landing on the deck, not hitting the carrier's stern. Average pilots have a tendency to hook onto the second wire.

Tonight on the *Saratoga* the second and third wires are "inop," not working. The middle wire got handled wrong during the daylight landings and part of it frayed. The shock-absorbing cylinder on the forward wire is leaking. The Readiness/Tooth-to-Tail problem and the Great Divorce are all present, and the result is an absence of cable mechanics. To land successfully, a pilot must hook the sternmost wire or go round and try once more. A lieutenant commander, carrier-qualifying after a few years on shore, hooks the rearmost wire three times in succession. His plane is manhandled to the elevator and descends to the hangar floor. He is through for the night.

The other pilots are not so precise. They slam onto the deck, engine roaring, miss the wire, race toward the bow, painfully climb into the air again. Some are hooking the wire every other time. Some have hooked it once in four tries. Standing in Primary Fly, a platform at the rear of the carrier's superstructure over-looking the flight deck, one can almost feel the confidence of the pilots ebbing as they miss and take off again into the night.

A commander standing near me recalls how once, on patrol off Vietnam, in a night landing he landed hard, missed the wires, and as his plane raced across the deck, all his lights went out. As his plane clawed its way back up into the dark, he was left with nothing but his emergency flashlight by which to read his vital instruments. Fortunately, he was flying by the book and had his flashlight correctly hooked to his life belt and turned on. Night carrier flying is for real, even when not under fire.

Now, beside me in Primary Fly, an argument is in progress between two lieutenant commanders about one of the pilots. (Often you learn as much by just standing and looking as by asking questions.) The discussion is between the flight officer responsible for the *Saratoga*'s air operation and the commander of the squadron whose pilots are qualifying for night carrier operations. The flight officer thinks one of the pilot's skills are not enough for him to attempt another night landing. He wants that pilot to fly back to the shore and land. His squadron leader wants the pilot to have more opportunity to qualify.

"He's not coming round to land on this carrier again."

"He did all right this morning. Look in the log book. He's just a little rocky."

"You saw his approach speed last time." There is a Doppler radar in the Primary Fly console that records the approach speed of the landing aircraft. A too-low approach speed and the plane drops out of the sky into the sea. Or it drops out of the sky and creams the carrier as it turns into a big flaming ball.

"He picked it up at the end."

"Yeah, and missed completely. He is not coming round again."

"He's got plenty of gas for a couple more passes and still make the beach. Give him one more."

"No. He's going to cream this ship."

The pilot gets ordered back to the beach.

I leave Primary Fly and descend into the bowels of the *Saratoga* to the radar and computer room, the electronic warfare center. As I show my ship's pass to marines guarding various layers of the ship, I muse on how little carrier operations have changed over the years. I first was flown onto a carrier during the Korean War. Since then the planes have grown faster, more complex, heavier, and larger. So have the carriers. But their method of operation, their tactics, have remained basically the same. I am concerned over the efficiency of weapons systems that merely grow larger while their pattern of use remains the same. Are they iceboxes in a world of refrigerators? I'm not saying this to pick on the carriers. I have the same feelings about large air bases and elaborate military headquarters: that these expensive, highly visible concentrations of national wealth and power are becoming more of a vulnerable liability than an effective weapons system. All this is reinforced by the new face of naval warfare seen in 1983, as the British fought to retake the Falklands.

The twenty-fifth of May, 1983, had dawned much as previous days off the Falkland Islands, bitter cold, windy, and for the British ships, dangerously clear. Crews on board a British radar picketship actually saw the red glow of an Exocet missile as it skimmed the sea at supersonic speed toward the main body of the naval task force. The missile was headed for one of two British aircraft carriers, the *Invincible*, a vital part of British seapower. The *Invincible* and the other fighting ships in the task force fired their weapons at the incoming Argentine missile and, more important, fired "chaff," strips of aluminum cut to the proper lengths, to confuse the missile's radar. The antimissile missiles missed; the chaff worked.

Several observers later claimed to have seen the Argentine missile almost hesitate, trying to figure out the real from the bogus targets. Two miles away, the *Atlantic Conveyor*, the primary resupply ship of the British Falklands forces, was carrying helicopters and other supplies critically needed by the troops ashore. Because she was seen as tail, not tooth, that ship had not been issued antimissile weapons or chaff, though the vital supplies she carried would make her loss as serious to the British forces as if they had lost a fighting ship. The Exocet found the *Atlantic Conveyor* and fatally struck home, making the battle for the

Falklands even closer. Three weeks earlier a destroyer, the $175 million *Sheffield*, in spite of the antimissile gear it carried, had been sunk by another $500,000 Exocet.

The Falkland battle confirmed what many had believed, that inside a ship's electronic warfare center, its radar and computer rooms, is where the ship's captain will win or lose his war. A year before the Falklands campaign, I was on a sister ship of the HMS *Sheffield*. The young officers on board the ship complained to me that the location of the radar and computer center was too vulnerable: It was on the upper deck right behind the bridge. "It's the senior officers who design the ships," they explained. "They think they are going to be moving between the electronic warfare center and the bridge. You won't see anything from the bridge." That proved true. Ship captains in the Falklands found that they fought their ships from the electronic warfare centers.

The electronic warfare center of the *Saratoga* is a series of darkened rooms located in relative safety on a lower deck. Here, bank upon bank of computer screens, each about a foot in diameter, keep track of the outside world around the carrier. The scene is even more cramped and complex than that in a major metropolitan air traffic control center. There are screens that track submarines under water, screens that track distant, high-flying aircraft, others that track lower-flying aircraft and missiles in the vicinity of the ship, screens that control the firing of guns, screens that control the firing of missiles, screens that show all these data at once. Most of those in the center are keen on their work because the week before they watched two Russian reconnaissance "Bear" aircraft track their ship "for real." I ask if they will please run a simulated three-missile low-level attack on the carrier for me. They will be glad to, though would I please remember that they are a new crew and have not yet had much chance to practice missile defense.

One of the computer programmers calls up a practice three-missile attack on the carrier. I watch the little dots on the screen before me move toward our ship and get identified as hostile, while on their screens nearby two petty officers try to bring the *Saratoga*'s own missiles to bear on the hostiles. In this computer game they get two out of three. That's all right; as they said, they are new and aware they need more training.

Forward in the radar control room is a captain's swivel chair with several sets of consoles pressing in around it, like the multifaceted eyes of a huge spider. These particular consoles are designed to bring all the battle information together so the captain can fight the carrier. I ask the men if the captain comes down to train with them. "Now and then," they report, but without much conviction. Later, I ask Captain L. G. Perry if he thinks in an emergency he will be fighting his ship from the bridge above the flight deck or from the radar and computer room.

"The bridge," he replies without hesitation.

A recently retired admiral is on board the *Saratoga* at the same time as I am. Don't I think, he asks, that the British admiral fighting in the Falklands would have preferred two large carriers like this rather than the two small jump-jet carriers he possessed?

I reply politely that that is not really the question at issue. With weapons costs so great, would the British admiral have preferred one carrier like this or two such carriers as he had? The admiral ponders that one and answers with a noncommital "Humph."

The question is not just one of cost. The more war-fighting assets you gather in one place, the more lucrative target you make for the enemy, the easier it is for him to find that target, and the more effort he will expend to kill it. And today, if you can find it and want to kill it, you can kill it. Again, I should repeat, this is true not just of big ships like this carrier but of big headquarters, big air bases, and, unfortunately, large concentrations of marines in one building in Beirut. The face of warfare is changing faster than the minds of many warriors.

For example, in 1983 the Navy complained at having to keep one of its large carriers off the relatively tranquil coast of Lebanon. The admirals were right; the risk was out of all proportion to the gain. While off Lebanon, the carrier could not perform its strategic nuclear mission, the purpose for which its gigantic keel was laid. A small carrier could have supported the Marine presence in Lebanon at much less risk. What is more, several small carriers would have permitted rotation of ships. Then the crews could have seen their families more often and morale would have been raised and readiness improved.

At present the Navy justifies its need for carriers in two ways: first, as part of the strategic nuclear strike force; second, as a method of applying conventional power about the free world periphery. The problem is that these two missions require very different sizes of ships. The dominant union in the Navy, the brown-shoe carrier admirals, have, as we have seen, historically regarded the strategic nuclear mission as vital to the Navy's interests. However, the admirals also justify the purchase of supercarriers that can handle the heavy aircraft needed for nuclear war by saying such ships are necessary to help maintain peace about the periphery. Yet when a peacekeeping mission arrives, the admirals argue that large carriers are too vulnerable in such a role and that such use detracts from their strategic mission. And Congress, which would like to have mobile forces to use in limited conventional wars in places of vital interest to the United States, like the Middle East, finds that instead of such forces the Navy has added three supercarrier groups at $17 billion apiece.

So the admirals and the civilian naval leaders press toward the 600-ship Navy (up from 479 ships in 1980), in the face of the evidence from the Falklands about the effects of even the early smart weapons. And they do not increase proportionally the effectiveness of the submarine fleet, still believing missile submarines somehow "not really Navy." While receiving the lion's share of the defense funds for the 600-ship Navy, the admirals have deferred spending for new communications aircraft needed to control the missile submarines at sea.

In a corner of a London club a senior British admiral and Ministry of Defense official are asking me questions. They have read some of my pieces and share my concerns about the problem of massing forces—naval, air, or ground—in the satellite age. Do I know a high U.S. Defense official, F. D., they ask?

Yes, I do. Fairly well. The two Britishers would like to set up a private, "backdoor," channel of communications to this Pentagon official about an American naval weapons project, Arapahoe, an idea in which the British Navy believes, but which it doesn't have the money to push by itself. However, they are willing to help the American Navy test the Arapahoe concept; and they would like F. D.'s "help in getting the ball rolling." I have felt for some time that Arapahoe should be tested, so I agree with the two men and set up the backdoor channel. But three years later the Arapahoe project still has not developed.

Arapahoe provides a new approach to getting supplies into a war area, particularly Europe or the Middle East. The old World War II convoy system merely provides the enemy with a gigantic target. The other side, easily locating the supply ship convoy by satellite, can concentrate against it submarines with guided torpedoes and bombers with guided missiles. Arapahoe, in contrast, puts on each freighter an antisubmarine helicopter package— one or two antisubmarine helicopters, some missile spoofers, and a cratelike hangar to house all this. Then the freighters are sent out at random across the ocean. Because there is no concentration, and therefore no big target, the enemy has to divide his forces to intercept the freighters. And when the submarine finds the freighter, the helicopter has a good chance of destroying the sub. Whereas in attacking the convoy the enemy might lose one submarine for every ten freighters, a winning ratio for him, under Arapahoe he might lose one sub for every three freighters, a losing ratio for him.

To me, the idea makes total sense in the age of accurate weapons, when not becoming a lucrative target has become vital. Further the idea is, or should be, playing into America's warfighting strengths, for it is flexible and puts a premium on individual action by thoughtful junior commanders. Instead of being part of a vast concentration of forces rigidly controlled by a senior commander who keeps the reins in his hands, each little unit of ship and helicopter has its own fate in its own hands, relying on the brains, courage, training, and discipline of the junior officers and men on board. "An entrepreneurial weapons system" is the buzz phrase for such projects. However, senior admirals fight Arapahoe precisely because it diminishes their control.

A year and a half later I was talking about Arapahoe to a Navy captain, one who has risen through the fighter pilot route. That problem is worse than I realized, he said, an illustration of the sad confusion within the Navy. It is all part of Intraservice, rather than Interservice, Rivalry. In the Navy, insiders refer to this rivalry as "the unionization of the Navy." The submariners in their union aren't speaking to the carrier admirals. The shore-based fliers are in another union and the "black-shoe Navy"— destroyers and missile frigates and cruiser men—are in another. On top of that, the Atlantic and Pacific fleets have different doctrines, and officers tend to go to the same fleet each time they draw sea duty. The Navy divides up its monies to satisfy the claims of those conflicting unions as much as for reasons of national defense.

No particular union wanted the responsibility for Arapahoe. Worse, each power center saw the project as a threat to the way it was planning to deal with hostile submarines. The shore-based fliers planned to use long-range aircraft. The carrier admirals said they were going to do the job with escort carriers. The destroyer, black-shoe, union said that ASW (Anti-Submarine Warfare) was a mission for their ships. Some genius thought of giving Arapahoe to the Naval Reserves. The Reserves, a minor and weak union, was interested in the idea; but the top Navy brass reminded the Reserve brass where their promotions came from, and the Reserves also dropped the program. To all the naval "unions" Arapahoe meant not a challenging new method of keeping open the seas and aiding American allies, but fewer large fighting ships and, therefore, slower promotions for themselves. The British Navy actually offered the American Navy a ship and $200,000 to help develop the program; still the American admirals could find neither money, people, nor time for Arapahoe.

The fate of Arapahoe and the problems of carrier size and poor communications with our missile submarines are important not just as horror stories. They illustrate what happens when the three services use their basic control of funds to frustrate the wishes of Congress or the Joint Chiefs. The final chapter of this book outlines a politically difficult but otherwise simple method of funding the missions—mobile tactical forces, strategic warfare, counterterrorism—rather than funding the services. This would not dilute civilian control over the armed services, as opponents claim, but rather prevent them from dividing the pie to suit their internal dynamics rather than the needs of the Giant.

It is difficult to think for any length of time about strategic nuclear weapons and other major weapons systems and remain "unmoved, cold, and to temptation slow." The weapons assert a hypnotic mastery over many, appearing to them as having "abolished history." Their awesome power causes some people to treat them as children do a new wonder, as something divorced from previous life. Over the years I have been struck by how often the discussion of nuclear weapons reveals more about the speaker's or writer's unconscious beliefs than about the weapons themselves.

There are those who argue nuclear wars can be successfully fought and won. They march into the briefing rooms of the military or academia with books full of options; these options are further subdivided, a, b, and c. Most who reason so I find bloodless and repressed men and women. These cerebral defense experts and leaders believe, no matter how much their own actions may belie such beliefs, that all the problems of the world can best be settled by rational thought. Questions of history, the world's complexity, and the human spirit they put to one side. For them the lives of the saints never happened. The proper application of power will always bring about the desired result.

Former Under Secretary of State George W. Ball has brilliantly described such men and women and their effects on military policy: "Even more influential than soldiers in shaping America's weapons policy has been an elite group of economists, mathematicians and political reactionists who, beginning in the 1950s, preempted the bomb as their special intellectual property, established themselves as a proprietary priesthood, and sought to impose logic on inherently irrational nuclear conflict. . . . The conduct and consequences of a nuclear exchange are, and must remain, pure speculation."

On the other side of the nuclear divide reside the total disarmers. In their passionate protestations of a higher rationality I hear the desperate pleas of those who fear they are about to lose control over their unconscious selves. Frightened by the violence of their turmoil, they fly to the world of Rousseau, where man is essentially good. If generals and barbed wire and nuclear weapons could be done away with, we could then reinvent the world and live in peace. They scorn any rational thought about warfare, believing such thought evil in itself. Joyce Carol Oates has accurately limned this attitude: "It is very tempting . . . this disavowal of intelligence, this sub-religious gesture of surrender to the senses and emotions, to death."

Naturally, I hope that those of us advocating slow, practical steps toward strategic forces that are both ready and strong but not overly threatening—and that are limited by arms control agreements of mutual benefit—are the Solomons or George Washingtons of this time. However, in moments of discouragement I see us as no more effective than Prince Hamlet, or worse, Polonius.

NINE

Report
from the Field

The prevention of nuclear war and the defense of the United States, like Caesar's Gaul, divides into three parts. These are: (1) our strategic nuclear forces; (2) treaties of arms limitation and control that benefit all parties; and (3) our conventional, or nonnuclear, forces. These last are those parts of the armed services that, without using nuclear weapons, can respond to a variety of threats, ranging from plane hijackings through the Russian attempt to place missiles in Cuba during the Kennedy administration to a possible Soviet invasion of Western Europe. If such pressures can be countered only by America's resort to nuclear weapons, then the United States must either back down or initiate nuclear war.

In the fall of each year, under a variety of names—Griffins Galore, Bold Guard, Cold Fire, Carbine Fortress, Saxon Drive—troops and tanks race down the streets, poke through the woods, and tear up the fields of West Germany—testing the forces of NATO. Overhead jets fright the ear as they streak 500 feet above the ground. The basic name for these annual exercises, now over thirty years old, is Reforger. Their object is to train everyone, from privates to generals; to test Readiness; and to demonstrate a united determination to defend Europe.

To follow these exercises for a number of years is to watch the ebb and flow of American ability to fight a conventional war. Today you see improvement everywhere. Gone are the vacant faces, black and white, with the slightly slack jaws and dead eyes that in the mid to late seventies peered out from the tank hatches and infantry fighting vehicles. In those perilous times such men, high school dropouts reading at barely the fifth-grade level, numb to discipline, alien to responsibility, and overwhelmed by the complexity of their equipment would, after two years in the Army, often be commanding tanks and squads. There was no one else.

From the end of the Vietnam War until 1978, soldiers were murdering their officers and destroying their equipment, drugs were rampant, weapons and facilities were neglected and poorly maintained. Studies conducted during World War II had shown that only 16 percent of those with merely an eighth-grade education or less made outstanding combat performers, while 64 percent of those with a high school degree or better did well in combat. Yet until the rising civilian unemployment of the 1978 recession caused an improvement in the caliber of military volunteers, roughly 40 percent of the Army's yearly intake read at only the fifth-grade level. And with most of the press uninterested or actually hostile to the military, few were reporting these facts.

The armed services themselves were lying—there is no polite word for it—about how ready their forces were. Captain Peter Moore, who resigned from the Army in the late seventies, described what happened in his infantry battalion in Germany: "The infantry companies in my brigade gave the basic rifle marksmanship test annually to soldiers assigned the rifle. . . . A large part of each company would flunk, but each company training office would fabricate a set of scorecards showing that everyone passed. . . . The unit would be deemed perfect in marksmanship."

In 1979, at the bar of an officers' club, two discouraged majors, both West Point graduates, sought me out to tell me about their experiences as part of a unit flown to Europe during the fall NATO maneuvers. The tanks, Sheridans, that their brigade drew out of the warehouses when they got to Germany would neither run nor shoot. But the records attached to the tanks said they did both; and the brigade commander didn't want it on his record that they did neither. So the Sheridans were winched onto tank transporters and trucked to the German firing range.

There they were winched off the trucks, towed into firing positions, hooked up to generators, since their own electrical systems were not working, and fired. Then they were winched back onto the transporters, trucked back to the warehouses, winched off the trucks and back into storage, and certified once again ready for combat. "Those tanks were in such bad shape that we thought someone would get killed firing them. So he and I"—the major talking indicated his fellow officer—"fired all of them ourselves."

About the same time the general commanding an Army division in Europe told me his men had achieved hits 95 percent of the time with the hand-held, infrared guided antiaircraft missile, the Redeye. His battalion commanders all confirmed this, without so much as a wink. Later, out on the range, I found out the reason for the good scores. The little flying drones at which the men were shooting had been slowed down to sixty miles an hour. At speeds closer to that of an attacking aircraft, too many soldiers had missed the targets. I was reminded of all those hamlet evaluation statistics that showed us winning in Vietnam.

In 1977 I spent a morning on maneuvers with a tank company of the 2nd Armored Division, which was down to one tank and half its attached infantry vehicles after three days. (Think what would have happened if someone had shot at them.) The lieutenant in command had not slept for those three days. He had no trained sergeants to work while he slept. As I stood on a crossroads with him in the rain, white-banded umpires came up and declared him out of action. What men he had left were facing the wrong way and shooting up his own side. Yet five miles away, the general who commanded his brigade had assured me earlier that morning that 95 percent of his vehicles were in operation. And back at the Pentagon the Carter-appointed officials were insisting that the volunteer army worked.

Until 1982 the United States finished last or next to last in the Canadian Cup, the live-fire contest established in 1977 between the top tank companies of the various NATO nations. At one time the senior American officers became so discouraged by the United States' continuously miserable showing that they considered dropping out of the competition. During the same period U.S. Air Force target scores in key events dropped below those of the British and the West Germans. Then, in 1983, the United States' new M-1 tanks finished second, while an American tank company with the old M-60s tied for first. By 1984, instead of dreading the challenge of the competition, different captains and colonels would tell me privately that this year, by God, their outfit, which was the best damn tank unit in NATO, was going to win that cup. I had not heard words of that kind spoken with passionate sincerity for sixteen years—since 1968, before the Tet offensive.

In 1976 the Army War College polled a group of outstanding junior officers about the problems of the Army. Seventy percent agreed with the statement that reports about how ready a unit was to fight were "unreal, inflated and biased . . . [and] held in disrepute by the Army personnel most familiar with [them]." Another report two years later from the Army's own Military History Institute says: "The willingness to compromise personal integrity, to lie to superiors, and to do so shamelessly in the certain knowledge that subordinates, peers and the very superiors they sought to please would all know they were lying has been corrosive in the extreme."

Among the non-American forces in NATO, forces that will supply 80 percent of the aircraft and 85 percent of the ground troops in the first week of a European conflict (a fact the U.S. Congress often conveniently forgets), there is a code phrase. That code phrase is "the Gretchen Frage." The Gretchen Frage, Gretchen's question, is a German expression that means "What is the essential reality of the situation?" It comes from Goethe's *Faust*, in which, after a lengthy and highly abstract philosophical discussion by Faust about good and evil, Gretchen asks Faust where he personally stands with his God. Faust cannot answer. When NATO officers, other than Americans, say, "That's the Gretchen Frage," they mean "Will the American Army fight? Are the morale and training of the average U.S. soldier good enough to hold up under the pressures of combat?" Or, as a British general bluntly put it to me, "Do you think your undisciplined city boys can take on their disciplined farm boys?"

I do not wish to make it seem as if all the problems lie with the Army alone. Here is part of a letter from the late 1970s sent anonymously by a group of fighter pilots to the Air Force Chief of Staff. I was given a copy one night by a group of majors and captains with whom I had been flying for a couple of days.

"Well I quit," the letter begins.

I don't mind the duty or the hours. That's what I signed on for.
I've been downtown and seen the elephant. I have watched my
buddies roll up in fireballs. I understand. It comes with the
territory. I can do it . . . but I won't. I'm too tired, not of the
job, just the Air Force. Tired of the extremely poor leadership
and motivational ability of our senior staffers and commanders.
. . . Our operational squadrons aren't worth a damn. They die
wholesale every time the Aggressors deploy. [The Aggressors are
a crack U.S. squadron that uses Russian tactics to train other
squadrons.] Meanwhile you lie about the takeoff times so it
isn't an operational or a maintenance late. . . . You lie about
your operational capability because you are afraid to report you
don't have the sorties to hack it. I listened to a three star General
look a roomful of us in the face and say that he "did not
realize that pencil-whipping records was done in the Air Force."
It was embarrassing. TAC fixed the experience ratio problem by
lowering the number of hours it took to be experienced. . . . It's
the party line, no issues, no controversy, yes sir, no sir, three bags
full sir . . . integrity a mockery.

Our Vietnam defeat and the Great Divorce produced grave
Gretchen Frage problems in all three armed services. Yet the
improvements in our conventional forces are also undeniable
and impressive.

In 1982 I attended a German Rotary Club luncheon at Bad
Mergentheim, a lovely medieval town near Würzburg, which was
in the middle of the maneuver area. Afterward several town
leaders came up to me and asked me to be sure to report how
much the American Army had improved—the vehicles not driving across their crops, knocking down their houses, tearing up
their orchards; the soldiers no longer stealing their farm animals
and chasing their daughters.

In 1984 a German panzer colonel I have known for ten years
who had been sharply critical of the American infantry and
tankers used the word "unbelievable" in describing the improvement in the American tank regiment with which his regiment
had been teamed. Driving between Tauberbischofsheim and
Bad Mergentheim at night over secondary roads I approached
from the rear and then passed a tank column of the 5th Mechanized Infantry Division. Each tank had someone looking backward
to wave me by when safe. I had not dared "jump" an American
tank column at night since the late sixties.

In 1980 the tank company I rode with lost eleven of its twenty tanks in three days of maneuver through mechanical failure. The company I rode with in 1983 lost only two tanks in three days. Then in 1984 both the two tank companies I watched had all their tanks in action by the middle of the second week. And the one infantry company I was with also kept all its Bradley fighting vehicles in action throughout the entire maneuver. There were sergeants and even gunners with five, six, even eight years inside the tanks. In 1985 most of the tanks one saw broken down beside the road had soldiers with tools working on them, while others directed traffic. Four years before, there were far more broken-down vehicles and soldiers were sitting on them smoking.

Electronic warfare is another area in which to study the state of Readiness. In 1980, the Electronic Warfare Intelligence (EWI) battalion I visited had no one in it who spoke Russian well enough to monitor Soviet military radio traffic. Nor did they have tape recordings of the maneuvers of Warsaw Pact forces on which to practice. In 1984, the EWI battalion I visited had the required language experts speaking Russian or German, and they practiced by analyzing tapes of actual Soviet maneuvers. The new "Quick Fix" direction-finding equipment (which locates enemy units more speedily and accurately) had arrived; and further, the information gained was being used by senior commanders. The Blue Force commander sent his Rangers by helicopter at night to destroy the Orange Force main supply center, located by radio intercept. Two years earlier, neither the equipment, doctrine, techniques, nor will would have been present for such an operation. The next day the Orange Forces retaliated by knocking out the Blue Force headquarters with a simulated guided missile fired on the basis of their signal intelligence intercepts and direction-finding, a maneuver first.

Even Interservice Rivalry, while still debilitatingly present, has declined. In 1982 the Hawk antiaircraft missile company that I visited had no idea when or if they were about to be attacked, or what planes were friend or foe. Their own long-range radar had broken and they had only telephone communication with their battalion headquarters. By 1984 the firing batteries of the 652nd Hawk Battalion were receiving on their TV screens inside their equipment-jammed trucks pictures of all the aircraft flying in Western Europe. These came to them by a series of data links from 4th Allied Tactical Air Force headquarters.

That same year, inside a dripping tent about a quarter of a bus-length in size, hidden in a pine forest, I stood on the damp pine needles and watched while General Glenn K. Otis, commander of the Army forces in Europe, persistently questioned a very unhappy Army captain. The captain was the air space coordination officer of a maneuvering division and had given the troops in his area the wrong location of the air corridors through which friendly Air Force planes would fly. Two years before there was no such officer in a division headquarters, nor would a senior Army general have cared enough about Air Force problems to make the fact they had been neglected the centerpiece of his visit.

When the Air Force wished to prepare its senior commanders in Europe for the air/electronic battle, it created the Warrior Preparation Center. The center, with its complex computers and sixty visual terminals, was constructed in two years at a cost of $15 million and is housed at Einsiedlerhof Air Station outside of Kaiserslautern in two closely guarded former warehouses. When senior Army officers in Europe learned of the project, they realized its value and offered to pay half the construction costs out of Army funds if the land battle could be included. The result was a joint service project: The center's computers simulate the ground war, the air war, the electronic war, and the intelligence problems all at once. When an Army corps and a tactical air force play in a maneuver, the Air Force and Army officers, some 350 of them, plug into the center the actual vans and equipment they would use in combat. The "free" maneuvers—that is, there is no set script about who will win or lose—are played against intelligence officers and civilians who are experts in Russian tactics and strategy, some of them former officers in the Soviet and satellite forces.

The Air Force fighter pilot in charge of the center showed off the ground battle simulation with the same pride with which he displayed the air battle. He explained that the computers even simulate the delays that will occur when the Army has lost all its new M-1 tanks in battle and has to bring the old M-60s out of warehouses to fight. The computers take into account the hours the surviving M-1 crews will need to learn to operate the M-60s efficiently. When an Air Force pilot enthusiastically explains tank crew cross-training and an Army commander admonishes an officer for not providing aircraft no-fire zones, Army/Air Force cooperation has dramatically increased.

The basic reasons for such improvements are more money and the better caliber of recruits joining the services since the 1978 recession. When defense officials and officers say that things are much better, they are telling the truth. When they say this is the best Army, Navy, or Air Force that the United States has ever fielded, they are talking nonsense.

How good things are today depends on your benchmark. Measured against the late seventies and even 1980, things are much better. Back then, only 68 percent of the armed forces' recruits were high school graduates. In 1984, 93 percent of the recruits were high school graduates and 4 percent had some college. The armed services, particularly the Army, used the fresh supply of abler people as an opportunity for ruthlessly weeding out the misfits. Earlier, the marginally able had to be retained to fill numerical quotas. However, while the caliber of those entering has improved, it remains true that one out of five soldiers in the Army is in category IV, the lowest acceptable category; some are barely able to read and write.

If one takes 1964 as the base, one finds decline rather than progress. To begin with the most obvious, the 1964 Army was almost twice as large as today's. Then, the Army was not accepting any category IVs, and 20 percent of those serving had some college. The Army had veteran noncoms many of whom had seen service in both World War II and Korea; and with the draft, a cross section of the country was present in the ranks. Twelve percent of the soldiers were black in 1964, as compared with 31 percent today; and 1 percent were female, compared with 10 percent today. Then, at that time the American forces alone possessed tactical nuclear weapons to back up their military might. On the ground, the Russians had 140 divisions largely equipped with World War II weapons, as against the 170 divisions with modern weapons that they have today.

Further, 1984, the year officials use in pointing to the excellent results of the all-volunteer force, appears to have been the peak quality year. Already standards are starting to slip as the number of volunteers begins to decline. The Army, traditionally the service that has the greatest difficulty attracting qualified volunteers, has decided to level off its strength at 781,000, instead of expanding as planned, because it can no longer find qualified recruits. The other services continue to expand; but there still exists no central authority to assign manpower where it is most needed.

Though we have improved since 1976–1978, we have far to go to return to 1964 standards. On the tank firing range, a muddy trail through fields and woods, U.S. crews get a passing score if they can identify a target and fire at it in forty seconds. In the real world you get about ten tense seconds. The crews I watched in 1980 were being scored as taking forty seconds though they were taking over a minute. On a close-to-identical range, German crews were averaging three seconds between the time the target popped and the time they fired. While we now have sergeants in our tank companies who average five years' experience, when I visited the antitank battalion of the 125th Panzer Brigade I found the junior sergeant had seven years' experience and the average was seventeen years. We have not fielded armed forces with such experience since before Vietnam.

One must also rank today's soldiers against the complexity of today's weapons. Take the tank, for example. In constant dollars, today's tank costs three times as much as a World War II fighter. And with its infrared sights, laser range-finders, and gun and missile weapons systems, that tank is a more complex weapons system than the World War II fighter and is more difficult to maintain. Yet that World War II fighter was commanded by a lieutenant who had, in theory, the equivalent of two years of college. Today's tank is commanded by a sergeant, as in World War II, but that sergeant who quite probably has less education than his World War II counterpart. The Israelis take their ablest and most aggressive draftees and select the top 5 percent to go to a special school for tank commanders. In 1980 our tank commanders averaged below the top 40 percent of all draftees on the general aptitude tests. To disguise these deficiencies in crew selection and professionalism, we devise easier tests for our men.

Finally, one must look behind the statistics at what is happening inside the units themselves. Take the soldiers—one out of five—in category IV. Those in this category are apt to have reenlisted in the Army, and since seniority is an important factor in military promotions, these men are often noncommissioned officers in command of the newer, often brighter soldiers. This creates a series of problems. The brighter recruits resent serving under the generally less able sergeants. The officers would like to retain the brighter new recruits by promoting them; but the way is blocked by the sergeants who enlisted back in the seventies. Whether the less able sergeants are allowed to stay or are removed, turmoil and resentment build inside a unit. Morale has certainly improved, but officers still must spend a great deal of time working around a problem that should not have been there in the first place. Asked today what their number-one problem is, officers no longer talk about crime and drugs, which is certainly progress. Their constant new concern is: "My privates are brighter than my sergeants."

To learn how well the Army and Air Force are equipped to fight a conventional war you have to go into the field and look. To best watch the NATO fall maneuvers you employ the same strategy by which you picked the SAC bomber *Biggs 99* in which to fly. You try to keep people guessing where you will turn up. The armed services lay on elaborate press flights to Europe and have tours available when you get there. Though the tours can be enlightening, mostly you see what "they" want you to see. There are other ways to go.

It's 1982 and I am in an old, large, hot hangar at Fort Bragg, North Carolina, about to fly across the Atlantic with the 2nd platoon of the antitank company of the 3rd Brigade of the 82nd Airborne Division. We are flight 160: sixty-nine of us Pacs, as passengers are called, and six jeeps with antitank missiles mounted on them, and some miscellaneous baggage. The troops are in their battle-green camouflage uniforms, the "green machine" dress. Outside, an Air Force plane waits for us, an extended C-121B, of the 60th Wing of the Military Air Transport Command, capable of aerial refueling. Four hours ago we were to leave immediately. We are still here. However, I have been able to convince the MPs searching our baggage for forbidden drugs that a lone reporter's scotch is not included in the confiscatory category. After all, the flight will take eleven hours.

As we are finally about to load up it is found that the vehicles for the 1st Platoon have been loaded on the plane for the 2nd Platoon and vice versa. The combined Army/Air Force paperwork to rectify that error may take another three hours. Fortunately, two sergeants solve the problem by switching just the six drivers from the two platoons from one plane to the other and handing the names of the switched men to the lieutenants. Again the truth is in the details. Trained sergeants who can make important decisions about their men have returned to at least this part of the Army. It must be remembered that the airborne traditionally gets the pick of the draw.

Shortly after the sergeants' solution, we load up and strap ourselves and our baggage into the bucket seats running lengthwise against the plane's fusilage. My legs are cramped up against the tires of the antitank jeep lashed down in front of me. A couple of troopers kindly change with me so my legs can stretch out beneath a jeep. Once we take off, the men arrange themselves on top of baggage, jeeps, and supplies and immediately fall asleep. Walt Whitman's description of the Union soldiers straggling back to Washington after the first defeat at Bull Run floats in my mind: "Washington gets all over motley with these defeated soldiers. . . . They drop down anywhere, on the steps of houses, up close by fences, on sidewalks, aside in some vacant lot, and deeply sleep. And on them sulkily drops the rain."*

Flight 160 lands to refuel and change aircrews at Goose Bay, Labrador. On the next leg, from Goose Bay to Frankfurt, the plane is commanded by a female captain, twenty-six years old, out of the first MAC class to graduate women as transport pilots. She flies well and has all the proper pilot attitudes, wisely setting the autopilot to grab a little sleep for part of the flight because "the action is tonight with those handsome German pilots." Like that of mercy, the quality of pilot is not strained; it changeth not with sex. She has no problems either flying the aircraft or commanding her all-male crew. Though she does cause some wistfulness among the paratroopers as they see her for the first time on disembarking. "Man, when do we get one of those."

---

* Sleep has always been a major military problem. Portions of Wellington's force at Waterloo, after marching for two days, were literally "out on their feet," soldiers holding each other up in the ranks. Many of the paratroopers landing in the night before D day, men in superb physical condition, report falling asleep in the middle of that desperate battle. I myself remember falling asleep in the middle of a tank action, with machine gun bullets hitting my tank. Physical fitness is another form of Readiness unfortunately often neglected and even ridiculed. There is no point in expertly flying mobile forces about the world if many go to sleep in battle. Or if those who must keep them supplied fall asleep.

While flight 160 was laid over for two hours in Goose Bay, airmen and soldiers got off the plane and shared the same ancient, paint-peeling lounges. On board the aircraft, airmen and paratroopers ate the same food, and that food was as good as that on board the B-52 *Biggs 99*: plenty of milk, juice, thick sandwiches, fruit, and candy bars for quick energy. Inside the Other America of Defense this marks an enormous change. As recently as four years ago the Air Force treated its members to better waiting rooms and food than it gave the soldier Pacs.

In 1953, during the Korean War, after covering the fledgling maneuvers of the just-formed NATO, I flew back from Frankfurt, Germany, to Westover Air Force Base in Massachusetts, again on an ordinary Air Force transport flight picked at random. Our plane, a Boeing Stratocruiser, lost two engines over the Atlantic and limped into an emergency landing in the Azores. Those in the aircrew, and the Air Force passengers on board and their families, were whisked to comfortable lounges in sedans. The Army passengers—enlisted men, officers, and their wives and children—waited in the rain for a bus, which took them to an unheated and unstaffed, filthy mess hall.

Today cooperation between the Army and Air Force is certainly better than it was in Korea and Vietnam and is probably the equal of the cooperation during World War II. I take my figurative hat off to Air Force General Robert ("Monk") Dixon of the Tactical Air Command (TAC) and Army General William DePuy of the Training and Doctrine Command (TRADOC). These two men, working together in the late seventies, finally forced their reluctant services to begin a greater measure of cooperation.

As an outgrowth of that cooperation, a team of ten officers, five from the Army and five from the Air Force, was set up. Not only does this group, called the Air Land Force Applications Agency, meet continually, but Army and Air commanders review and accept its work. The chief of the agency's Air Force team is graded for his future promotions by the Army commander at TRADOC; and the senior Army member is graded by the Air Force general at TAC. Unfortunately, the Navy and Marines, when invited to join this interservice effort, did not even bother to reply. But while cooperation now is on a level with that of World War II, there remains a further question: In the light of today's weapons and the complexity of today's battlefield, is merely as good as World War II enough? Here are two paragraphs from the official document that governs how we will decide what targets our fighter aircraft will attack in Europe to aid the ground forces:

> Apportionment is the determination and assignment of the total expected effort by percentage and/or priority that should be devoted to the various air operations and/or geographic areas for a given period of time. (ATP 33 (A)) Apportionment must be accomplished at the highest command level. (In the Central Region, this is Allied Forces Central Europe (AFCENT/Allied Air Forces Central Europe (AAFCE)). This determination is based upon priorities established during consultations among subordinate commanders and the theater commander. The strategy, objectives, and priorities of the latter will be a primary factor in the apportionment decision.
>
> Allocation is the translation of the apportionment into total numbers of sorties by aircraft type available for each operation/task. (ATP 33 (A)) It is accomplished at the level of command where the proper army/air force interface occurs. In the Central Region, this is at the Allied Tactical Air Force (ATAF)/Army Group level.

There is an important but unmentioned fact about this "translation of apportionment." In the central part of Western Europe, where this "interface" will occur "at the highest command level" with explosions, confusion, and people dying, the Air Force and Army headquarters are not even located near each other! And as for naval aircraft, they are not even mentioned. This means that 40 percent of America's fighter aircraft, planes that we count on for the defense of Europe, have missions to which their services, the Navy and Marines, give a higher priority than they do to the defense of Europe. They seldom, if ever, train for the NATO mission.

So what really happens on maneuvers? The Navy is absent. Can the Army and Air Force work together? Remembering how often soldiers were lost in Vietnam, one wonders, Can the Army even find itself? In 1982, General Bernard Rogers, NATO supreme commander, wanted to locate and congratulate the Danish battalion taking part in the maneuvers. Rogers flew around in his helicopter for several hours and never found the Danish troops, who were not where their corps commander believed them to be. Back in 1976, General J. Steinhoff, then the NATO air commander, estimated that after five days of maneuvers, friendly forces had shot down all his planes.

Two days after staggering sleepily off flight 160, I watch some barges ferrying soldiers across the Rhine. I ask a German antiaircraft gunner on one of the ferries if a helicopter flying by is *"Feind oder Freund."* (It has been said that my German is NATO's second-greatest challenge.)

"Freundlich," replied the NCO in charge positively, before the man could answer.

How did he know? "If they are enemy, the lieutenant will tell me."

A couple of hours later I ask one of the American antiaircraft gunners guarding an American supply column if the planes sweeping over the column are enemy or friendly.

"Friendlies."

"How do you know?"

"They have orange triangles on them."

"In real life how would you tell?"

"Anything I can hit is too close. I'd shoot them."

Just outside one of the new bedroom suburbs near the Pied Piper's town of Hameln in Niedersachsen, a British unit has skillfully set up and camouflaged a Rapier antiaircraft guided missile company.* The Rapiers on this little rain-wet hill are tracking on radar a bunch of incoming helicopters and fighter planes. Are they friend or foe? No one is quite sure because the code word to identify planes today has not reached us yet.

But from the way the fighters and helicopters are maneuvering, they seem about to attack our bridge. We theoretically blast them from the skies. The helicopters land their troops in a soccer field and they race toward the bridge. They are friendlies, come to help us defend the bridge. A tough German tank colonel watching this little play punches me on the shoulder and remarks, "NATO is so fucked up its only hope lies in the responsibility of every soldier to disobey orders."

---

* The Rapier did not perform too well in the Falklands. Still, the Rapier and the French Roland are better than any antiaircraft missile currently with the U.S. forces. At one time America was going to buy Rapiers. But the deal continually hung fire because the Army and Air Force could not agree whose responsibility it was to pay for the Rapiers that would guard air bases.

Two nights later it is bitter cold, and though the rain has stopped, the banks of the Kusten Kanal are slippery with ice. Completely blacked out in the dark, the gigantic bridging trucks of a German engineer company are putting in a bridge. Rutting, snorting, and splashing like gigantic courting rhinos, the huge amphibious trucks of the German bridging company roar down the bank and splash into the water. "Gas, gas, gas," their captain yells at them at the top of his lungs, urging them to hit the water fast so that the giant vehicles won't stick to the bottom of the canal. Some trucks make it. Others stick and are winched in. Once afloat, they are drawn by their propellers into the canal's middle, turned around, and bolted together. In daylight this process would probably take about forty-five minutes. Now, in the dark, without the use of any light, it takes three and a half hours.

Though this bridge is critical to the whole maneuver, the German captain is the most senior officer there. The bridge comes in on time. Next year an American unit puts in the bridge. It is hard to count in the dark but there appear to be at the least two generals and five colonels present. No one is really in charge and the bridge comes in way late. This again is Overcontrol, the "Russification of the American Army."

To keep warm that night at the Kusten Kanal, I sit inside a German Leopard tank of the 3/3/3 (3rd Company, 3rd Battalion, 3rd Panzer Brigade), listening to the radios while waiting for the German bridge to go in. A flight of planes flies back and forth over the dark bridgehead. Does anybody in any of these German tanks have any idea whether they are friend or foe? No. The American Army and Air Force are not the only lost folk on the modern battlefield.

It's a pleasant autumn day during the 1984 maneuvers in central Germany along the Donau, *Altweibersommer*, with the sun burning through the morning mists in the valleys. I spot the unique radars of an American Hawk antiaircraft missile battalion on one of the hazy blue-green hilltops. Since a Hawk battalion, with its complex electronic equipment, is a good place to observe both Readiness and Interservice Rivalry (that is, Air Force/Army coordination), I turn my car up the dirt track toward the missiles. Two well-camouflaged soldiers with pine boughs in their helmets and M-16s in their hands rise out of their shallow holes and order me to stop.

Hawk battalions are priority targets in the first instants of actual combat, and in peacetime secret agents try to steal their electronic black boxes, so they are quite properly more jittery about security than tank or infantry units are. Therefore I stop quickly. Both the soldiers are women. When I finally make it through security to battalion headquarters itself, half the officers manning the complex radar scopes and firing computers are women. I had found the same high ratio of women two days before when I visited the waterlogged site of an EWI (Electronic Warfare battalion) on the other side of the Donau.

One of the reasons the Army, like the Air Force, is handling its complex equipment so much better than formerly is the increased use of women. This creates for the Army, and parts of the Tactical Air Command, a little-understood Readiness/Tooth-to-Tail problem. Congress has legislated that women not be placed in combat jobs. Surveys show that Americans as a whole do not want women involved in battle, and the vast majority of enlisted women do not wish to be in combat. (Most female officers have a very different view on this issue, wishing to move into as many military roles as they are physically able to handle.) Yet this anti-aircraft Hawk battalion, and units doing fighter-aircraft maintenance at forward bases, and electronic warfare units, and large, rear headquarters—all places that were relatively safe in World War II—are the priority targets on today's battlefield.

The enemy has to knock out this Hawk battalion above the Donau before their planes can concentrate on the tanks and infantry in the woods below along the river. In the "real thing," this Hawk battalion and the soldiers in it, male and female, will be a higher-priority target than those all-male tank units. The Hawk unit is one of the easiest for the enemy to locate and kill because of the unique "signature" of its radars. The Soviets employ specific antiradar missiles designed to strike at Hawks.

Hawk battalions are earmarked to move with airborne forces to trouble spots about the globe, like the Middle East. One of the captains in the battalion (female) explains that American units cannot shut their radars down quickly and restart them, as the Israelis can, because their equipment is not as modern. This lack of "jinking ability" increases their vulnerability. During the fighting in Lebanon the Israeli Air Force went first for the Syrian antiaircraft missiles.

U.S. Air Force doctrine calls for all-out attack against enemy air bases and their maintenance facilities in the first phase of any battle. The Soviets are believed to follow the same doctrine and are known to have created special parachute units whose mission is the destruction of headquarters, supplies, and air bases. Equally at risk are the electronic warfare listening posts, often in advance of the front, whose unique radio antennas make them easy to spot. All these areas and locations contain a high percentage of servicewomen.

If the United States is forced to fight in Europe or elsewhere, such as the Middle East, death will be an equal opportunity employer. More female soldiers, sailors, and airmen will die in the first five minutes in any next war we are forced to fight than were killed in World War II, Korea, and Vietnam combined. In fact, since females are clustered in the high-priority targets, initially women will die out of all proportion to their numbers in the armed services.

Recently, concerned that women were being too exposed to danger, the Army closed off from them a previously open key occupational specialty, Fifty-four Echo, the nuclear, chemical, and biological warfare designation. This caused the Army's ability to handle nuclear weapons to break down, because there were not enough qualified men available to replace the female soldiers. Pressure from commanders in the field forced the order to be rescinded. Nuclear weapon storage areas are the most important targets on the battlefield. Over and over I hear from both high-ranking officers and civilian defense officials some such phrase as "Yes, we realize women will die in the next war." Yet at the same time I find everyone hiding behind the rubric that women are not in combat jobs.

Here the Readiness questions arise. What criteria will be used for such military necessities (and horrors) as triage? Where those so severely wounded they have little chance of living are left to die, while those with more chance are operated on first? Will women and men be subject to the same standards of judgment as they lie, mangled, on their stretchers? Do we possess doctors and medical technicians who, surrounded by horror and out on their feet, can make unisex judgments at such a time? Those who will make such choices next time need rules agreed to in advance.

What about combat fatigue? The Vietnam War was so mild compared with World War II or Korea that the armed services haven't much recent experience with this fact of battle. The Israelis found that combat fatigue vulnerability was more prevalent in combat support units than in actual fighting units. These support units are where the women are now. Will the numbers of combat fatigue cases rise among both men and women as they see substantial numbers of women blown apart? Even if average American officers, male and female, will fight on while women are maimed and die around them, will average American enlisted men and women?

And the public and Congress, how will they react to seeing lots of dead and dying servicewomen on their TV screens? Will they cripple the Giant by demanding at that moment that women be removed far from battle, leaving no one trained to handle the complex military equipment?

When Congress discovered that there were women in the aircrews flying the paratroopers to Grenada during the attack there, many members demanded this stop. One of the lessons of Vietnam is that we need a broader national consensus on the composition and use of our fighting forces. An Israeli unit with large numbers of women in it was overrun during the 1968 war. Having experienced the wounded-woman problem, the Israelis are pulling back from their widespread use of women soldiers close to the battlefield. They are reluctant to discuss their actions; but after having been out ahead of us in the use of women in the late sixties, they are now decidedly more traditional.

The female soldiers in the Hawk battalion raise Readiness questions. The blips on their radar screens pose an entirely different but equally important problem of Interservice Rivalry. The data coming down from 4th Allied Tactical Air Force Headquarters through a complex series of links were the product of a number of Army/Air Force committees "interfacing" with each other at various levels of command. These decided which data should be passed through. Information on friendly and hostile helicopters was often absent from the screen, and the Hawks had problems passing data from their radars back into the system. When it came to deciding what to protect and which targets to fire upon first, they were left largely unguided.

If antiaircraft missiles, where the coordination is at its best, are in such a nebulous state, what about the antiaircraft weapons with the tanks? Soldiers who would fire these weapons are totally in the dark about the air battle. Army/Air Force cooperation today is better than ever before; but is cooperation itself an adequate answer? Is not the belief that there will be, now or in the immediate future, a separate land battle and a separate air battle a recipe for defeat? To me the idea appears as ridiculous as the pre–World War II belief that there would be separate tank and infantry battles. Isn't what is needed not more cooperation, however much improved, but actual command over a unified battle?

The coming accuracy of missiles and enhanced radar coverage force all planes near the battle line to operate "down on the deck," within, as a maximum, 200 feet of the ground, in order to survive. Inside that crowded space are going to be Army helicopters, Air Force fighters, perhaps in the future Navy fighters, maybe some bombers from SAC trying to sneak in beneath the enemy radar screen. Through this same area are going to streak Army missiles and artillery shells with proximity fuses that explode when in radar range of an object. Antiaircraft missiles will be chasing targets from both below and above. On the ground, troops will be under attack from the land and air. All around will be that ancient complicator of problems, bad guys trying to kill you.

Will cooperation work then, although in the far simpler up-to-now it has not worked? Most of these units cannot even talk to each other. Few of the officers in them have been to the same schools. Nor have they rehearsed this problem before. Only in 1982 did a few Army helicopters participate at Nellis Air Force Base in the superb Air Force Red Flag maneuvers, which are conducted against simulated Soviet missiles and aircraft. The Air Force and the Army in Europe are not truly under one command. Instead, a committee requests them to fight in certain ways and to destroy certain targets.

Even the air battle itself is fragmented. The Air Force plans to fight the modern air battle from a computer-filled airborne command post with giant radars sprouting from its top and bottom, known as AWACS (Airborne Warning and Control System). Such a mobile headquarters makes a difficult target to kill, and its radars carried aloft can penetrate farther into enemy air space to divine the intent of the enemy's aircraft. Further, such headquarters can be quickly flown to trouble spots about the globe. The Navy has even agreed that at certain times naval planes can be controlled—not commanded, controlled—from the AWACS. The radios, computers, and Identification Friend or Foe (IFF) devices don't mesh; but we won't flog that horse again. The Marines have not even gone this far.

If we had billions and billions of dollars and millions and millions of aircraft, we could afford to let them fight in separate service packages, outnumbering the enemy at every point along the periphery. We do not have those numbers, nor will we ever be able to afford them. Future victory requires that the superb mobility and lethality of aircraft be mated with tactical and strategic flexibility. The entire air battle must be under one command.

With the air battle in disarray, what progress is there in efforts to unify the air and ground battles? Here again, the airborne command post, AWACS, tells a sad story about Interservice Rivalry and the limits of mere cooperation. When the AWACS was being developed, the then Chief of Staff of the Air Force, General David C. Jones, secretly sought out one of the Army's most senior and highly decorated generals, James Hollingsworth. Jones had grown concerned over the ground defense of his forward air bases in Europe. Now he wanted to enlist Hollingsworth's help in obtaining Army funds for AWACS. With Army support, Jones felt, both the land and air battles could be depicted on the computers of the airborne headquarters and both battles fought as one. Would Hollingsworth use his prestige and back-channels within the Army staff to gain Army funds and doctrine support for this Air Force project?

Hollingsworth, a man of courage and flexibility, had already decided that airborne headquarters were the future, even for the Army. He thought over Jones's unusual proposal and agreed to try to help him do it. He went back-channel to the Chief of Staff of the Army, the Vice Chief, and a few other key power centers and pressed them to join the Air Force project. Jones used his clout to ready the Air Staff to accept Army cooperation. (This "neutral reporter" was shamelessly lobbying the West German Defense Ministry to inform Washington that they would not purchase the AWACS unless the ground and the air battles were both depicted on the airborne computer screens.) In spite of Hollingsworth's skillful urgings, the Army, fearful of losing control over portions of the ground battle to the Air Force, refused to have anything to do with the project. As a result the AWACS computers depict only the air battle, and, as we have seen, not all of that.

When the AWACS is used in Europe during a maneuver, you can see the automobiles on the autobahn because they are going faster than 100 kilometers an hour and that is what shows up on the airborne computer screens. (Technically this is known as setting the "gate" of the radar.) But you can't see the slower-moving tanks and often you can't even see the helicopters.

Defense officials who are pressed about deficiencies such as these tend to deny their reality or claim the deficiencies don't matter because we are ahead of the Soviets in modern weapons, such as antitank missiles, electronic warfare, and particularly tactical air power. "We need not match the enemy tank for tank," President Carter's Secretary, Harold Brown, reported. "We retain a qualitative edge." The problem with this answer is that we are not that far ahead overall; indeed in some areas we are behind. Also, even if we have better weapons, they will not produce victory unless used correctly by able and motivated people.

When I go on the speaking circuit, I am practically always asked what I think is the greatest military strength possessed by America. "Tell me now, Samson, wherein thy great strength lieth?" And I reply, "In the intelligence and aggressiveness of our people and the strength of our beliefs in our government." I can see by looking at the audience that this is not a satisfactory answer, particularly to those between twenty and forty. "We are asking you a serious question," one college student complained from the floor, "and you talk about 'fire in the belly.'"

The answer expected and wanted, I have discovered by questioning back, is that we are ahead in technical areas; that there is some scientific breakthrough that gives us the military advantage. Perhaps we lead in precision weapons, in atomics, in tanks, in fighters? Alas, these presumed superiorities are either not there or not that decisive. The Russians are not supermen, they are behind us overall, but they aren't Fuzzy-Wuzzies either. We thought the Vietnamese were Fuzzy-Wuzzies; the Israelis thought the Egyptians were Fuzzy-Wuzzies; both proved dangerous misconceptions.

The belief that weapons can be designed that will turn mediocre soldiers into winners is one of the products of the Great Divorce.

It is a rationale for not supporting a draft. Don't let my college graduate son serve. Give those poor unfortunates in the service some wonder weapon. It doesn't matter that they are too stupid to read maps; we will give them a bleeper in their helmet that tells them by satellite where they are. In the early days in Vietnam one was continually told the helicopter was going to win the war for us. Good weapons are a vital part of defense. But good people in trained units with high morale using sound tactics in pursuit of a rational strategy come first. (I am aware that I sound banal and risk turning people off when I write such words.)

For example: To help the infantry stop tanks, the U.S. Army relies on a wire-guided antitank missile called the Dragon, which is fired from the soldiers shoulder. The claim is that these Dragon missiles in the hands of our soldiers will be the answer to the fact that Russian tanks outnumber us in Europe better than three to one. Improved antitank guided munitions are coming, and the dominance of the tank is fading. However, right now and for the next few years the "wonder weapon" Dragon has problems. As they say out in the field, "The Dragon is not soldier-proof; and the soldier is not Dragon-proof."

When an infantryman fires a Dragon he has to keep the launching tube's optical sights on his target. If he does that, the missile will automatically correct its course and hit the tank. But the Dragon kicks so much on launch and flies so erratically that guiding it in flight is exceptionally difficult. Furthermore, I have never met a single soldier who has fired a Dragon, though commanders will tell me that everyone in their unit is Dragon-qualified. That means they have practiced on the Dragon trainer. This is a Tooth-to-Tail and Readiness problem again. The Dragons are so expensive the Army cannot buy extra ones for people to learn on by firing them in training. In addition, the Dragon is so heavy it can't be fired standing up. Nor can it be fired inside a room smaller than the Hall of Mirrors at Versailles. Nor can this answer to the tank be fired lying down. Its back-blast is so great that, if fired lying down, it burns off the soldier's buttocks. The Dragon must be fired from a special sitting position. Also, the weapon is so delicate that even when well cared for it must be sent to the rear every seven days to have its sights recalibrated. And there is no way to tell by looking at the weapon if its sights are in line.

A few years back, on some muddy patch of ground in Germany,

I watched a group of soldiers training to fire the Dragon. Even on the electronic simulator, without the shock of the back-blast, they had trouble hitting the target. I asked the sergeant training them, a weathered old-timer, if he had ever fired the Dragon. No, he said, in his soft Kentucky drawl, he hadn't. But he had once seen one fired. He had been to a special Dragon school and at the end of the course the top man in the class, a Marine captain, got to fire one Dragon. "Did he hit the target?" I asked. "No," replied the sergeant again, "the poor fellow didn't." By now the soldiers had clustered round us, leaving their simulated Dragon tubes. "He was a real big man, sir, real big. But that Dragon kicks a bit. Oh, sir, you should have seen what it done to his neck."

What sort of physically well-conditioned, highly motivated and disciplined person do you think it will take to sit up in combat and hit a moving tank with a Dragon? How often will he be found in a volunteer army in which, even during the depression-induced spurt of enlistments, one of five soldiers reads at barely the eighth-grade level?

Electronic warfare, such as the fixing of targets by electronic means, is another area where we are presumed to be far ahead of the Soviets. On the surface this idea makes sense. America is where the communications revolution started; it has a vast communications industry. The truth is that, again, while we may have good weapons on the drawing board, the Soviets are ahead in the field. "Five years" is the figure given me by two generals, one at NATO headquarters, one at a forward air base. The Russians have two mobile radio direction-finding units in each division and are about to go to four. We have none. The Russians have two mobile radio and radar-jamming units with each division. These models are superior to those which so successfully tied up the Israelis in 1973. We have none. The Russians have mobile listening stations operated by trained crews who can distinguish between targets. For example, they can tell the difference between targets you want to destroy, like tank battalions, and targets you want to listen to, to gain intelligence, like division and wing headquarters.

And even where we have the equipment, Interservice Rivalry and conservatice mind-set often combine to destroy its value. Eight hours elapse between the time an Army unit requests an FLIR (Forward Looking Infra-Red) target-finding mission from the Air Force and the time the data get back. Then the information comes through in the form of coordinates and data printouts that many of today's commanders do not understand. Infrared pictures take twenty-four hours between request and delivery.

I stood in Germany three years ago staring at a set of FLIR pictures that some captains had gotten declassified for me so that I could see what they looked like. To my inexperienced eye the pictures all looked like snow on an old-fashioned black-and-white TV set. But right in the middle of one photo was this small bright splotch, standing out like a cancerous mole on the face.

"What's that?" asked the colonel who was monitoring this meeting to make sure I didn't learn too much.

"That's what we are trying to explain to you, sir," said one of the captains. "That's your headquarters, hidden yesterday inside a farmhouse. Remember, we told you all those generators would make it stand out."

"I don't believe that," said the colonel. "They must have found out some other way, then taken the picture."

Later I asked one of the captains if he could tell the difference between a tank and a truck with FLIR.

"Oh, yes. And between a tank with its hatches open or closed. Sometimes I can even spot the commander's tank. And tell if the tanks have been refueled or not."

"People ask you for this information much?"

"No."

As for our superiority in the air, the numbers certainly show that we have bought a great deal of tactical air power. Roughly one quarter of the American defense budget goes to tactical air power in any given year, and that excludes the helicopters. Until President Reagan's shipbuilding program, tactical air was the largest single item in the military budget since Vietnam. Air forces are highly mobile, and the maneuvers, like Crested Cap, held every few years to demonstrate our ability to move fighters rapidly to Europe, appear to NATO observers efficient and effective.

But here Interservice Rivalry strikes, with 40 percent of all the tactical air assets assigned almost irretrievably to the Navy and the Marines.* These would not even arrive in time for the

---

* "Assets" is a current bit of service jargon I hate. It reflects the false concept of defense as a business, and so disguises that defense is about fighting, not business management.

violent first two weeks of a European war, the period most analysts believe would be decisive. When they got there, they would never have trained with the NATO forces. Of the roughly 6,000 aircraft available for tactical use, only a little over 2,000 would probably join the initial fight.

Even for the planes there now and those that would get there in the first two weeks, important questions remain. In this world of missiles and increasingly accurate weapons, how many of the gigantic bases the planes need would still be operating in Europe? And of equal importance, how well would the aircraft perform when they got there? Even if they were not shot down, as they are now on maneuvers, would they be able to find targets?

Joint Army/Air Force doctrine calls for a forward observer team on the ground, called a FIST team (Fire Support Team), that will direct planes to targets. In Vietnam, however, Air Force after-action studies showed that it took a pilot five and a half minutes to find the correct ground target. And that was with the aid of an airborne forward observer. It took longer than that with just ground forward observation. But in the 1973 Yom Kippur war the Israelis found that they were out of communication between ground and air in less than a minute as a result of jamming.

At an air base in Germany, drinking coffee with a bunch of pilots, captains, majors, colonels, all of whom have flown over North Vietnam, I ask one, "Colonel, do you expect to be talking to the FIST team after the first half hour?"

"Hadley, I don't expect to be able to talk to my wingman after the first five minutes." The other pilots rock back and forth on their chair legs or nod agreement. They look slightly nervous in talking to a stranger about what they hash over only among themselves.

"Do you really expect many FIST teams to be alive after the first day?" I ask an Army colonel I have known well, both in Vietnam and before. We are walking through his brigade area in Germany late one night.

That is a complicated question, he replies. Our published doctrine, which the Soviets most certainly read, calls for the FIST teams to be at the front lines with each infantry and tank company. So the Soviets know that by locating our FIST teams they will know just where the front is. The FIST team's unique ground-to-air radios make them easy to spot with DF (Direction-Finding) equipment. Indeed, he adds, with our poor, easily jammable communications and with the Russians' excellent DF equipment, they will probably have a better idea where our front line is than we ourselves. (He was not the only American commander to tell me this.) It is to the Russians' advantage to keep the FIST teams alive and merely jam their radios so that they cannot communicate. On the other hand, the artillery radio with the FIST teams is pretty good; so some artillery messages are going to get through Russian jamming. Therefore perhaps the Russians plan to locate and kill the FIST teams. He is not sure.

Even if the planes get to the front lines without being shot down by friendly fire and find the right targets, the battle has not yet begun. When the Russian divisions advance, they advance inside something called the bubble. That's a protective covering of SAM 6 missiles for high-altitude work and ZSU 23 antiaircraft guns for low-level work. The ZSU 23 is by far the best antiaircraft gun in the world. "The Soviets are decisively ahead in control of the air," a high German defense scientist told me bluntly; and many of our aviators agree.

In the Yom Kippur war the Israeli fighters could not penetrate the far-less-sophisticated bubble with which the Russians had supplied the Egyptians. The way the U.S. fighters are supposed to penetrate this bubble is to come in under 200 feet while the Army jams the radars and takes out the AA guns. But the Army lacks the equipment to do this, and the complex maneuvers and timing have never been rehearsed. Special Air Force squadrons, called Wild Weasels, containing some of the hottest, most thoughtful Air Force pilots, are meant to have high-speed antiradar missiles to take out the Russian defenses. Those missiles are still in the development stage.

Suppose that everything works (which on the evidence is totally unlikely) and for two days we and the rest of NATO have fought the Russians, East Germans, and Czechs and the rest of the Warsaw Pact to a standstill. On the third day the old Tooth-to-Tail problem will defeat us. Again, looking at the Yom Kippur war, it seems certain that in this age of accurate weapons, the losses will be horrendous. NATO war plans call for each U.S. division to fire 5,000 tons of ammunition on the first day and

3,000 tons of ammunition a day thereafter. At these rates of fire, artillery gun tubes will last one week. But U.S. forces do not have the skilled mechanics to replace the gun tubes. Nor do we have enough trucks and drivers to bring the ammunition forward.

With agony in his face, one of the officers responsible for solving this problem tells me he will be 500 rounds short for each gun in his division by the start of the third day. NATO studies show that American forces in Europe will have run out of anti-tank helicopter ammunition at the end of the second day. The Navy does not plan to get its first resupply convoy started toward Europe until after the second week.

And as for tanks, if we lose them at merely the same rates as the Israelis did, we will need (at the beginning of the third day) 300 new tanks for each of our 360-tank armored divisions. We do have some extra old tanks in warehouses. But these are on the wrong side of the Rhine, and we lack the tank transports and crews to move them forward. Which doesn't really matter since the Rhine bridges certainly will not be standing. Anyway, the radios for these replacement tanks are in another warehouse, miles away, and they don't fit inside these tanks. As a result of the Yom Kippur war, the Germans have greatly increased their forward, already-in-position supplies of tanks, ammunition, and men, too. We have not.

When the 115 tanks of a German tank brigade now go into mock battle, 350 tons of spare tank parts move with them on trucks. When a U.S. tank brigade goes into mock battle in Germany, its far fewer spare parts stay put in a warehouse. Why? Congress classifies the trucks that move spare parts as tail and economizes by not buying such equipment. The very word "tail" implies a safe rear somewhere. With long-range missiles, secret agents, paratroop forces, and precision weapons delivery by aircraft, where is this safe rear? Can the rear be safe, particularly if it is fixed in one place, like a warehouse?

The majority of the American supply dumps in Germany are west of the Rhine. The U.S. Army plans to fight the decisive NATO battle close to the border between the two Germanys, which is way east of the Rhine. Congress has refused to supply funds to move the supplies to the other side of the Rhine, and the Defense Department again has not pushed what it classifies as a tail problem. If U.S. forces run out of ammunition after the first day and a half, is moving the supply dumps a tooth problem or a tail problem?

Nor will our European allies be able to supply us with the replacement weapons that we need. Two years ago on maneuvers I was standing in a dripping pine forest along the southern slope of the Hartz Mountains, behind the command truck of a Belgian tank battalion. Shaking the water off themselves beside me were the Belgian colonel commanding the tank battalion and an American captain. The captain was the liaison officer from the American tank brigade on the Belgian's right. To fill time during a lull in the maneuver, I asked the two men what weapons and ammunition their two tank battalions had in common. The captain and the colonel went through their weapons one by one: tank guns, mortars, antitank rockets, machine guns. None were the same.

"What about the pistols you are both wearing?" I asked in forlorn hope. Their pistols were different, too. In battle, if one battalion ran out of ammunition, there would be no way the other could help. And in common-use items, or "interoperability," as it is called in the trade, things are actually getting worse. In 1982 the American Army adopted a 155 artillery piece with a slightly longer chamber than those used by the rest of NATO.

To turn from looking at a little picture to some supporting numbers, as of 1977 there were in NATO:

41 different types of naval guns
31 different types of antitank weapons
6 different types of recoilless rifles
36 different types of fire-control radars
8 different surface-to-air missile systems
6 different antiship missiles

There is a bitter jest throughout NATO that American plans for the defense of Europe are based on flying imaginary troops in nonexistent planes into already-destroyed air bases at the command of headquarters no longer in action.

There is a final argument to excuse the weakness of the Giant in conventional warfare. This holds that the strength of the forces in Europe does not really matter, since their purpose is merely to act as a trip wire that will trigger the use of nuclear weapons, first on the battlefield, then if necessary against the satellites, finally against the Soviet Union itself. This is the "trip-wire argument," that the main purpose of American troops in Europe is to prevent a war from starting, because the Soviets know that if they attack our troops they will trigger a nuclear holocaust. Partisans of this view believe we could actually cut our own and other NATO conventional forces back and save money. This is a point of view that made some sense when NATO had a virtual nuclear monopoly. But the Russians have gone from the 649 warheads they had in the early 1960s to around 4,000 warheads in their ICBM force alone. The problem of the trip-wire argument in today's nuclear plenty is that using conventional forces only as a trip wire greatly increases the probability of nuclear war. Besides, important distinctions of time and degree are overlooked.

If at the end of three days the armies of the Warsaw Pact stand victorious on the English Channel, having taken few casualties and not used nuclear weapons, they have won. We are unlikely to use nuclear weapons to dislodge them from the parts of Europe they hold. If they ever thought, especially in time of crisis, that they could win so much at so little risk, then they might well be tempted to move. But if, on the other hand, at the end of those same three days, the Warsaw Pact armies are just twenty miles inside the inner German border, advancing slowly at best, while both sides take horrendous losses and the Soviet satellites, seeing no easy victory, seethe with unrest, that is a very different outlook. The risks of nuclear war are certainly great. But paradoxically, so is the outlook for negotiation and peace. The stronger the trip wire, the longer we can avoid using nuclear weapons. In fact, with strong conventional forces we should be able to avoid that choice unless forced to it by others using such weapons first.

A little theory is helpful here in understanding NATO's present nuclear dilemma. The problem of defending Western Europe through the threatened use of nuclear weapons involves two aspects: The first is called extended deterrence, the second, the nuclear firebreak. Plain, old-fashioned deterrence, which has kept the nuclear peace so successfully, rests on the ability of the United States and the Soviets to cause each other unacceptable damage if we or they are attacked. Note that deterrence is a psychological concept. If you do something to me, I will do something back to you. This means that to be effective, nuclear weapons must be usable enough so that the enemy is restrained by his belief that they will be used, but awesomely different enough so that one dares not use them.

Extended deterrence is the concept that tries to evaluate how much besides your homeland you can defend by threatening nuclear war. "If you do that you risk nuclear war" has so far helped to keep peace in Europe. This has been true while at exactly the same time the destructiveness of nuclear weapons has prevented their use. We have not left the world of paradox just because we believe the Middle Ages to be behind us.*

The limits of extended deterrence are debated endlessly, and shift as the balance of power shifts. Obviously you can't stop your wife from leaving by threatening to nuke her. Nor can you force Iran to free hostages. Some believe that, today, threatening to defend Western Europe by using nuclear weapons makes about as much sense. Others believe that the threat of nuclear weapons applied to something as major as an all-out attack on Western Europe remains a peacekeeper.

The nuclear firebreak is the obverse of extended deterrence. To achieve a nuclear firebreak, one tries to make the gap between waging nuclear warfare and fighting all other forms of warfare as wide as possible. A major problem of defense policy is to create military forces and align them with political realities to achieve both the extended deterrence necessary for an effective foreign policy and a nuclear firebreak. A second continuing problem for both defense and arms control has been to make certain that measures taken to reduce the risk of nuclear war do not set the stage for a great big, bloody, conventional war. Among the many excellent reasons for avoiding such a large conventional war is that the last one ended in the use of nuclear weapons.

Recently several military savants have tried to limit the threat of nuclear war by advancing the theory of "no first use." This doctrine holds that America should swear not to be the first to use nuclear weapons. Like so much of the reasoning that led us

---

* An excellent exploration of present-day nuclear theory and the consequences thereof is Leon Wieseltier's *Nuclear War, Nuclear Peace* (New York: Holt, Rinehart and Winston, 1983).

into Vietnam, this idea is excellent in theory, devastating in practice. How much more will the Soviets or our allies trust us just because we swear we won't use nuclear weapons first? To answer that, ask how much easier you would sleep if Chairman Gorbachev had so sworn? Suppose that at breakfast tomorrow your love and constant companion—who, God willing, are one and the same—looks you in the eye over the coffee cup and says, "No matter how I act or what you hear about me, sweetheart, I swear I will never betray you first." Is a great wave of security going to flood over you as you pass the salt? Nations are like people; they require trust and enforcement and rewards to make them behave as they have sworn.

To the extent that other nations believed we would never use nuclear weapons first, they would be encouraged to take the sorts of major risks that could lead to a major conventional war. The threat of nuclear power, like all threats, deters most when something is left to chance. The exact amount that should be left to chance to make a nuclear threat most effective as deterrence is the subject of endless debate. The presence of tactical nuclear weapons in both Western and Eastern Europe introduces a greater element of chance into how the West will respond to a conventional or nuclear attack on Western Europe. In an effort to tidy up the ambiguities that have kept the peace, a logical and legalistic mind may actually make nuclear war more likely. As Secretary of Defense Lovett often remarked, "Beware of legal beavers."

In most of the war games in which military officers and civilian defense experts take part, it is the civilian experts who are more likely to initiate the nuclear war. I have wondered why this was so since the 1960s, when as a reporter I first noticed the now well-documented trend. I believe it is because the professionals, having handled and trained with the weapons and dealt with the practical aspects of their use, view their destructiveness as reality, while for the civilians, the weapons still have a more academic cast.

The United States has roughly 6,000 nuclear warheads in Europe—down from 7,000 until 1980—stored in roughly 176 different locations. Each weapon requires five people to maintain and guard it. Occasionally, in the British or German zones of NATO, I run into obvious Americans in British uniforms and realize I am close to a secret base. I believe plans for the use of

nuclear weapons in defense of NATO are on about the same
level as their supposed secrecy. I have been told that if I think
the papers on air-power employment are jargon, I should see
the highly classified pages on the nuclear employment, MC 14/3,
based on the Athens guidelines of 1962, also known as POC
(Programs of Cooperation).

With nuclear plenty and the arrival of accurate short-range
missiles, both our own and the Soviets', NATO's ability to defend
Western Europe by tactical nuclear warfare is changing. NATO's
forces are not. Fighter aircraft remain poised at their bases, ready
to deliver nuclear weapons; and now they are being augmented
by missiles. What are we spending that money for? Since the
weapons we buy determine the type of war we must fight, is
planning to fight a tactical nuclear war to our benefit? A modern
battlefield is deadly, complex, wide-ranging, and complete with
saboteurs and airborne troops, which means that nuclear weapons,
if used, will probably have to be used early or they will be
destroyed or captured. Is early use of nuclear weapons what we
want? If not, why do we keep buying and deploying forces to
fight such a war?

If tactical weapons are primarily there for deterrence, could
not many of them be placed on submarines or ships offshore—
particularly now, when precision guided cruise missiles, which
go easily onto ships, are becoming reliable weapons? Nuclear
weapons would be more secure at sea and would accomplish the
same deterrent mission. This would free up some 30,000 Army
and Air Force men for conventional forces: That's two armored
or infantry divisions. It would also free many jet fighters from
the nuclear mission, and these could help win the conventional
European battle. Would such a course make Europe safer and
nuclear warfare more likely or less likely? Unfortunately, today's
Defense Department is too paralyzed by Interservice Rivalry and
Faulty Organization to find answers to such questions.

The defense of Western Europe now rests on conventional
forces that are lacking and a nuclear threat in which it is becoming more difficult to believe. American strategy is not based
on philosophy, or doctrine, or world outlook, but on the weakness of the Giant. After billions of dollars spent on defense and
on NATO, we are back with the choice we sought all along to
avoid, the choice between relying on ground and air forces that
cannot win and starting a nuclear war that is not winnable.

TEN

To Replace
Straw with Steel

This book began with the disastrous attempt to rescue our hostages in Iran. To answer questions raised by that failure we have examined the realities inside the Other America of Defense from before World War II through victory in that war to the creation of the present fragmented Defense Department. From there, we traced certain persistent themes through the forgotten war in Korea, the creation of NATO, the expansion of the defense bureaucracy, to our defeat in Vietnam. Then, after a quick glance at the future, we ended with a report from the field on the Giant's true condition.

Those inside the Other America of Defense, "the military" and their families, live in separate enclaves, they shop at company stores, they speak a company language, they attend company schools, where they study company policies alien to most of us. On active duty, they and their families are sustained by an ethic markedly different from that in other parts of America. When they retire, they often retire to enclaves of their own kind. To a degree this has been true in all western democracies; but in twentieth-century America this trend, the Great

Divorce, has been accentuated. As a result, lacking hands-on knowledge of the military, Congress and often civilian elites have pressed on the armed services many "reforms" that have impeded rather than helped our defenses.

For example, the *New York Times* in July 1983 ran an editorial on the cost overruns of the Navy F-18 fighter. The editorial quite correctly criticized the enormous overruns, but the *Times*'s solution to the problem typified those unconscious attitudes fostered by the Great Divorce. The paper advocated the creation of an independent "weapons testing board." Once again, the answer to a presumed defense fault was to add yet another layer of civilian bureaucrats on top of the military. One can imagine how the *New York Times* editors would react if, because of errors in their reporting on the Grenada invasion, they had been ordered to add a layer of admirals to correct all future dispatches.

The problems with the F-18 (an aircraft that Navy fliers had initially rejected and that had then been forced on them by the Defense Department civilians) stemmed precisely from an excess of committees. The F-18 theoretically was to be a cheap carrier-based fighter with limited electronics to be used for visual dog-fighting, a plane to complement the complex, electronics-loaded F-14. (In my mind, that was a poor idea to begin with, another example of backward reasoning: not trusting the scientific future, you build on the cheap; warfare is a game for knights of the sky.) While the F-18 was being designed, no other new naval aircraft was in the works. So all the committees and boards that had a hand in its design hung their pet projects on it. There was no tough, knowledgeable SOB in command of the F-18 program whose promotion was coming from someone who, rightly or wrongly, wanted a cheap, fast airplane. On the contrary, a heavy airplane would lock the country for decades into the big super-carriers needed to handle it, a favored Navy weapons system. Those who made it bigger, heavier, and more costly would probably receive such tangible, earthly rewards as rapid promotions. And for the contractors, a loaded design means loaded profits.

In such a situation the F-18 soon became burdened with everyone's favorite hardware and rapidly became more expensive than the F-14. More important, it also became a plane that does not fly well. If the men who are going to fly and may die in it had been making the decisions, that plane would have been different.

Another reason the F-18 continues to be built is that parts for its engines are made in the state of former House Speaker Tip O'Neill and Senate powerhouse Ted Kennedy. No new Washington committee gyrating wildly as the thousandth unnecessary hind wheel on our chariot of defense will change that fact of the weapon's cost. Indeed, removed from hands-on work and day-to-day decisions, a "weapons testing board" would be perfectly placed for contractors and politicians to mount a maximum lobbying campaign. Each time such a solution is put forward, those able men and women in the Other America of Defense feel downgraded, and more of them leave the armed services.

As we seek to improve the Giant's posture we must be careful that we are responding to his needs, not our beliefs. When the facts about the My Lai massacre began to leak out, the Army launched a successful broad-gauge investigation of itself, led by an Army general, William Peers. Among the far-ranging results of this probe was the removal of the West Point superintendent, who as a divisional commander in Vietnam may have been involved in the My Lai cover-up. Contrast this with the conduct of the House of Representatives over the ABSCAM sting operation. After a number of congressmen and a senator had gone to jail for taking bribes, a subcommittee of the House Judiciary Committee called for an investigation of the FBI for smearing their noble brother congressmen. One recalls those estimates, which seem to me conservative, that the removal of congressional interference with military procurement would save upward of $10 billion a year.

The first major reform necessary is for those both inside and outside the Other America of Defense to work to heal the Great Divorce. This is no mere shibboleth nor an effort to avoid the hard problems of organizational change by calling for attitudinal and behavioral adjustments. Not even the most inspired reorganization of our Defense Department will greatly strengthen the Giant unless able faces appear in the rearranged organizational boxes. Nor will our armed services ever function effectively if much of America indulges in the luxury of seeing the military as an unwanted stepchild. This request that the civilian elites recognize the armed services as an important part of America is not raised to denigrate today's officer or noncommissioned officer corps. The Great Divorce has hurt the intake and retention of able officers and NCOs. That's a fact of political life, of national life, just as the filling of the infantry with the less able draftees was a fact of Vietnam and World War II. The able inside the Other America of Defense are the first to express alarm over present statistics on intake and retention. Indeed, service cries of alarm are often stilled by their civilian superiors, who proclaim for political purposes that all is fine. This was particularly true of the Ford and Carter years, when information about the desperate straits of all three services was suppressed by the civilian management of the Pentagon.

During the Falklands war, Henry Fairlie, the British reporter and observer of the American scene, ruminated:

> I could not be unaffected, as the British troops set sail for the Falklands, by the words of American reporters. "The Welsh Guards, one of the finest regiments in the British Army... The Scots Guards, perhaps the best fighting unit in the world today ... The Gurkhas, the fiercest fighting force..." All true, in a way.... But why do American reporters never use such phrases of the American armed forces? If it is said that this is due to the loss of prestige which American forces suffered in Vietnam, then that only strengthens my question; because the military did its job in Vietnam.
>
> In the late 1960s, I told the editor of *The New Yorker* that I would like to attempt profiles of institutions. He was interested in the idea. What institution would I like to start with? "The U.S. Marines," I said.... I will never forget his reply, "We do not like war here.... it hurts people, so we don't like war and pieces about the armed services." How terribly, terribly sweet. There are the offices of *The New Yorker*, protected by the armed services of the United States, and he will not run a profile of the U.S. Marines.

It is hard to be more eloquent than that about the pernicious effects of the Great Divorce. Still, let us "cleave ever to the sunnier side of doubt." In today's America, women and blacks both have recently shaken off traditional role limitations. Granted that females and blacks still have a ways to travel before they reach full equality with white males, still, a comparable shift in American attitudes toward the worth of our armed forces would do much to improve military strength.

In the nuclear age, when America no longer enjoys the luxury of being protected by her oceans, we now need armed forces, exactly as those in Europe have needed them throughout history. This is an unpopular thought, which many people fight, just as they did at the creation of our nation. Alexander Hamilton warned that America would have to bear "the vicissitudes that have been the common lot of nations." But America has tended intellectually to remain a Jeffersonian democracy, with Jefferson's distrust of all things military.

Historically, Americans have tried to solve their problems by leaving them behind. "Broadening the context" is the modern jargon. Most of those persecuted for their religion in England or Holland or Germany decided to remain at home and hide, or work for tolerance. The Pilgrims and successive waves of early settlers elected to risk emigration instead. And in the New World, if life did not work out or there were too many in the family for the family farm to feed, one set out for the frontier. America honors such men and women, and quite rightly. They were the pioneers who risked dangers to open up new territories. But they were also people who had elected to leave behind their old problems. So we grew up as a nation admiring people who solved problems by turning from them and moving on. We elected such people as our leaders, adjusted our philosophy and morality to such a world, and trained our children to be like them. "Americans are always moving on" is the refrain of one of Archibald MacLeish's finest poems.

As we became a more mature nation we turned to science and technology to help us solve our problems. We all recognize the figures of speech that still move us: "the new world of the atom," "the frontier of space." But in a profound sense we are misled by these stock phrases, this attitude of always turning toward the frontier, this belief that problems can be solved by giving them a wider context. We are no longer the "New World" but a large, important, and energetic part of the rest of the planet.

"When America ended its isolation after World War II," Henry Kissinger has written,

> an atomic monopoly gave America a margin of security unprecedented in history. As late as 1950 the United States produced 52 percent of all the world's goods and services. America by itself represented the global balance of power. American alliances were in effect unilateral guarantees; recognized problems could be overwhelmed with resources.
>
> By the late '60s these conditions were disappearing. Nuclear parity was upon us. As Europe and Japan recovered and other nations industrialized, America's percentage of the total gross national product was declining. By 1970 we produced about 30 percent of the world's goods and services; today the figure is around 22 percent.
>
> Henceforth we would have to live in a world of relative security, capable of reducing dangers but unable to banish them.

Living in constant danger like the rest of the world, we require, as other countries do, armed forces in being to guard both ourselves and our vital interests. There is no new frontier to which we can travel to avoid commitments.

No matter how times change, able men and women seek the action. If attitudes about the military alter and the services themselves make certain overdue reforms in their personnel policies (for example, stop transferring their ablest people every two years), the drive of the next generation for success will, of itself, help heal the Great Divorce. The country has been moving to strengthen the Foreign Service by giving more ambassadorships to professional diplomats rather than to political appointees, but the Defense Department has been moving in the opposite direction.* The proliferation of civilian

---

*Recently, however, the Reagan administration has put a dip in the upward curve of Foreign Service ambassadorial appointments.

committees at the Pentagon's apex, and excessive congressional oversight, have downgraded the advice of the professional military. One does not have to redesign human nature or erase the American dream to start to strengthen the Giant. All that need change are certain prevalent social beliefs about the worth of those in the service and the emotional and psychological rewards of a military career. Those of us who remember General Marshall's eyes can testify with certainty on the rewards.

The armed services need able professionals; they also need able recruits. This requires establishing a fair and just draft. The draft has always been a watershed issue for nations. Who should serve and for how long? and Who may stay home? are questions charged with emotion. The draft has divided citizens from one another since Rome's decision to recruit "barbarians" into her legions; on through the French revolutionary government's imposition of twenty-five years of military service on all male citizens; the New York City draft riots of 1863, with over 1,000 dead; and finally to Vietnam and the hill at Kent State University. Today the draft is not just an issue in itself, but also a code word for the type and amount of defense this nation needs, just as it was in the isolationist years before Pearl Harbor.

This legacy of the draft's past unfairness poisons today's debate. Those who avoided Vietnam service through loopholes (or, more correctly, loop-highways) in the draft, being in the main honorable men, now feel guilty. They relieve these feelings either by venomous attacks on all things military, including the draft, or by becoming superpatriots, military experts, who often make Attila the Hun sound like Mother Goose. Here they repeat history. A recent biography of Theodore Roosevelt concludes that much of his bellicosity derived from shame over his father's having purchased a draft exemption during the Civil War. Nor can my own generation be entirely exempt from such conflicted feelings. Recall that General Lewis Hershey, who directed the Selective Service during World War II, once remarked, "In the Civil War it took $300 to escape service. In this war it requires sufficient funds to attend college."

There are those who argue that the draft is unnecessary because the country is now getting a sufficient number of able volunteers. It is true that the armed services have improved from 1980, but what will happen when prosperity returns? When prosperity returned in 1976, enlistments dropped by 20 percent. As good times began to roll in 1984 the number of pilots leaving the Air Force and Navy rose by 20 percent. The number of those turning eighteen grows smaller each year. Unfortunately, around 1990 those numbers will be thinned even more—perhaps by 20 percent—because of AIDS. Our armed forces today still lack any semblance of being a cross section. One out of five Army soldiers remains in category IV, the lowest acceptable category. The ratio of students to instructors in military schools is 1.5 to 1. In civilian colleges, it is 15 to 1. The less educable the students, the more instructors you need—another part of the hidden costs of not having the draft.

The middle class, both black and white, is conspicuously absent, as well as the sons and daughters of the "elites." The quality of the troops we have available for combat is statistically disguised because the women being recruited into the armed services are decisively more intelligent than the men. After a three-year tour with troops in the years between 1970 and 1980, a young officer was physically and emotionally drained from trying to maintain discipline and lead and train men of whom the majority are uneducated and unmotivated. And the better the officer, the greater the drain.

The noncommissioned officers, the sergeants and corporals who are the backbone of any Army, suffer the same fate. In the first place, their worth is diminished in their own eyes and in the eyes of those they lead because recruits are paid such large amounts of money. These sums are necessary to attract people to volunteer into the armed services; but the erosion of the differential between the pay of the basic soldier and that of his noncommissioned leader causes NCOs to leave the service.

Congress and the political appointees in the Department of Defense are always under great pressure to solve the problem of too few people in the armed services by lowering the standards for those taken in. (During the Korean War, as the services moved to draft fathers to replace their combat losses, Congress proposed instead that the already minimal intelligence standards be further lowered.) Politicians quite naturally would rather fill the services with the less able, who tend not to vote, than improve the services by drafting able people, who might vote against them.

As an example of why the able must be present, here is a part of the instructions on the operation of the latest electronic-warfare radar jammers:

> To prevent permanent damage to the helix structure, if the helix interception becomes excessive, the intercept protection circuitry must react and reduce the intercept current to an acceptable level within a few microseconds. This is done by interrupting the TWT beam with the control anode. The anode modulator must then switch the anode from ground to cathode potential (several thousand volts) in those few microseconds while handling several kilowatts of power. Figure 9 shows the variation of both helix and anode intercept current during this on-off transition. (The 90 to 80 percent and 20 to 10 percent areas must be traversed quickly or destruction of the helix or anode will result.)

Some sophisticated and abstract arguments claim that by spending several billions more for pay, or by providing certain career benefits, or by causing the sun to always shine on Tuesdays, we could patch up the present AVF (All-Volunteer Force). That has not been historically true. It is not true today, when the situation in the field, while improving slightly, is far worse than is generally perceived. It will, I believe, be even less true in the future, as PGMs bring increased danger, loneliness, and complexity into a battlefield that knows no secure rear areas. Even in World War II, contrary to popular myth, American commanders were markedly nonaggressive and junior officers and noncommissioned officers, except in a few special units, lacked dash and professional skill. What makes us think that in the far more complex and deadly world of today we can continue to get by with inferior troops?

During the Berlin crisis of 1962 President Kennedy felt himself restricted in the ways he could respond because of the great weakness of the U.S. reserve forces, particularly the state-oriented National Guard. The whole question of American reserve forces is complex and politically explosive, as Congress uses the reserve forces as its private plaything. By and large, a great deal of extra effort had to be expended to bring National Guard units up to fighting standards in World War II and in Korea. Today, with few able people passing out of the armed services and into the reserves, the situation is mostly worse. I say "mostly" because flying units of the Air Force Reserve and Air National Guard, where professional airline pilots get in a little further flight time, are ready enough to provide true combat reserves. A just draft would not of itself improve our Guard and Reserves; but at least having a pool of able trained people would allow a chance at improvement. If a short deadly war is to be the reality, with both sides exhausted after the first weeks, trained reserves are an important part of the Giant's strength.

Those who favor maintaining the military power of America through the AVF are driven by the logic of their position to push for the expanded use of women in the armed services. This is why some conservatives, whom one would expect to think of women in traditional terms and argue against more women in the services, instead favor their increased use, even in combat-related roles. Every Reagan appointee in the Pentagon I have talked with favors enlarging the role of females in the service. "I have no problem contemplating an Air Force 50 percent female," one such official told me.

Those who favor a draft often oppose the increased use of women, believing the military machine would run better with the majority of the slots now held by women filled instead by the able men the draft would provide. Others believe that even with the draft, the deadly intensity of modern battle would so suck dry the small pool of able, motivated men that increased use of females would still be necessary. Female officers point out the lack of logic in having women pilots flying the AWACS command aircraft, which is a primary target, and not the jet fighters protecting the AWACS. They also ask such questions as: Why can the intelligence agents flown behind the lines be female, and not the helicopter pilot flying the agents?

I am in favor of the employment of women in the widest

variety of military jobs possible. With the limited manpower/ womenpower pool of the next twenty years, there is no way the country can meet its military responsibilities without large numbers of women in the armed services. This is particularly true if we continue with the AVF but would remain true if we had a draft. My problem is that I find the country largely against women in combat roles. Yet as we saw in the last chapter, women are in the combat environment now in significant numbers, and will die in combat in significant numbers. To employ women effectively inside the Other America of Defense, the country as a whole must first face the question of what happens when the dying starts.

Our reliance on the AVF rather than the draft raises fundamental questions about America's political health. Among these questions are: Would not the war in Vietnam have ended sooner if the sons of Harvard, Yale, Berkeley, Stanford, et al. had served there and brought back the truth of their firsthand experiences? Then there is de Gaulle's statement that he could not have ended the Algerian war if his army had been entirely composed of volunteer professionals. He needed the draftees to report what was going on and keep the defecting officers loyal to civilian authority. I pass quickly over the fact that because it would avoid enlistment bonuses and pay incentives for the lowest ranks, the draft would be much less expensive than the AVF, to the final moral question: Should a great nation lay so much of the burden of defending itself upon the poor and the outcast?

I do not wish to oversell a just draft, to claim that with its restoration alone all our military problems will disappear. Even the Germans, with a fifteen-month period of compulsory military service, have a hard time training their soldiers to maintain and fight with today's complex equipment. But they do better—though I hate to say it—they do far better on identical items of equipment. And so do the Dutch, Belgians, Danes, and others, again on equipment similar to our own. And their reserves are far more ready.

If a just draft is instituted, one portion of the Readiness/ Tooth-to-Tail problem will become more complex. To be effective, armed forces, like sports teams, must train realistically.

How much realistic training will Congress permit in peacetime if not merely the professionals but average citizens are asked to take risks in the name of Readiness? The line between an unnecessary harshness and realistic preparation is often arguable. I have nothing but respect for the members of Congress who must face these questions of risk and excellence when the dead or maimed are from their own districts.

This problem first dramatically struck me one night in Texas during the Korean War. I was reporting on the regeneration of the 2nd Armored Division from its low of sixty officers and men and zero tanks in 1948 to become a fighting unit once more. The division engineer battalion and a tank battalion were constructing a pontoon bridge in the dark below the Lampasas reservoir. The vast majority of engineers and tankers sweating in the bridge had been civilians a few months before. They were, by the lottery of the first Korean draft call, largely from Texas, Oklahoma, upstate New York, and Pennsylvania. Their average age was twenty-four, and 19 percent had some college. (In Vietnam their average age would have been twenty-three; and only 1 percent would have had some college.) As the recent civilians wrestled the huge boatlike pontoons off the trucks, dragged and winched them into the muddy water, then bolted them into place, they could see couples dancing on the lighted porch of a roadhouse some 100 yards away. The couples were enjoying themselves to the jukebox tune "She was a nice girl, a pretty girl; but she had a roving eye." Those sweating in the dark, about to go to Korea or Europe, could plainly see the dancers, who in the lottery of life had been handed an easier and safer if not a better existence. I wondered then, and continue to wonder now, how much realistic training a democracy can impose on its citizens, particularly in peacetime.

On 17 January 1983, four planes of the Air Force Thunderbird aerobatics team crashed and exploded. Something had happened to the leader's aircraft, and the other three pilots, guiding on him, hit the ground with him. The nation recoiled in understandable horror, a reaction that was repeated when several weeks later a soldier was killed on an 82nd Airborne jump. There were calls in the press and Congress to abolish such units and such training. If that had been done, fighter tactics and airborne training would have suffered. Concern over casualties had already caused the Air Force to raise from 200 to 400 feet the altitude at which its famed Red Flag fighter exercises were conducted. In wartime, pilots expect to operate often below 200 feet.

To leave this discussion of the draft by turning to history: In 1864, in the midst of the Civil War, it looked as if Lincoln would lose the October elections in Indiana. This would lead to the loss of the White House that November by the Republicans and himself. To win in Indiana, Lincoln came under extreme pressure to halt the unpopular draft. He replied: "I have been pressed to stop the draft. But what is the Presidency to me if I have no country?" Those congressmen who, fearful of losing public office, resist enactment of the draft today should ask themselves the same question: "What is my office to me if I have helped lose this country by creating a Straw Giant?"

Reform of the Flawed Organization of the Joint Chiefs of Staff and indeed of the entire inefficient armed services' command structure is another necessary action. The Joint Chiefs supposedly set military strategy, with the Secretary of Defense determine the military budget, then divide the monies provided and finally oversee that plans are followed. But the Joint Chiefs, created by Congress as an impotent committee, have been unable to perform these functions. And this vacuum at the top has produced layer after layer of headquarters beneath, with numerous officers who coordinate vast amounts of paper in proportion to the size of the fighting forces. Here it is a pleasure to report that the Giant has taken the proverbial giant step toward replacing his straw. On October 2 1986, the Goldwater-Nichols Act became law. This legislation, which required political skill and courage to enact, was spurred by our obvious defense failures and shaped by the detailed military knowledge of legislators such as Senator Sam Nunn and Congressman Les Aspin. The initial spark that fired the process was the sweeping reform proposals advanced in 1982 by the then Chairman of the Joint Chiefs of Staff, Air Force General David C. Jones.

General Jones's initiative was important not just because of his plan's intrinsic worth; but also because he dwelt inside the armed services. The reforms are not seen by those inside the Other America of Defense entirely as another solution imposed by "us" on "them." There are areas where I would go further than Goldwater-Nichols or do things differently. But those are mere quibbles. It is not hyperbole to write that the bill is the most important piece of defense legislation since World War II. And this specifically includes the National Defense Act of 1947 that separated the Air Force from the Army and created the Department of Defense. Finally, the Defense of America stands as intended by those giant victors of World War II: Truman, Marshall, Stimson and Lovett.

Interestingly, the new legislation in many respects parallels the reorganization of the British armed forces undertaken just before they successfully fought the Falklands campaign. As one would suspect from Defense Department history, the legislation has been largely welcomed by the Army and Air Force. The Navy is mobilizing allies in the Senate to try and overturn major parts of the reform in the next session of Congress. However, after the recent defense disasters, several of the Navy's prestigious admirals with experience on the Joint Chiefs and in Joint Commands broke ranks to support the plan. Significantly, they are no longer in the Navy. Also Ronald Reagan's Secretary of Defense, Casper Weinberger, seemed not to understand the nature of the plan and fought the reforms. Indeed, the President, elected on a platform to strengthen defense, and a friend and political ally of Senator Goldwater, did not even hold a signing ceremony in the White House.

In advancing his proposals, General Jones wrote eloquently why his own experiences led him to advocate change:

> I have been a member [of the Joint Chiefs of Staff] for nearly eight years and its Chairman for most of the past four years, and have thus served as a member of the Joint Chiefs under four Presidents and four Secretaries of Defense. During this time, and before, many good men have struggled very hard to make the best of the joint system, and most, if not all, have experienced a great sense of frustration in dealing with both large and small problems.

Much of this frustration comes from having to cope with legislative and organizational constraints which reflect concerns of the past, inhibit attempts to meet the rapidly changing demands of today's world, and violate basic leadership and management principles. Yet, despite many studies that have periodically documented problems with this military committee system and made cogent recommendations for improvements, the system has been remarkably resistant to change. Committees can serve a useful purpose in providing a wide range of advice to a chief executive or even in making some key policy decisions, but they are notoriously poor agents for running anything—let alone everything.

Any institution that imbues its members with traditions, doctrines and discipline is likely to find it quite difficult to assess changes in its environment with a high degree of objectivity. Deep-seated Service traditions are important in fostering a fighting spirit, Service pride and heroism, but they may also engender a tendency to look inward and to perpetuate doctrines and thought patterns that do not keep pace with changing requirements. Since fresh approaches to strategy tend to threaten an institution's interests and self-image, it is often more comfortable to look to the past than to seek new ways to meet the challenges of the future. When coupled with a system that keeps Service leadership bound up in a continuous struggle for resources, such inclinations can lead to a preoccupation with weapon systems, techniques, and tactics at the expense of sound strategic planning.

Furthermore, officers come from and return to their Services which control their assignments and promotions. The strong Service string thus attached to a Joint Staff officer (and to those assigned to the Unified Commands as well) provides little incentive—and often considerable disincentive—for officers to seek joint duty or to differ with their Service position in joint deliberations. Indeed, it is hard to argue that Joint Staff duty is a path to the top. With the exception of Army General Earle Wheeler, not a single Director of the Joint Staff or one of its major components has ever become Chief of his Service or Chairman of the Joint Chiefs of Staff.

To reinforce Jones's words on service strings, here are a few examples: The Joint Staff is the staff of 400 officers that serve the three Joint Chiefs. In 1982 and 1983 the Navy, which includes the Marines, did not "promote early" a single officer serving on the Joint Staff. Early promotion, or promotion "below the zone" as the services call it, is the most coveted award all three services give to those they deem exceptionally able. In the same period the Army and Air Force had from one to four officers on the Joint Staff who were promoted "below the zone."

Further, "within the zone," where the ordinarily able get promoted, the percentage of naval and Marine officers promoted on the Joint Staff lags behind the percentage of such officers promoted not only from the naval staff but from the fleet as a whole. In other words, the Navy and Marines are not even assigning their average officers to the Joint Staff. They are assigning their mediocre officers. In contrast, the percentage of Air Force and Army officers on the Joint Staff promoted "within the zone" equals those in the Army and Air Staffs promoted on time. Here is another area in which we have slipped way backward since World War II.

Yet in the face of Jones's statement—and such evidence as the disasters in the Iranian desert and Beirut—Admiral James L. Holloway III, a former Chief of Naval Operations, stated: "...We must be extraordinarily cautious in approaching any decision to make significant changes. The present system works...it has served us well in its same basic configuration through two conflicts and years of cold war with the Soviet Union." The Marine Corps Commandant, General P.X. Kelley (he who was "surprised" by the truck bomb in Beirut) saw the reforms as the end of America: "[They] would create chaos... to the point where I would have deep concerns for the future of the United States." And a former Marine Corps Commandant, General Wallace M. Greene, Jr., testified before Congress that all that was needed was "more willingness on the part of all hands to make the present JCS machine work. Make a real effort!" (exclamation point his).

While I welcome General Greene's tacit admission that someone has been jamming the gears (and none knows better than he who threw the wooden shoes), such talk is dangerous nonsense. Those who believe the system worked must have been living on a different planet from all of us since the close of World War II. History repeats itself with the service that feels its basic mission threatened opposing further unification.

The Navy did this at the Defense Department's creation, then the Army was in opposition in the late fifties, now the Navy and Marines have returned as the frightened service of the opposition. Fortunately, Congress, which in the past had used such service complaints as an excuse to continue the impotent organization they could easily dominate, this time found the strength within itself to put the health of the Giant first. The House seems determined to keep the reforms in place for a few years to see how they work. The Navy has powerful friends in the Senate who appear determined to repackage the old straw. The present Chairman of the JCS, Admiral William Crowe, Jr., has shown both political skill and a willingness to give the reforms a try. In the best of all possible worlds this "sailor" may be able to open the Navy to reform as Forest Sherman once did. After all, it was a Republican President, Nixon, who brought China and America together.

In essence, Goldwater-Nichols accomplishes the following. The Chairman of the Joint Chiefs is made the senior military officer, responsible for providing advice to the President, the Secretary of Defense and the National Security Council and developing strategic plans and budgets. His advice, not that of a log-rolling committee, goes before the President through the NSC. The Chairman also gains control over the Joint Staff, the 400 officers who serve the JCS. To aid the Chairman and act for him in his absence, a new position is created, Deputy Chairman, senior to the Chiefs of Staff of the three services. If any of the three service chiefs disagreed strongly with the rec-ommendations of the Chairman they would have the right to take their disagreements to the Secretary of Defense, or, on certain grave issues, the President.

The Chairman needs a deputy because he must continually be attending Congressional hearings, NSC meetings, be away on inspection trips or meeting with allies. While he is out of town, or even just out of the Pentagon, meaningful work often stops. Under the present system, during one week of vital planning for the Iranian operation, there were seven different Acting Chairmen of the Joint Chiefs. Each one had to be "brought up to speed"—have what had just gone on before and what he was expected to do explained to him before he could act. How, with such a system, can we expect any other result than failure? How can senior naval officers claim "the system works"?

The law also tackles the vital problem of who gets promoted for doing what. This is a crucial reform. Today when a courageous colonel or commodore argues the nation's interest rather than that of his (or her) service, he or she knows that they most likely forfeit their chances of promotion. Here we have marched backward from the days of World War II, when Marshall made an interservice outlook a criteria for Army and (Army) Air Force promotions. Officers on interservice staffs should not have to put their families and future at risk when they act against the perceived interests of their service. I could run off a list of names that would mean little to anyone outside the Other America of Defense of outstanding officers who were forced into early retirement because their services considered their action in some joint matter disloyal.

To reward rather than punish officers who think and act jointly, the legislation creates a new career path for officers, the "joint specialty." No officer is to be promoted to General or Admiral unless he has served successfully in a position on a joint staff that requires this joint specialty.* To make sure joint specialty officers and others who have served on joint staffs are promoted fairly, all boards considering their promotions must contain an officer appointed by the JCS Chairman. If that person reports hanky-panky the Chairman can intervene. In other words, an officer from one service can have a say in the promotion of an officer in a different service and make it stick.

The joint staffs are not just the staff that serves the JCS but those that serve such other major commands as NATO, the Pacific Area, the Southern Command, the Middle East—ten in all. To be brutally frank about it, the staffs of these commands, possibly excepting NATO, are of not too high a caliber.

---

*There can be waivers for this requirement for those with critical specialties. This is important particularly for the Navy submariners who have a true problem. There are so few of them and their training is so lengthy that it is difficult at present for them to put in the time necessary to qualify for a joint specialty.

Up to now, able officers have fought shy of service on them for fear of offending powers that be in their own service. However, now that successful service on joint staffs becomes a preferred route to promotion, the ballgame changes; the able will bid for joint staff work. The British had reformed their system to give the Chairman of their Joint Chiefs a major voice in senior promotions in all three services just before the Falkland campaign.

Goldwater-Nichols's other major reform strengthens the powers of the theater commanders, who command American forces in various areas of the world, places them directly under the Secretary of Defense and brings them into the budget and planning process. These commanders are known as CINCs (pronounced as in kitchen "sink") and supposedly command all the forces in their area—Army, Navy and Air Force. For example, the NATO commander in 1987 is General Jack Galvin, not only a decorated veteran of Vietnam combat, but also completely fluent in German and Spanish, and the author of an excellent book on the American Revolutionary Soldier. He is known as CINCEUR, Commander in Chief Europe. During the Vietnam War the instructions from the Joint Chiefs went to Vietnam by way of CINCPAC in Hawaii. While, in theory, the CINCs have command of everything in their area, actually there are strings on their forces: planes and submarines are committed to strategic nuclear attack, aircraft carriers are part of the strategic reserve, airborne units have special intelligence missions. Forces vanish from under the CINC just when they are most needed. Even though he is the man who will command the battle, the CINC has had only a limited official say in what forces he needs and how they are to be trained and where they will fight.

Before the reforms the services, rather than the CINCs, planned much of these battles and kept a large measure of control over supplies and forces that the CINC might need. The exclusion of the CINCs from defense planning has grown out of service fears of being dominated by a rival service. This divided responsibility between area commanders and services causes such fiascoes as the deaths of the Marines in Lebanon. These Marines were in theory commanded by an Army general in Heidelberg, through a series of admirals in Italy and at sea, and the battalion's officers had not even had an intelligence briefing on terrorist truck bombs. To bring the CINCs into top-level planning helps mate the tooth to the tail; and aids in fixing responsibility.

Another example: When the *Stark* was hit by the Iraqi missile in the Persian Gulf on May 17, 1987, the reforms were just being implemented. The chain of command over the *Stark* had run from CENTCOM commanded by a Marine general at McDill Air Force base in Florida, out to a junior admiral at CINCPAC in Hawaii, then to the Naval task force commander in the Persian Gulf and then to the *Stark*. Now the Marine general was able to command the task force bypassing the admiral in Hawaii. One whole layer of coordination and confusion had been removed. This also meant that a Marine was commanding a Navy ship, undoubtedly confirming the worst fear of certain admirals about the new law. Had the attack occurred a few months earlier, those fleet units would have been under the command of an Army paratroop general.

The Goldwater-Nichols Act also makes certain other important reforms. Among these are the insistence on a three-and-one-half-year term of joint duty, removing exclusive Navy control over certain missions, and mandating study of roles and missions. But here I am decidedly faced with the problem of what to include and exclude, the difficulty to which I referred in the preface as my "Fink-Nottle dilemma." Reform of the JCS, the promotion system and the authority of the CINCs are the guts of the bill.

I do not wish to seem to oversell these reforms. There are still going to be bureaucratic battles and people trapped in service parochialism, as there have been all along. The services still face the task of realigning roles and missions in the coming age of accuracy. Congress is still an unrepentent micromanager and meddler; in the year following Goldwater-Nichols the number of reports required by Congress from the military actually increased. But blow trumpets blow! The system now works to minimize parochialism, rather than rewarding the disease.

Let me reiterate that these reforms are not a method of

abolishing the services. I believe in strong services and service loyalties. I have found that it is precisely those services, or portions of the services, that are most secure and strong in their identity that are the most willing to compromise and negotiate meaningfully with other parts of the Department of Defense.

To augment the reforms of Goldwater-Nichols the method of funding the major missions of the Defense Department should change. Part of the shift, the more powerful JCS Chairman, his Joint Staff plus the Secretary of Defense and the enhanced CINCS will be able to accomplish on their own. Other parts require legislation and perhaps reorganization of portions of the House and Senate Armed Services Committees. This will be hard because once again political self-interest and the national interest will fight for control of the hearts and minds of the politicians involved; and in that battle the outcome is always in doubt.

Congressional reform becomes more difficult yearly because of Washington's major growth industry—serving on a Congressional staff. Between 1970 and today committee staffs have grown from around 700 to around 2,000. As early as May 1941, General Marshall wrote: "Yesterday I had five Congressional calls, three visits at the request of important members of Congress which could not well be refused by me, and about 12 Congressional telephone queries. Meanwhile, I have to confer with the Secretary of War, with the Secretary of State, with the President, with members of the staff, make some inspections and attend to the business of the Army. A democracy makes certain requirements that have to be treated in a philosophical manner; but the manner is now progressing beyond the point of feasibility."

General Edward C. ("Shy") Meyer, the recently retired Army Chief of Staff, put it politely in describing today's turmoil: "The explosion of lawmaking and regulation writing in the 70s has greatly complicated the development of a coherent defense posture.... The growth in Congressional staffs has had an impact on the time available for the individual Chief to direct his service.... The Chiefs have even less time for strategic reflection."

What Congress must do both to increase civilian control over the Defense Department and the military's own efficiency is fund the major defense missions directly, rather than through the three services as at present. Now, if Congess wishes to put X number of dollars into the strategic warfare mission, that money passes from Congress to the Secretary of Defense and then onto the three armed services, who may or may not spend the dollars as Congress intended. We have seen how the Navy puts money into carriers that Congress and the Secretary of Defense intended for submarine-launched missiles. And how during the Vietnam War, monies appropriated for other purposes were shifted to Vietnam to disguise the true costs of that war.

Under mission funding, the monies appropriated by Congress for each major mission would pass from the Secretary of Defense to the Chairman of the Joint Chiefs and from there to the Commander in Chief, CINC, of that mission. Civilian control is increased because Congress and the civilian secretaries can watch that the money is being spent as intended.

Some in the services are bound to resist funding by mission as a threat to service autonomy. The proposal does cut across the traditional boundaries of the services and somewhat reduces service autonomy. But it is most emphatically not a method of abolishing the three armed services, of putting everyone into one service, the so-called "purple suit" approach. Service differences are vital for morale, and the last thing the armed services need right now is to have their morale further tampered with.

Funding by mission gives the CINCs of the missions— NATO, Strategic Warfare, antiterrorism—both funds and authority to do that with which they are charged. In other words, to bring their tooth and their tail together. For example, at present, both Army and Air Force are struggling to get the other service to pay for desalinization equipment for the Rapid Deployment Force. This is because the money for that force passes through the services first and both the Army and Air Force have uses for those dollars to which they assign higher priority. If those funds had gone directly from Congress, through the Secretary of Defense and the JCS Chairman, to the CINC of the Rapid Deployment Force, then the Army and

Air Force would fight to build the plants. The service that built them would have its available funds increased rather than decreased.

At present, the Air Force is reluctant to explore and exploit the possibilities of space for fear that any monies spent there will come out of more favored weapons such as bombers and fighters. The Army, having been burned in the past during the Vanguard/Redstone controversy of the late fifties, is not about to "waste" its money on space. The Navy sees space as a threat to its mission of sea surveillance—oceans they plan to watch with ships and planes can be watched by satellite. As a result the amateurs of the Kettering Observatory in Great Britain, not the United States Air Defense Command, uncovered the Soviet's successful testing of a killer satellite. If monies went directly to the space mission the services would turn from worrying that space will subtract from their budgets to considering how to get a piece of the space action.

Healing the Great Divorce, instituting a just draft, funding by mission system, are the major necessary actions to replace straw with steel. Along with these, all interested parties must remain vigilant that the reforms of Goldwater-Nichols have a chance to operate; and are not weakened or even overturned by parochial service intrigue and Congressional self-interest. There are other improvements the armed services should and could take by themselves, such as an end to KAFCA. Combat leadership will always correctly remain the final key to high command. However, in today's complex world, such areas as military intelligence, procurement, and service with foreign troops should also be routes to the top. When you visit the outer reaches of such places as the Army Material Command, you realize usually that you have reached bureaucratic darkness. Yet those there can make or break a future weapons system.

The constant shifting of officers from assignment to assignment should lessen—a goal the services often claim they are about to reach. Brigadier Julian Thompson, who commanded the British commando forces in the Falkland Islands, had been in his command for almost his entire service life. Colonel

James Terry Scott, who commanded the airborne brigade invading Grenada, had been in his command four days. That part of Goldwater-Nichols which sets three and a half years as the length of time for service on joint staffs should reduce turbulence at the top and that should be felt throughout the armed services. The cursed "ticket punching" that began in the late fifties, where officers have to hold a wide variety of jobs to get ahead, is seen by all inside the Other America of Defense as a major cause of the Giant's weakness. But, though the Navy exhibits less personnel turbulence than the other services, all three are caught in some absurd game of musical chairs.

Writing later of his efforts to end the constant rotation of officer assignments during his period as Army Chief of Staff in the early eighties, General Meyer reported: "Efforts to extend command tours were met with great alarm by the Army, and it goes back to the self-centeredness that was engendered by the six-month [Vietnam command] tour." Meyer also found the wives in effective opposition; they didn't want their husbands overseas for longer periods. Summing up his largely unsuccessful efforts, Meyer concluded that "the voice of the twenty-year careerist was heard louder than the voice of the soldier."

I have one proposal of my own to help heal the Great Divorce: that is, broaden the present basis of the ROTC programs given at many universities. Most universities offer groups of courses under such titles as industrial relations, or business administration, which are taken by those who seek business or industrial careers. Industry hires from these pools. Similarly, those heading for the Foreign Service often major in international relations. Why cannot there be a similar armed service course of study, in which those who wish to pursue a military career in the regulars or reserves could enroll?

Such a course of study would cut across many departments: history, psychology, economics, languages, and so forth. In the summer, those in such a program could do actual military service. Individuals in this extended ROTC program would receive a stipend based on the degree of their future commitment. This is done now with medical students who agree to serve in the armed forces after graduating from medical school.

The military are cold to such a proposal because they would like to go back to the days when their officers were actually professors in the universities that had ROTC programs. Such an arrangement still exists in many universities and should remain; but it does not answer all needs. On the other side, many of the elite universities fight the idea of a major in military affairs as something less than real education. What is needed is a little give and take on both sides, some recognition that both academia and the military suffer from the Great Divorce.

In 717, Leo the Isaurian, a shepherd's son who through his own efforts had risen to high command in the Roman Empire, defeated the Arabs before the gates of Constantinople. The Moslem surge into Europe stopped there. Leo was outnumbered five hundred to one. He revitalized a dispirited and often defeated army. He rallied the civilian population, stored food, repaired Constantinople's ancient walls, on which he then mounted catapults. He used a new weapons system, fast galleys carrying Greek fire which was squirted out of bulls' intestines. This set the Arabs' ships aflame before they could close with Leo's ships. He induced many of the Egyptian Christians manning ships in the Arabs' fleets to defect. Leo spread rumors, which the Arabs believed, that a force of fearsome Franks was about to fall on their rear. He instituted successful guerrilla operations against the Arabs' supply lines. And his diplomats persuaded the Bulgars to attack the Arabs in the East. Unity of purpose and command (and some luck, the winter was unusually severe) brought victory against odds that seemed to make defeat inevitable. Constantinople, which had been regarded as a Straw Giant, stood for seven more centuries.

BIBLIOGRAPHICAL NOTES

PROLOGUE: DISASTER IN THE DESERT

The account of the Iranian rescue mission is based largely on a series of interviews conducted by the author. In addition, the following sources have been used: *All Fall Down*, an account of the Iranian crisis as seen from the Carter White House by Gary Sick (New York: Random House, 1985); *Delta Force*, by Colonel Charlie A. Beckwith, U.S.A., Retired, an account of the Iranian mission by the leader of the commandoes who were going to rescue the hostages (New York: Harcourt Brace Jovanovich, 1983). Logan Fitch, the deputy commander of the rescue force on that mission, has also published a memoir in *Penthouse*. The Pentagon published an official after-action report on the mission called the Holloway Report after the chairman of the committee convened to look into the disaster, Admiral J. L. Holloway III. Certain parts of the report were kept secret and some of these I have seen. In addition, a number of the participants in the mission wrote after-action reports and I have been fortunate to read more than twenty of these.

"Nitrogen under pressure": The whole question of the failure of the helicopter rotor blades and the problem of erratic warning lights is gone into thoroughly in the Holloway Report.

Shakespeare's caustic profile of a staff officer comes from *Henry IV, Part I*, I, iii, 52–63.

For information on the invasion of Grenada, see the *New York Times* of 6 October 1985, which goes into the details of the Senate Armed Services Committee report on that operation.

For an analysis of Flawed Organization, see "The Organizational Structure of the Department of Defense in the 1980s: An Analysis Based on the Defense Organization's Study of 1977," 1980, by Archie D. Barrett, Senior Research Fellow at the National Defense University Research Directorate of Washington, D.C., January 1982.

Information on the different attitudes toward Readiness and Tooth-to-Tail in the Israeli and American armies comes from after-action reports of the 1973 Arab/Israeli war.

The fact that the White House requested the tail numbers of the helicopters lifting the final survivors of Vietnam off the roof of the American embassy in Saigon comes from a series of interviews with the participants. Other information on Vietnam comes from the experiences of the author while a reporter there in 1970.

GETTING TO THE BEGINNING

A discussion of the historic gap running between civilian elites and the military can be found in Allan R. Millett and Peter Maslowski's comprehensive history of America's military forces, *For the Common Defense* (New York: Free Press, 1984). Amplification based on the period just prior to World War II is contained in Charles A. Beard's *President Roosevelt and the Coming of the War, 1941* (New Haven: Yale University Press, 1948).

Historian Thomas Fleming offered insights into Colonial America's professional armed forces during a conversation held in June 1983. Supporting his view is the description of Andrew Jackson's cabinet, taken from chapter two of *Power's Human Face* by Arthur T. Hadley (New York: William Morrow, 1965). Samuel P. Huntington's *The Soldier and the State* (Cambridge, Mass.: The Bellknap Press of Harvard University Press, 1957), pp. 35 and 144, contains some further thoughts on the peculiar nature of the military in American society.

Huntington's *The Soldier and the State* contains an excellent discussion of President Thomas Jefferson's attitude toward the military. It also discusses the political moves against the establishment of standing military forces by Jefferson's allies.

The information on the gap between the intellectual elites and professional service officers in the thirties comes from newspapers and news magazines of that period.

Thomas B. Buell, biographer of Admiral King and Admiral Spruance, can be credited for information about both men's professional and personal reputations. Stories of Admiral King's competitiveness can be found in *Master of Sea Power: A Biography of Fleet Admiral Ernest J. King* (Boston: Little, Brown, 1980), pp. 5, 108; references to Admiral Spruance's clash with Admiral John McCain appear in *The Quiet Warrior: A Biography of Fleet Admiral Raymond A. Spruance* (Boston: Little, Brown, 1974), pp. 217–18.

An accurate and well-written fictional account of the Navy in the 1930s can be found in *Delilah—A Novel* by Marcus Goodrich, reprinted in 1978 by the Southern Illinois University Press. The original book appeared in 1941.

Descriptions of the bitter rivalry between TAC and SAC are found in Perry Smith's generally excellent study *The Air Force Plans for Peace 1943–1945* (Baltimore: Johns Hopkins Press, 1970), ch. 3. The first volume of *The Army Air Forces in World War II*, by Frank Caven and James L. Kate (Chicago: University of Chicago Press, 1958), gives one of the better overviews of the Army Air Corps' struggle to gain recognition from the ground Army officers.

Over the years, the International Institute of Strategic Studies (IISS) has issued a number of excellent studies of pre–World War II air forces development in both the United States and Great Britain, and I am indebted to them for many of the insights and quotations here, such as that of Marshall Trenchard.

The account of General MacArthur's disbanding of Brigadier General Chaffee's Experimental Mechanized Force appears in Millett and Maslowski, *For the Common Defense*, p. 382. In 1969, *Armor Magazine* published a series of articles on the early history of the then Tank Corps. In *Combat Commander* (New York: Prentice Hall, 1970), Major General E. N. Harmon recalls that when he decided to join the mechanized forces rather than stay with the horse cavalry, he was told by the cavalry bureau to expect no further help in gaining promotions from their office.

For further information about tank preparedness, see pp. 204–5 of Mark S. Watson's *U.S. Army in World War II, The War Department, Chief of Staff: Prewar Plans and Preparations* (Washington, D.C.: Historical Division, Department of the Army, 1950) The author's own experiences begin to enter the picture at this point.

Keith Douglas's description of fighting in a Grant can be found on p. 109 of *Alamein to Zem Zem* (London: Editions Poetry, 1946). The book also contains a selection of Douglas's poetry. Douglas, who was killed shortly after D day, is virtually unknown in America as a poet. However, most Britishers see him as the World War II Wilfred Owen.

General George Marshall's establishment of an Advance Planning Group is detailed in Smith, *Air Force Plans for Peace*, p. 12, and also in Watson, *U.S. Army in World War II*, cited above. For fuller details, see *On Active Service in Peace and War*, by Henry L. Stimson and McGeorge Bundy (New York: Octagon, 1971, reprint of 1948 ed.). General Marshall's early thoughts on reorganization can be found in *George C. Marshall: Education of a General*, by Forrest C. Pogue (New York: Viking, 1963).

General Kuter's letter to General Arnold concerning the Air Staff's estimated figures of German aircraft production is taken from Smith, *Air Force Plans for Peace*, p. 108. In a footnote Perry Smith cites the date of Kuter's letter as 6 August 1943.

The secrecy which shrouded the construction of the atomic bomb, denying even Vice President Harry Truman knowledge of its existence, is documented in Truman's *Memoirs, Volume I: Years of Decisions* (New York: Doubleday, 1955), p. 10.

The Green Door problem appears over and over again in various military histories. The perilous consequences of secrecy at Pearl Harbor are discussed in Gordon W. Prange's *At Dawn We Slept* (New York: McGraw-Hill, 1981), chs. 57–61; the effects of undisclosed information on the fate of the cruiser *Indianapolis* are sketched in Raymond B. Lech's *All the Drowned Sailors* (New York: Stein & Day, 1982), ch. 2, and in Buell's biography of Admiral King, *Master of Sea Power*, pp. 348–49.

General Weyand's analysis of what the North Vietnamese actually intended appears in Don Oberdorfer's masterly study, *The Tet Offensive* (New York: Doubleday, 1971), pp. 136–41.

The first chapter of Ronald H. Spector's *Eagle Against the Sun* (New York: Free Press, 1984) provides a number of perspicacious insights into the state of the American military mind just prior to Pearl Harbor. This same book is also eloquent on the confusion in both the Hawaiian and Philippine islands immediately following the attack on Pearl Harbor and Manila.

The feuding and lack of command coordination between the various forces in the Pacific which led to such communications as that between General MacArthur and Admiral Hart are detailed in *The Pacific War*, by John Costello (New York: Rawson Wade, 1981), pp. 651ff, and John Toland, *Infamy—Pearl Harbor and Its Aftermath* (New York: Doubleday, 1982).

The reorganizations of the Army and Navy triggered by the series of defeats following Pearl Harbor are detailed by John Keegan in *Six Armies in Normandy* (New York: Viking, 1982), pp. 42–43, and Buell's *Master of Sea Power*, pp. 119, 152–53.

The controversy between the Army Air Corps and the Navy over the best method to deal with the German submarine menace is well described in Stimson and Bundy's *On Active Service in Peace and War* and in "Robert A. Lovett: *The War Years*," Ph.D. dissertation by Jonathan F. Fanton, Yale University, 1978.

For considered comments on the history of unification and the advantages and disadvantages of separate, autonomously commanded armed forces as compared with a unified Defense Department, see Smith's *Air Force Plans for Peace*; Millett and Maslowski's *For the Common Defense*, ch. 3; and C. W. Borklund's *The Department of Defense* (New York: Praeger, 1968).

I am indebted for insights into President Franklin D. Roosevelt's handling of wartime command to Eric Larabee. Larabee's own study of Roosevelt as supreme commander is scheduled for publication in 1986 and should be a major contribution to the history of World War II.

Interesting details of the Army/Air Force/Navy battle to control the seas can be found in Stimson and Bundy, *On Active Service in Peace and War*. Further details can be found in "Robert A. Lovett: The War Years," by Fanton.

Accounts of JCS disputes over manpower during World War II come from several histories. The first of these is *Eisenhower's Lieutenants*, by Russell F. Weigley (Bloomington: University of Indiana, 1981), pp. 568–70. Max Hastings also comments on America's manpower problems and includes a general discussion of the quality of invading forces at D day in *Overlord* (New York: Simon and Schuster, 1984), pp. 46–58. A third useful source on the topic is Millett and Maslowski's *For the Common Defense*. Finally, see ch. 4 of "Robert A. Lovett: The War Years," by Fanton.

The whole question of casualties and strategy during the bitter middle phase of the World War II European campaign is brilliantly covered in Weigley's *Eisenhower's Lieutenants*.

The excerpt from Patton's diaries concerning replacements and munitions comes from Weigley, *Eisenhower's Lieutenants*, p. 567.

Information on the 2nd Armored Division comes from *A History of the Second United States Armored Division, 1940–1946*, Lieutenant Colonel E. A. Trahan, G.S.C., editor (Atlanta, Ga.: Albert Love Enterprises, 1946).

Figures recording the relationship between soldiers' educational levels and outstanding combat performance are taken from Table 8 in *The American Soldier: Combat and its Aftermath* II, by Stouffer et al. (Princeton, N.J.: Princeton University Press, 1949).

General S. L. A. Marshall's findings on the percentage of riflemen in an average infantry company who actually fire weapons during combat appear in his book *Men Against Fire: The Problem of Battle Command in Future War* (Gloucester, Mass.: Peter Smith, 1978), pp. 54–59.

Corroborating accounts of Operation Cobra are taken from Weigley, *Eisenhower's Lieutenants*, pp. 151–52; from Hastings, *Overlord*, pp. 249–66; and from a number of other sources, including the personal experiences of some of those involved. General Montgomery's reference to Air Marshall Leigh-Mallory as a "gutless beggar" is recorded in the 21st Army Group Papers (WO 205/5D) PRO.

Lieutenant General James Hollingsworth is quoted in Harry G. Summers, Jr., *On Strategy: A Critical Analysis of the Vietnam War* (Novato, Calif.: Presidio, 1982), p. 46.

Soldiers, Statesmen, and Cold War Crises, by Richard K. Betts (Cambridge: Harvard University Press, 1977), p. 95, is the source for General Marshall's reminiscence on America's inability to "give the Russians hell." Both General Omar Bradley, in *A General's Life* (New York: Simon and Schuster, 1983), and Weigley, in *Eisenhower's Lieutenants*, dwell at length on the rapid decline of the American armed services at the close of World War II, as do Millett and Maslowski in *For the Common Defense*.

For a detailed account of "Lightning Joe" Collins's interpretation of orders to "roll with the punch," see Weigley, *Eisenhower's Lieutenants*, pp. 535–36. Interesting corroboration comes from Major General E. N. Harmon in *Combat Commander*. Harmon writes (p. 236): "Mounting the . . . attack required some rather serious finagling with military orders."

THE CHAOTIC CREATION

Neil Sheehan's insightful book *The Arnheiter Affair* (New York: Random House, 1971) contains his criticism of newspapers' inability to bring the truth to print (p. 266).

Admiral King's defense of the Navy's welfare before Congress is quoted on pp. 30–31 of Borklund's *The Department of Defense*. This book is also excellent for a general chronology of events, both onstage and backstage, during the creation of the Defense Department.

The difference between actual American power and what many Americans, including the President of the United States, believed to be American power in 1945–1946, can be found in "Afghanistan in the 1946 Iran Analogy," by Barry M. Blechman and Douglas M. Hart in *Survival*, November–December 1980, pp. 248ff.

General Omar Bradley recounts the Navy's attack on the policy of strategic nuclear bombardment in ch. 52 of his autobiography, *A General's Life*, written with Clay Blair. Earlier, in ch. 51, Bradley discusses the Army's perspective on the postwar future of the armed services.

General Marshall's quote comes from *Features/Columnists*, by General Edward C. Meyer, Chief of Staff, U.S. Army, Part II, Main Edition, 31 March 1986, p. 2.

An account of combat naval commanders and their unfixed opinions of a unified postwar military organization is offered in Borklund, *The Department of Defense*, pp. 25–27.

For a picture of James Forrestal's often disillusioning, dehabilitating struggle to strengthen the Defense Department, see ch. 51 of Bradley, *A General's Life*. See also ch. 2 of William R. Kintner's *Forging a New Sword* (New York: Harper, 1958).

The outline of the JCS chain of command established in 1947 is elaborated on in Borklund, *The Department of Defense*, pp. 78–101. The quotes from President Truman are from the same source. Further information on internal JCS battles was provided during a series of interviews conducted by the author.

The Eisenhower Diaries (New York: Norton, 1981), edited by Robert H. Ferrell, reprints the general's thoughts concerning special interests promoted during unification. The entry is dated 24 July 1947.

The first use of tanks in World War I, by the British at Cambrai, is described in *A Military History of the Western World* II, by Major General J. F. C. Fuller (New York: Funk & Wagnalls, 1955), pp. 272, 279–80.

It is Perry Smith in *Air Force Plans for Peace* (p. 76) who tells the story of General Arnold's delayed use of a Mercator projection map.

An excellent overview of the process Forrestal went through in changing his mind about the need for further unification of the Defense Department is provided in Kintner, *Forging a New Sword*, pp. 26ff.

The entry in Eisenhower's diary concerning James Forrestal is dated 2 February 1949.

Much of this information comes from interviews conducted immediately after the events by the author.

For further details of Louis Johnson's tenure as Secretary of Defense, see the section of Bradley, *A General's Life*, entitled "The Johnson Phase," pp. 501–5.

KOREA AND NATO: SUCCESSES AND FAILURES

Much of the information in this chapter comes from the notes and reports made by the author at this time as military correspondent for *Newsweek* and also for his weekly radio program on military affairs.

General Bradley offers an account of Offtackle on pp. 499–501 and 524 of *A General's Life*. General MacArthur's and Secretary of State Dean Acheson's descriptions of America's line of defense in the Far East appear on p. 528.

An important source on Korean War history is *Korea: The Untold Story*, by Joseph C. Goulden (New York: Times Books, 1982). Pages referred to for information contained in this chapter are pp. 20–21, 33 (KMAG), 57, 67, 76, 109–10 (first American infantry sent), 136. See also *Korea: The Limited War*, by David Rees (New York: St. Martins, 1964), and *This Kind of War*, by T. R. Fehrenbach (New York: Macmillan, 1963). For an account of the war itself, General Matthew B. Ridgway's *The Korean War* (New York: Doubleday, 1967) is outstanding. Omar Bradley's *A General's Life* also provides an interesting overview from the perspective of the Joint Chiefs of Staff.

On 30 June 1950, Eisenhower made the entry in his diary concerning Washington's initial, confused response to the Korean invasion.

For information on the call-up of the National Guard and Reserve during both the Korean War and the Berlin Crisis, see *Survival*, February 1983, pp. 30ff.

The changes in President Truman's civilian high command which were effected in late 1950 were covered by the author.

Admiral Ewen's comments on the dismal.lack of communication between air and ground troops were first printed in a *Newsweek* article (8/7/50).

Public documentation of the problems the Defense Department faced in managing the Korean War through its confused bureaucracy can be found in *The Semi-Annual Report of the Secretary of Defense, January 1 to June 30, 1952* (Washington, D.C.: G.P.O. 1952), pp. 2–66.

Information on the secret agent war and intelligence come from private documents in possession of the author.

The information on the CIA/Air Force battle over who would pilot the U2s that delayed photographing the Cuban missile sites comes from interviews in the possession of the author.

General Grant's comments on the military and political situation in 1862–1863 can be found in *Personal Memoirs* I by Ulysses S. Grant (C. L. Webster & Company, 1894), p. 262.

Admiral George Miller's criticism of President Carter's military budget appeared in an article by George C. Wilson in the *Washington Post* (1/15/78).

For a controversial but provocative overview of where the deficiencies in NATO's creation have led and a look at possible ways out, see "New Conventional Force Technology and the NATO Warsaw Pact Balance," by Dr. Steven L. Canby in *Adelphi Papers* No. 199, London, IISS, 1985.

Over the years, Alton Frye, Washington Director of the Council on Foreign Relations, has been a particularly perceptive critic of NATO's dilemmas and also a thoughtful proponent of various plans and proposals to move NATO into a more rational defense posture. Throughout this and the penultimate chapter of the book will be found reflections of his insights and ideas, for which I am most grateful.

PROMISE AND PERFORMANCE: THE GAP WIDENS

The off-the-record comment made about Defense Secretary Charles Wilson is recorded in General James Gavin's book *War and Peace in the Space Age* (New York: Harper, 1958), p. 155.

H. Struve Hensel's analysis of the Defense Department's organizational philosophy was published in the *Harvard Business Review* in February 1954. The excerpt reprinted in this chapter comes from p. 104.

The point that Pentagon leaders have routinely come and gone before getting a handle on their jobs is an accurate and oft-made one. While supporting figures related to turnover are drawn from a 1977 *Washington Post* article by Clayton Fritchey, "A Change of Hats for the Chiefs?" (11/12/77, p. A19), a comparable analysis was published over twenty years earlier in a *New York Times* article by Hanson W. Baldwin, "The Pentagon Turnover" (11/2/55).

An unpublished paper by Thaddeus Holt, former Deputy Under Secretary for International Affairs, on the composition and function of the military in the late 1960s contains figures on the number of "splits" produced by the JCS between 1955 and 1959.

Former JCS Chairman General David C. Jones's controversial article on the need for reorganization within the JCS appeared in *Armed Forces Journal International*, March 1982. Excerpts from the article, "Why the Joint Chiefs of Staff Must Change," come from pp. 62–72.

General Bradley offers a glimpse of Sandstone on pp. 495, 509, and 514–15 of his autobiography, *A General's Life*.

President Eisenhower's displeasure with Air Force General White's public, critical comments on the other armed services was recorded in his diary on 5 August 1957. John Foster Dulles, the original spokesman for the doctrine of massive retaliation, frequently outlined its principles and implications for America's defense posture and capabilities. Typical of his phraseology are the quotes in this chapter, which come from the *Department of State Bulletin* XXX (12 January 1954), pp. 107–10; and from Townsend Hoopes's biography of Dulles, *The Devil and John Foster Dulles* (Boston: Little, Brown, 1973), p. 127.

The Russians' success in launching the first space satellite and the internal Army vs. Air Force battles at that time are verified by General Gavin on pp. 14–18 of *War and Peace in the Space Age*.

A summary of Operation Paperclip, the program that brought German rocket experts to the United States, is provided by Frederick I. Ordway and Mitchell R. Sharpe in their book *The Rocket Team* (New York: Crowell, 1979), pp. 287, 292, 357, 362.

At the time the author conducted a number of interviews on the missile programs of all three services and that of the USSR. The fact that the Army was ordered by Defense Secretary Wilson to launch no missile with a range exceeding 200 miles is confirmed by General Gavin in *War and Peace in the Space Age*, p. 160.

A scholarly and detailed overview of American nuclear targeting doctrine can be found in "Targeting for Strategic Deterrence," by Desmond Ball (*Adelphi Papers* No. 185, London, IISS, 1983).

The cross-targeting of Soviet installations is reported in "Choosing a Strategy for World War III," one of Thomas Powers's many important articles on strategic arms. This piece was published in *The Atlantic*, November 1982; excerpts are from p. 92.

The description of the developing of the initial SIOP doctrine is from the author's notes at the time, supplemented by "Targeting for Strategic Deterrence," by Desmond Ball, pp. 8–11.

I am indebted to a number of friends in the Strategic Air Command for descriptions of the state of readiness inside SAC in the late fifties and early sixties. Things were not always as bright as they portrayed them in their reports to me, but they were decisively better than they are today.

President Kennedy's description of the doctrine of nuclear deterrence is quoted from Summers, *On Strategy*, p. 57. Further comments by Summers on Kennedy's ambivalence about the military appear on pp. 71–77.

The story of President Kennedy and the lieutenant immobilized by a Soviet blockade was reported by several participants, in interviews with the author.

The information on the Falkland Islands campaign comes primarily from Max Hastings and Simon Jenkins, *The Battle for the Falklands* (London: Michael Joseph, 1983), supplemented by interviews conducted in Great Britain by the author immediately after the event with some of the participants and staffs involved.

Comments made to McNamara about bombing the Viet Cong come from author's interviews.

See Clausewitz, *On War* II:2, Michael Howard's translation, p. 133, for his thoughts on the relationship of economics to combat.

Daniel Ellsberg, who later released the Pentagon Papers to the *New York Times* and became an ardent critic of the Vietnam War, was one of the principal architects of this winnable-nuclear-war targeting doctrine. See Desmond Ball, "Targeting for Strategic Deterrence," and also the same author's *Politics and Force Levels: The Strategic Missile Program of the Kennedy Administration* (Berkeley, Calif.: University of California Press, 1980).

For a profile of McNamara as Secretary of Defense and a thorough analysis of his decisions concerning the TFX/F-111, see *The TFX Decision*, by Robert J. Art (Boston: Little, Brown, 1968). Further information about the hidden service agendas buried within the TFX competition was provided during interviews with a number of the participants.

The transcript of the hearings of the Permanent Subcommittee on Investigations of the Senate Committee on Government Operations of the 91st Congress on the TFX contract provides overwhelming and repetitive detail about what may or may not have happened during the TFX purchase maneuverings. Part I, 24 March 1970, is perhaps the most revealing.

The move of troop E of the 1st Cavalry is described by then 2nd Lieutenant Samuel L. Myers (later general) in an after-action report written in 1930 and finally published in *Armor Magazine* in 1976.

The true story of the fortunes of Hadley Tank Company ("No tank like a Hadley tank"), a fictitious tank company created to obtain credit cards and show up the Pentagon, is detailed in "I Was a Military Industrial Complex," by Arthur T. Hadley, *Playboy*, May 1979.

Facts in this chapter concerning measurements and capability of Minuteman missiles were verified in *Jane's Weapon Systems*.

The stated directive for establishing the ICBM program is given in the *Air Force Plan (Revised) for Simplifying Administrative Procedures for the ICBM and IRBM Programs*, 10 November 1955, p. 5. Other information comes from interviews by the author.

Pork-barrel politics are written up frequently in the press. Among the articles used for this chapter are "Budget Knife Only Nicks Road and Harbor Projects," by Howie Kurtz, *Washington Post*, 1/26/82, pp. A1, 8; John Fialka's *Wall Street Journal* article on the Infantry Fighting Vehicle, 2/17/82, pp. 1, 20; "To Pentagon, Oversight Has Become Overkill," by Fred Hiatt and Rick Atkinson, *Washington Post*, 7/4/85, pp. A1, A12.

The author is indebted to Dr. Lewis Sorley of Anzonic Services Corporation for his observation on the relationship between the caliber of America's volunteer soldiers and the quality of weapons designed for their use.

General Frederick Morgan's assessment of committees is quoted from his book *Overture to Overlord* (New York: Doubleday, 1950), p. 77.

A brief discussion of "double-dipper" hearings appears in Mike Causey's *Washington Post* article of July 21, 1977 (p. B2). Also see "Confluence of Interests Often Unites Hill, Industry," an article written by Peter J. Ognibene which appeared in the *Washington Post*, January 3, 1978.

VIETNAM—THE GIANT STUMBLES

In the early days of the French action in Indochina up through the Dien Bien Phu period, I was covering the White House and National Security Council for *Newsweek* and much of this information is derived from my notes of the time.

Summers's *On Strategy*, chs. 1–6, contains a thorough analysis of the strategic drift into Vietnam.

Gavin's assessment of the proposal to put American ground troops in North Vietnam is described fully in ch. 3 of the general's book *Crisis Now* (New York: Random House, 1968), written in collaboration with Arthur T. Hadley.

There are a number of sources for the various pieces of information on Special Forces and the Kennedy administration. For figures verifying the tremendous and rapid expansion of Special Forces, see Betts, *Soldiers, Statesmen, and Cold War Crises*, pp. 128–29. Comments on the best of the officer specialists in irregular warfare can be found in David Halberstam, *The Best and the Brightest* (New York: Random House, 1972), pp. 202–5, and General Bruce Palmer, Jr., *The Twenty-five-Year War* (Lexington: University of Kentucky, 1984), pp. 22–23.

Secretary of State Henry Kissinger describes a new breed of military officer in his book *The White House Years* (Boston: Little, Brown, 1979), pp. 34–35.

McNamara's statement concerning America's military program in Vietnam is documented in Gavin, *Crisis Now*, p. 54.

President Kennedy's decision to deny blanket permission to the horde of officers planning fact-finding tours to Vietnam is recounted by David Halberstam in *The Best and the Brightest*, p. 255.

Summers's appraisal of U.S. failure to leave ARVN in charge of counterinsurgency comes from *On Strategy*, p. 173. Other general information on U.S. offensive strategy is taken from ch. 10, pp. 108–24. While in Vietnam myself I heard a number of officers forceably make the same point.

The insight that intelligent staff officers swallowed their doubts because they felt they had been wrong in World War II comes from *Soldiers, Statesmen, and Cold War Crises* by Betts.

The Joint Chiefs dispute with McNamara and McNaughton is detailed in Betts. The information about Lyndon Johnson lying on the rug and about the request for the tail numbers of the helicopters lifting the last Americans off the embassy roof in Saigon comes from interviews by the author.

The convoluted chain of command that hampered the carrying out of orders in the field is described by General William C. Westmoreland in *A Soldier Reports* (New York: Doubleday, 1976), pp. 75–76.

The death of Richard W. Pershing is reported in "Letters from Quang Tri," by Paul Hofheinz and Morris Panner, *The New Journal* (Yale University), March 2, 1984, pp. 18–25.

Statistics on black casualties are reported by Rick Atkinson in the *Washington Post*, 12/12/84, p. A14. For insights on the initial black casualties I am indebted to General Bruce Palmer, who cites as his source Martin Binkin and Mark J. Eitelberg, *Blacks in the Military* (Washington, D.C.: Brookings Institution, 1982), pp. 32–33.

People Sniffers are described fully in *The Tunnels of Cu Chi*, Tom Mangold and John Penycate (New York: Random House, 1985), p. 202.

Percentages of congressmen with battle experience were reported by Don Winter in the *Washington Post*, 4/6/80, p. E1.

A description of General LeMay's challenge to an Army Chief of Staff is given in Palmer, *The Twenty-five-Year War*, p. 27.

General Palmer's comments on the lack of command and direction in Korea's air wars appears on p. 30 of *The Twenty-five-Year War*.

The seductive trap caused by the considerations of tactics rather than strategy provides one of the themes of *On Strategy*, by Summers.

An account of the Marine Corps' attempt to go back on its promise to pool aircraft with the other armed services is sketched in Westmoreland, *A Soldier Reports*, pp. 343–44.

The picture of the exhausted RAF squadron leader expected to "yomp" for days in the cold is mentioned in Max Hastings and Simon Jenkins, *The Battle for the Falklands*, p. 239.

The insights on and analysis of the impact of the Vietnam War on the Army as an institution come from an excellent unpublished paper by Dr. Lewis Sorley, "It Tolls For Thee." For his quotation about the dead count of Viet Cong, Sorley credits Jeffrey A. Jay, "After Vietnam: I. In Pursuit of Scapegoats," *Harper's*, July 1978, p. 19. "US Army Unit Readiness Reporting" is also cited by Sorley as the source for quotes about Army personnel and their disregard for the credibility of readiness reporting.

A brief profile of the young, able General Upton can be found in Millet and Maslowski, *For the Common Defense*, pp. 255–57. A more detailed description of Upton and his work can be found in Huntington, *The Soldier and the State*, p. 232.

The fate of the Bru is chronicled in *Free in the Forest*, the second volume of Gerald C. Hickey's *Ethnohistory of the Central Highlands* (New York: Yale University Press, 1982).

Abraham Lincoln on his defeat for a Senate seat is quoted in John G. Nicolay and John Hay, *Abraham Lincoln: A History* (New York: Century, 1890), vol. IX, p. 377.

THE ACCURACY REVOLUTION

In September 1977, at Bruges, Belgium, the International Institute of Strategic Studies (IISS) devoted its annual conference to the effects on strategy and the strategic balance of the arrival of more-accurate weapons. I am indebted to all the conference participants, particularly those who delivered papers, for the development and clarification of my own ideas about the effects of the accuracy revolution. In particular, Walter Stutzle, then chief of the planning staff of the Ministry of Defense in Bonn, and Philip A. Karber, a vice president for national security programs at the BDM Corporation in Virginia, have helped me clarify my thoughts over a number of years.

Information about the fate of the Than Hoa and Paul Doaumier bridges comes from after-action reports of the time, as do the facts about the Israeli 190th Armored Brigade and the planes lost during the 1973 war. The information on the sinking of the *General Belgrano* comes from Hastings and Jenkins, *The Battle for the Falklands*. In addition, an excellent summary of the effects of the Yom Kippur War on Western defense thinking can be found in *Military Lessons of the Yom Kippur War: Historical Perspectives*, by Martin van Creveld (Washington, D.C.: The Center for Strategic and International Studies, Georgetown University, 1975).

The vulnerability of surface ships to attacks by PGMs is discussed in *Adelphi Papers* No. 122, pp. 1–10, 22–30, London, IISS, Spring 1976. See particularly "The Impact of New Maritime Technologies," by Hubert Feigl, Senior Staff Member, Stiftung für Wissenschaft und Politik, Ebenhausen, in this issue.

The problem of dividing up the sea-control mission between the Air Force and the Navy is investigated at length in the 16 August 1982 issue of *Aviation Week*.

Current status of the American Harpoon antisubmarine cruise missile was reviewed in *Aviation Week*, 8/16/82, p. 25.

For a wealth of corroborative detail on the Air Force's lack of commitment to the use of smart bombs I am indebted to Graham T. Allison and Frederic A. Morris.

Speaker of the House Sam Rayburn's remark on the inexperience of Kennedy's administrators is taken from Halberstam, *The Best and the Brightest*, p. 41.

The 1st Cavalry Division's casualty figures were verified by the Center of Military History, U.S. Army.

Professor Michael Howard's response to charges that smart weapons are a threat to the free world alliance was printed in a letter to the editor of *The London Times*, 11/3/81. Other insights on the capabilities and uses of smart weapons come from discussions held at the 19th and 26th conferences of the International Institute for Strategic Studies.

Marshall Akhromeyev's quote was reported in the *New York Times*, 18 October 1985.

The figures on MX costs and, to some degree, the configuration of the missile itself keep changing constantly. The set of figures used in this book derive in about equal measure from the author's interviews and official Air Force fact sheets and testimony before Congress on MX missile development.

One possible configuration of the Minuteman was photographed and described by *Aviation Week* in the issue of October 28, 1985.

A great deal of information on Soviet nuclear forces can be found in *Adelphi Papers* Nos. 187 and 188 by Stephen M. Meyer.

TODAY'S STRATEGIC FORCES—EXPENSIVELY UNREADY

The author's account of his test flight in a B-52 appeared in the *Washington Star*, 7/1/79, pp. B1, 4–5.

SAC headquarters' description of the SRAM is found in "Fact Sheet USAF, April 1, 1978, p. 30." The technical specifications of the Minuteman missiles are also from the SAC fact sheets. The information about fan problems is from author's interviews.

It is Dr. Lewis Sorley who discusses Europe as a way station for troops going to Vietnam, p. 44.

Polled responses on U.S. military expenditures are drawn from a survey conducted by Lawrence Kaagan and Daniel Yankelovich for the 24th Annual Conference of the International Institute of Strategic Studies, The Hague, September 1982.

The hypothetical jet fighter used to illustrate the trade-off between readiness and total force levels is derived from a model created by Richard K. Betts in an article entitled "Conventional Forces: What Price Readiness?," *Survival*, IISS, January/February 1983, p. 25.

Recruitment statistics on women in the armed forces are verified in a document entitled "WEAL Facts," provided by the Women's Equity Action League, Washington, D.C. Other valuable, nonstatistical information was offered during an interview with a director of WEAL, Carolyn Becraft.

The problem of survivability for Minuteman and submarine-launched missiles is analyzed by Thomas Powers in *The Atlantic*, November 1982, p. 95.

A theoretical discussion of the vulnerability of the command links in the strategic nuclear defense system, bolstered by excellent real-world details, can be found in ch. 3 of Desmond Ball's "Can Nuclear War Be Controlled?," *Adelphi Papers* No. 169, London, IISS, 1981.

The author's rhetorical question on the use of nuclear arms first appeared in *The Nation's Safety and Arms Control* (New York: Viking, 1961), p. 38.

A detailed picture of the sinking of the British ship *Atlantic Conveyor* is painted in Hastings and Jenkins, *The Battle for the Falklands*, p. 277.

Plans and funding for the 600-ship Navy are described by Michael Getler, " 'Too Late to Stop' Fleet Buildup, Says Navy Secretary," *Washington Post*, 12/2/82; and by David North, "Emphasis in Navy Budget Shifts Toward Expansion," *Aviation Week & Space Technology*, 2/15/82, pp. 22–23.

George W. Ball's comments on the influence of an intellectual elite on U.S. weapons policy are taken from his article "White House Roulette," *The New York Review of Books*, 11/8/84, pp. 5–8.

Joyce Carol Oates's remarks are taken from her acceptance speech for the National Book Award in Fiction, 1970.

REPORT FROM THE FIELD

Facts about the United States' poor performance in the Canadian Cup come from author's interviews and John Fialka's *Washington Star* article "U.S. Posts Dismal Record in NATO Competitions," 12/16/80. This piece was the second in a revealing five-part series entitled "Can the U.S. Army Fight?"

Further quotes from polled junior officers are taken from Dr. Lewis Sorley's paper "It Tolls for Thee."

Rising educational levels of military recruits were reported by Fred Hiatt in the *Washington Post*, 11/1/84, p. A16.

A comparison of the type of soldier being trained as a tank commander in the United States and his counterpart in Israel was made by General Paul Gorman during an interview with the author.

The information on the Rapier comes from interviews with British officers after the Falkland battle.

Defense Secretary Harold Brown's assessment of relative U.S.–Soviet military strength appeared in "Our Underequipped, Unprepared NATO Forces," an article written by the author for the *Washington Post*, 6/4/78.

The estimate that one quarter of the American defense budget is spent on tactical air power is taken from a Brookings Institute report. The figure, cited by Steven L. Canby, appears in a footnote on p. 36 of *Adelphi Papers* No. 109, London, 11SS.

Those interested in pursuing the possibilities and limitations of air power in the nonnuclear defense of NATO should study "Deterrence in the 1980s: Part II: The Role of Conventional Air Power," by Lieutenant Colonel D. J. Alberts, USAF (*Adelphi Papers* No. 193, London, IISS, 1984).

The revealing comparison made between the amount of spare parts brought into mock battle by a German and a U.S. tank brigade was printed in a *New Republic* article by the author entitled "Why Johnny Can't Fight," May 7, 1984, p. 20.

It was during an address to Congress on 10 March 1977 concerning standardization in NATO that Senator John Glenn reported on six areas in need of improved interoperability.

TO REPLACE STRAW WITH STEEL

Insights into the design of the F-18 came from interviews conducted by the author.

Publication of the district location in which F-18 engine parts are constructed was made in the *Congressional Record, Senate*, 7/11/78, p. S10380.

The story of the My Lai massacre and the subsequent Army internal investigation can be found in *Cover-Up*, by Seymour M. Hersh (New York: Random House, 1972).

Henry Fairlie's reflections upon the American armed forces' loss of prestige are taken from the *New Republic*, 7/12/82, pp. 8–12.

Henry Kissinger's analysis of America's changing role in the global balance of power are recorded in the *Washington Post*, 11/20/84, p. A15.

The ratios of students to instructors at civilian and military colleges were offered in a *New York Times* editorial, 12/30/76.

The congressional proposal that intelligence standards be lowered during the Korean War was reported in *Newsweek*, 9/11/50, p. 31.

The convoluted description of helix structure is excerpted from an article entitled "Airborne Jammers Get Smarter Over the Years," *Electronic Warfare*, January/February 1977, p. 52.

A discussion of President Kennedy's use of U.S. Reserve forces appears in Betts, *Soldiers, Statesmen, and Cold War Crises*, pp. 101–2.

Lincoln's statement in support of his position on the draft is to be found in *Statesmanship of the Civil War*, by Allan Nevins (Charlottesville: University of Virginia, Barbara Page Foundation, 1951), p. 58.

Joint Staff experience and promotion practices in the armed forces were addressed by Vice Admiral Thor Hanson, USN (Ret.) before the Investigations Subcommittee, House Armed Services Committee, June 16, 1982.

Statements on JCS reorganization by General Wallace M. Greene, Jr., USMC (Ret.) and Admiral James L. Holloway III, USN (Ret.) were made before the Investigations Subcommittee, House Armed Services Committee, April 29, 1982.

General Edward Meyer's discussion of the astronomical growth in committee staffs and the impact they have had on the Joint Chiefs was printed in *Armed Forces Journal*, April 1982, pp. 82–90.

The best discussion of the siege of Constantinople and the defense of that city by Leo III in 717 can be found in ch. 12 of Major General J. F. C. Fuller's *Military History of the Western World* I (New York: Funk & Wagnalls, 1954).

A captain in World War II, ARTHUR T. HADLEY covered the Pentagon and the White House for *Newsweek* during the Korean War and won prizes for his dispatches from Vietnam. He is a former editor of the *New York Herald Tribune* and has written for such magazines as *The Atlantic, The New York Times Magazine, Playboy,* and *New Republic.* He served as consultant to the Joint Chiefs of Staff and is the author of seven books, among them *The Nation's Safety and Arms Control.*